OXFORD WORLD'S CLASSICS

THE OXFORD SHAKESPEARE

General Editor · Stanley Wells

The Oxford Shakespeare offers new and authoritative editions of Shakespeare's plays in which the early printings have been scrupulously re-examined and interpreted. An introductory essay provides all relevant background information together with an appraisal of critical views and of the play's effects in performance. The detailed commentaries pay particular attention to language and staging. Reprints of sources, music for songs, genealogical tables, maps, etc. are included where necessary; many of the volumes are illustrated, and all contain an index.

JAY L. HALIO, the editor of *King Henry VIII* in the Oxford Shakespeare, is Professor of English at the University of Delaware. He has also edited *The Merchant of Venice* for the Oxford Shakespeare.

D0448827

THE OXFORD SHAKESPEARE

Currently available in paperback

The rest of the plays are forthcoming

OXFORD WORLD'S CLASSICS

WILLIAM SHAKESPEARE

King Henry VIII, or All is True

Edited by
JAY L. HALIO

OXFORD
UNIVERSITY PRESS

OXFORD

UNIVERSITY PRESS

Great Clarendon Street, Oxford OX2 6DP

Oxford University Press is a department of the University of Oxford.
It furthers the University's objective of excellence in research, scholarship,
and education by publishing worldwide in

Oxford New York

Athens Auckland Bangkok Bogotá Buenos Aires Calcutta
Cape Town Chennai Dar es Salaam Delhi Florence Hong Kong Istanbul
Karachi Kuala Lumpur Madrid Melbourne Mexico City Mumbai
Nairobi Paris São Paulo Singapore Taipei Tokyo Toronto Warsaw

with associated companies in Berlin Ibadan

Oxford is a registered trade mark of Oxford University Press
in the UK and in certain other countries

Published in the United States
by Oxford University Press Inc., New York

First published as an Oxford World's Classics paperback 2000
Reissued 2008

British Library Cataloguing in Publication Data

Data available

Library of Congress Cataloging in Publication Data

Shakespeare, William, 1564–1616.
[King Henry VIII]
King Henry VIII, or All is true / by William Shakespeare and John
Fletcher; edited by Jay L. Halio.
(Oxford World's Classics)
Includes bibliographical references and index.
1. Henry VIII, King of England, 1491–1547 Drama. 2. Great
Britain—Kings and rulers Drama. I. Fletcher, John, 1579–1625.
II. Halio, Jay L. III. Title. IV. Title: King Henry VIII.
V. Title: All is true. VI. Series: Shakespeare, William,
1564–1616. Works. 1982.
PR28178.A2H35 1999
822.3'—dc21 99–20892

ISBN 978–0–19–953743–3

2

Typeset by Jayvee,
Trivandrum, India
Printed in Great Britain by
Clays Ltd, St Ives plc

PREFACE

THIS edition aims to provide a modernized text of *King Henry VIII, or All is True*, based on the First Folio of 1623, along with appropriate textual notes, commentary, introduction, and illustrations. A special effort has been made to include information that may be useful to actors and directors engaged in staging the play. Although both Shakespeare and Fletcher had a hand in writing *King Henry VIII*, the play is included only among Shakespeare's works in the Folio of 1623 and not in the Beaumont and Fletcher Folio of 1647. For that reason, but mainly for simplicity's sake, I shall throughout this edition refer to the play as Shakespeare's, with the tacit understanding that while he may have been chiefly, he was not solely responsible for its composition.

All editors in the past fifty years, myself included, owe a great debt to R. A. Foakes, who edited the Arden edition (1957) and therewith benefited subsequent scholars with a wealth of scholarship, critical acumen, and common sense. Like him, all of us are also indebted to the work of earlier editors, beginning with Rowe and Pope, whose textual emendations and commentaries have been extremely useful. I owe a special debt to the editors of the Oxford *Complete Works*, and to William Montgomery in particular, whose text I have followed, except where I found myself disagreeing with it. As this edition does not pretend to be a variorum, the variants in a number of early and late editions do not appear in the Collation, nor are the comments of their editors included, except as cited in editions I have consulted.

I am grateful to Tom Clayton, Elise Goodman, and Lois Potter, who have read parts or all of the Introduction, and especially to the General Editor, Stanley Wells, who has read everything. Shakespeare Institute students Gene Giddens, Jane Kingsley-Smith, and Rob Conkie helped check the text and Collation. All have helped me correct errors and rethink positions, but final responsibility for what appears in this edition of course rests solely with me. I am also grateful to the University of Delaware Library, the Folger Shakespeare Library, and the Shakespeare Centre Library, whose facilities I have once again made good use of, and to their staff, whose service and cooperation remain unsurpassed. Frances

Whistler at OUP has as ever cheerfully and competently helped see this work to completion. Finally, I owe a considerable debt to Mrs Christine Buckley, copy-editor extraordinaire, whose wit and wisdom so often helped to provide greater clarity and accuracy in this edition.

JAY L. HALIO
Newark, Delaware, 1998

For
Elliott and Frances Halio

CONTENTS

LIST OF ILLUSTRATIONS

INTRODUCTION

THE last of the English history plays printed in the Folio of 1623 (our only text for the play), *The Famous History of the Life of King Henry the Eight*, to give it its full title there, is also one of the last plays Shakespeare wrote. Like the other play written in his so-called retirement from the stage, *The Two Noble Kinsmen* (as well as the lost *Cardenio*), it was written in collaboration with John Fletcher, although some scholars dispute this claim of joint authorship (see below under 'Date, Authorship, and Printing'). But that is only part of the controversy *King Henry VIII* (as it will be called here) has aroused. Dispute begins with the title, which appears to have been *All is True*, the title preferred by the editors of the Oxford *Complete Works of William Shakespeare*. Further and even more vigorous discussion centres on its critical interpretation. Is it a well developed play, adequately unified and coherent, or merely a pageant-play, its scenes strung together loosely but its main interest localized in the big court scenes and processions? These are some of the critical issues that this introductory essay will address, starting with Shakespeare's representation of Henry VIII's break with Rome, the beginnings of the Reformation in England, and his use of various historical sources.

Henry VIII, Shakespeare, and the Reformation in England

When Henry VIII succeeded his father, Henry VII, to the throne of England in 1509, he was already affianced to his brother Arthur's widow, Katherine of Aragon, daughter of Isabella and Ferdinand of Spain, and aunt to Charles V, soon to become King of Spain and Holy Roman Emperor. In 1503, after Arthur died, Pope Julius II on appeal from both Henry VII and Ferdinand had given dispensation to allow Henry and Katherine to marry, on the assumption that the union between Arthur and Katherine, which occurred when both were only fourteen years old, had not been consummated.[1] Henry and Katherine did not marry, however, until June 1509

---

[1] See Leo F. Solt, *Church and State in Early Modern England, 1509–1640* (Oxford, 1990), 113.

1. King Henry VIII in his council chamber. (From a contemporary engraving designed by Hans Holbein the Younger; reproduced in Halliwell's edition, xii. 75.)

when, according to Holinshed, Henry was persuaded to do so in order that Katherine's great dowry should not be lost.[1] For twenty years afterwards they lived as husband and wife. Katherine bore many children, only one of whom, Mary, survived birth and lived through infancy. Henry, meanwhile, had a number of mistresses, including Elizabeth Blount, who in 1519 bore him a son, Henry Fitzroy, named Duke of Richmond in 1525.

As Katherine grew past the age of childbearing, Henry became acutely conscious of the fact that he needed a legitimate son and heir to secure the Tudor line; except for Matilda in the twelfth century, England had not had a queen regnant, nor had a bastard ever succeeded his father.[2] Ironically, of course, not one but two queens ruled England later in the sixteenth century, the second of whom, Elizabeth I, became one of the greatest of all English monarchs. That was later. The Wars of the Roses in the preceding century,

[1] Holinshed, 800–1. See also Hall, 507.
[2] See Ridley, 152, and cf. Rex, 7.

which had been fought in large part over the right of succession, had decimated the English nobility and nearly ruined the kingdom. This recent history remained fresh in memory; hence, by the end of the 1520s, Henry felt that a male heir was of crucial importance, and he determined to get one.[1]

Although Henry's divorce from Katherine was not the sole cause leading to the Reformation, it was the most immediate one. As Shakespeare shows in his dramatization of events, Henry felt no malice towards Katherine; indeed, he seems to have loved her as his true and faithful wife—until around 1527, when he began to feel pangs of conscience, or so he professed, concerning the morality of his marriage.[2] Claiming that his brother and Katherine had in fact consummated their union, Henry argued that his marriage to Katherine was invalid, that they had been living in sin all these years, and that their punishment was the lack of a surviving male heir. He therefore appealed to the Pope for a divorce, or rather an annulment of the papal decree of 1503, which had permitted his wedding to Katherine to occur. And that is where his conflict with the Church of Rome began.[3]

Earlier, Henry had been a steadfast Catholic and had earned the title, 'Defender of the Faith', for his book called *Assertio Septem Sacramentorum* (1521), which he dedicated to Pope Leo X.[4] This was a defence of the seven sacraments against the attacks of Martin Luther and included not only statements about the indissolubility of marriage but also a reference to the pope as the 'Chief Priest and Supreme Judge upon earth'.[5] Henry thus enjoyed good relations with the papacy, gaining for his devoted servant, Thomas Wolsey, Archbishop of York and Chancellor of England, a

[1] See Ridley, 153, and Scarisbrick, 150.

[2] On Henry's qualms of conscience, see Hall, 753, and cf. Holinshed, 897, 906. See also Scarisbrick, 152–4. According to Holinshed (907), the Bishop of Bayonne (actually, the Bishop of Tarbes), then French Ambassador to England, first put doubts in Henry's mind about the validity of his marriage to Katherine while negotiations were going forward regarding the marriage of their daughter Mary to the Duke of Orleans, second son to the French king. If Henry's marriage to Katherine was invalid under church law, Mary would be illegitimate and thus unfit to wed royalty. The story may be untrue; Henry's confessor, John Longland, Bishop of Lincoln, may have first raised the question with Henry: cf. Saccio, 219.

[3] On the 'King's Great Matter', see Ridley, 157–80; Scarisbrick, 163–240; Elton, 103–25.

[4] See Hall, 629; Scarisbrick, 115–17; Elton, 76.

[5] Solt, 11–12.

cardinal's hat.[1] He might therefore have expected little opposition to his request for the annulment, but the situation that had developed by then both personally and politically was such that his hopes and expectations were destined for disappointment.

In the first place, Katherine turned out to be entirely uncooperative. She refused to admit that her marriage with Arthur had been consummated, or that she had been anything other than Henry's true and loyal wife. In one of his most moving representations of women, Shakespeare portrays Katherine as exactly that, winning sympathy for her on every count, up to and including her final illness and death. In the second place, the Pope, Clement VII, was no longer his own man but in effect the captive of Katherine's nephew, Charles V, whose armies had attacked the papal states and sacked Rome. Thirdly, Henry's appeal to church law as founded in Scripture was not conclusive. While he might cite the injunction against a man marrying his brother's widow in Leviticus 20: 21, another biblical verse, Deuteronomy 25: 5, said that 'When brethren dwell together, and one of them dieth without children, the wife of the deceased shall not marry to another, but his brother shall take her, and raise up seed for his brother'.[2] Only if the original marriage had not been consummated, however, could the union proclaimed in Deuteronomy occur, or so Henry's clerical advocates maintained.[3] And there the matter rested, while Henry tried to obtain what he needed from the Pope or, failing that, from the learned universities in England and throughout Europe,[4] or from Katherine, whose trial in 1529 he and Wolsey orchestrated and Shakespeare later dramatized.

What also urged Henry on to dissolve his marriage to Katherine was his attraction to, or infatuation with, Anne Boleyn, one of

---

[1] See Cavendish, 16–18; cf. Holinshed, 835, 837; Hall, 583.

[2] Cited by Solt, 13. On this issue, see Scarisbrick, 194–5, and Elton, 106–7.

[3] Rex, 7–10. Wolsey did not share this opinion but proposed another way out, regardless of whether or not the marriage with Arthur had been consummated. This was through the 'impediment of public honesty', which Julius II's bull had not addressed. But Henry wanted nullification on the basis of Leviticus, to which he was committed. Moreover, by 1527 Wolsey had become suspect. He could have saved the day for Henry, but was turned away. The King grasped not the wrong end of the stick, but the wrong stick (Scarisbrick, 191–6).

[4] For a summary of various positions taken by the universities, see H. Maynard Smith, *Henry VIII and the Reformation* (1948), 30–1.

Katherine's ladies-in-waiting.[1] Anne's sister Mary had already been one of Henry's mistresses, but Anne held off yielding to Henry's importunities, possibly in the hope of becoming something more than the king's mistress.[2] When the Archbishop of Canterbury, William Warham, who had been merely lukewarm to Henry's divorce proceedings, died in August 1532, Henry appointed a supporter, Thomas Cranmer, to the position. Shortly thereafter, another supporter, Thomas Cromwell, who had been Wolsey's secretary, began drafting a bill against appeals to Rome in an attempt to foil Katherine's manoeuvre in that direction. Only then did Anne submit to Henry's advances, possibly expecting marriage and eventually herself becoming Queen of England. When in mid-December she became pregnant, Henry secretly married her (25 January 1533).[3]

The Act in Restraint of Appeals was passed in March 1533, and subsequent legal proceedings led to Cranmer's declaration on 23 May 1533 that Henry's marriage to Katherine was null and void.[4] On 1 June, in a scene that Shakespeare recalls with much stage pageantry, Anne was crowned as the new queen.[5] In 1536, shortly before the fall of Anne of the thousand days, Katherine died, but Shakespeare chose to end his play before these events.[6] He ends, rather, with the events of 1533—with the birth and christening of Henry's new child, Elizabeth; Cranmer's prophecy of 'wonders' yet to come; and the King's joyful gratitude.

So much for the divorce and second marriage. Of course, the Reformation, in good part initiated by these events, encompassed a great deal more. Already during these years, Lutheranism had

---

[1] Events in the play are not chronologically accurate but arranged or altered for primarily dramatic effect, the subtitle 'All is True' notwithstanding. Henry's meeting with Anne followed rather than preceded the fall of Buckingham; moreover, she was not present at the Hampton Court feast that Cavendish (25–8) and Holinshed (921–2) describe, and that Shakespeare dramatizes in 1.4. (The Commentary includes chronological and historical corrections and notes.)

[2] Scarisbrick, 149–52; cf. Maynard Smith, 33.

[3] Rex, 17. See Hall, 788, 794; Holinshed, 928–9. Hall says the marriage occurred on St Erkenwald's Day (14 November). Most scholars accept January 1533, but see Diarmaid MacCulloch, *Thomas Cranmer* (1996), 637–8, who argues that *two* secret marriages took place.

[4] Hall, 796; Holinshed, 929–30.

[5] See Hall, 798–805; Holinshed, 930, 933–4; Rex, 18.

[6] Although 4.2 is like a death scene—Katherine is very near her end—she does not then die.

been exercising its influence in England, and Tyndale's New Testament had circulated and been vigorously opposed by John Fisher, Bishop of Rochester, and others.[1] On these events, Shakespeare remains silent. No mention is made either of Henry's title as 'Defender of the Faith' or of his subsequently becoming head of the Church of England. Issues of theology or the politics that became involved with theological controversy are not raised, except perhaps indirectly through the representation of Cardinal Wolsey. Here a less hostile view of the man appears than one might expect from reading Holinshed's or Hall's vituperative accounts. But what happened to Wolsey had the greatest implications for the Reformation in England. Had he survived as a political force, it is arguable whether the Reformation would have come to England when it did or as it did.[2]

The Fall of Thomas, Cardinal Wolsey. Wolsey's fall was as meteoric as his rise from a poor boy in Ipswich to Chancellor of England and, in the view of many of his contemporaries, the most powerful man in the realm, not excluding the King. His pride and power occasioned hostility from both the nobility and the commoners, who resented the pomp with which he displayed himself, so graphically portrayed in the chronicles by Hall and Holinshed.[3] In the first part of his reign, Henry entrusted more and more affairs of state to

[1] See Hall, 708, 729, 762–3, 771; Holinshed, 913; and cf. Elton, 74–7. For the various senses of 'Lutheranism' as used in this period, see Ridley, 186.

[2] Cf. Ridley, 186: 'By overthrowing Wolsey, Henry was pandering to the anticlerical movement which its opponents called "Lutheranism."' Maynard Smith (16–17) argues that while Wolsey did not precipitate the schism (Anne Boleyn did), his actions as Lord Chancellor and papal legate did much to pave the way. For example, he showed Henry how one person could rule both church and state, and how an exhausted exchequer might be replenished by plundering the monastic establishments. His haughty and dictatorial manner, furthermore, made the papacy and the clergy so unpopular, at least in the south of England, that the curtailment of clerical privileges and the repudiation of the papacy were welcomed.

[3] See, e.g., Hall, 567, on Wolsey's being made Bishop of Lincoln: 'This man was born at Ipswich and was a good Philosopher, very eloquent and full of wit, but for pride, covetousness, and ambition, he excelled all other'. Holinshed, 837, describes the way the Cardinal's hat was delivered to Wolsey in November 1515 with as much pomp 'as though the greatest prince in Europe had been come to visit the king'. He was generally hated for his ambition and for comporting himself as 'a proud popeling'. Cf. Hall, 583, and see Cavendish, 28, for further displays of Wolsey's pomp and power. On Wolsey's excessive exercise of power and the danger of praemunire (into which he eventually fell), see Holinshed, 877, and note to 3.2.341.

Wolsey, not only as his emissary abroad—to the French King, the Emperor, and the Pope—but also in domestic matters, including taxation, which as much as anything aroused public ire. As papal legate, moreover, Wolsey managed to supervene even the Archbishop of Canterbury.[1] He had, in addition, definite aspiration to become pope and lobbied hard for that position of power.[2] No wonder he was resented on every side.

Wolsey did not oppose Henry's desire to have his marriage to Katherine annulled and in fact worked towards that end.[3] But the political situation in Europe, in which the Pope was effectively Charles V's prisoner, forestalled his best efforts.[4] On the other hand, he was by no means eager to see Henry marry Anne Boleyn; quite the contrary, he recognized Anne's Protestant affinities and those of her family, and he rigorously opposed them. He would have preferred to see Henry marry the Duchess of Alençon, a union that would strengthen the alliance with France he had worked hard to arrange.[5] But it was not to be. Henry was already smitten with Anne and, once the annulment was secured, he was bent on making her his queen.

Wolsey's failure to obtain that annulment doubtless had much to do with his fall from Henry's favour. Henry had begun to mistrust his closest aide and confidant, especially as his efforts along with those of his companion legate, Cardinal Campeggio (Campeius in Shakespeare's play), failed to gain Katherine's consent to the divorce, despite repeated attempts on their part to win her over. She remained adamant, and Henry grew disgusted. By 1528, Wolsey no longer enjoyed the King's favour.[6] The next year, after the fiasco of the Blackfriars trial and Pope Clement's decision to remove the trial to Rome, Wolsey's fate was sealed.

Dramatic though the incident doubtless was, as recorded by Hall

[1] See Cavendish, 16; Ridley, 110, 127; Saccio, 213–14. As papal legate, Wolsey was the supreme ecclesiastical authority in England.

[2] See Holinshed, 871; Scarisbrick, 107–10.

[3] Ridley, 178–9.

[4] Scarisbrick, 155–6.

[5] See Holinshed, 906; Ridley, 178–9; Scarisbrick, 162.

[6] See Hall, 745. Following a long private conversation with Wolsey, Hall says, 'the King mistrusted him ever after'. The incident that occasioned Henry's mistrust relates to the interception of some letters Wolsey had sent threatening war against Charles V without first obtaining Henry's consent. But Scarisbrick, 228–31, notes other reasons for Henry's cooling.

and Cavendish, Shakespeare does not include the meeting of the court on 23 July 1529. On that occasion, Henry fully expected the Cardinals' decision. As the court assembled, the King was himself present along with crowds of spectators. But when Campeggio opened proceedings, he announced that judgement would not be given that day and adjourned the trial until October. The shocked silence was broken by the Duke of Suffolk who, striking the board with his hand, spoke out angrily: 'It was never merry in England whilst we had cardinals among us'.[1]

This was most likely the cue for further action by the nobility, who formulated a list of thirty-four charges against Wolsey and sent them to Henry. Henry did not act at once, but when the Cardinals visited him at Grafton so that Campeggio could take his leave of the King, Henry ordered Wolsey to accompany the legate to London, whence the Roman might proceed out of the realm. It was the last time Wolsey saw and spoke with Henry.[2] Meanwhile, Anne, who Cavendish says kept her state 'more like a queen than a simple maid', accompanied Henry and was regarded by the populace as the real cause for the divorce.[3] Katherine was sent away, and though Henry treated her with great courtesy, he never came to her bed again.[4]

Shakespeare treats Wolsey's arraignment and loss of office somewhat differently from the Tudor historians. He dramatizes Henry's discovery of Wolsey's immense wealth just after learning that the Cardinal had written to the Pope to delay action on the King's Great Matter, his divorce from Katherine (3.2). These are the immediate causes of his fall from grace. The bill of particulars against Wolsey is not enumerated; Wolsey's arrest follows just after the King hands him the inventory of his worldly goods that he inadvertently included among some state papers given to the King, an incident borrowed from an event that occurred many years earlier (see below under 'Sources'). Neither Wolsey's appearance

---

[1] Cavendish, 90; Ridley, 179. Hall, 758, dates the event 30 August and quotes Suffolk somewhat differently: 'by the Mass, now I see that the old said saw is true, that there was never Legate nor Cardinal, that did good in England'. Cavendish reports Wolsey's long reply to Suffolk but notes that Henry had already left the court after the Duke's first words.

[2] Cavendish, 92–7; Ridley, 182–3; Scarisbrick, 233–5.

[3] Cavendish, 94; Hall, 759.

[4] Cavendish, 92; Hall, 780; Scarisbrick, 152.

in Parliament nor his trial on the charge of praemunire is dramatized, but Suffolk and Norfolk mention other charges when they
approach him in the same scene to demand his surrender of the
Great Seal.[1] Wolsey did not live much longer after these events, but
Shakespeare does not dramatize his last days—his removal to
Yorkshire, his attempts to regain power, his arrest by Northum-
berland and journey to the Tower, where he never arrived, dying
en route in Leicester Abbey.[2] Instead, we have his 'long farewell'
to all his greatness[3] and Cromwell's announcements: that Sir
Thomas More has replaced him as Lord Chancellor, that Thomas
Cranmer is now Archbishop of Canterbury, and that Henry and
Anne have secretly married. It is to Anne that Wolsey attributes
his downfall in Shakespeare's play, though the enmity between
Wolsey and the nobility has been dramatized from the first,
beginning with Buckingham's fall and execution. The scene ends
as Wolsey exhorts Cromwell to serve the King and to be mindful of
ambition, nothing of which appears in the historical sources. A
final, mixed tribute to the great man appears in the dialogue
between Katherine and her gentleman usher Griffith in 4.2.

Reform of the Church. The historical sources, however, make a
good deal of the repeated efforts to reform the church, climaxed
later in Henry's reign by the spoliation of the monasteries. Shakespeare's play does not go that far nor, as noted, is it much concerned with matters of clerical reform[4] any more than with the
international political strife that raged during this period, including the Sack of Rome, which is not so much as mentioned. Even as
Wolsey remained Archbishop of York and sat in Parliament
following his dismissal as Lord Chancellor, debate continued on

---

[1] See Hall, 759–60; Holinshed, 909. In Cavendish's account, 98, Wolsey challenges the Dukes' authority to demand the Great Seal. This very likely inspired
Wolsey's dialogue with the Dukes in Shakespeare's play, although it is Holinshed
(912) who records the several abuses that the Dukes enumerate.

[2] Hall, 773–4; Holinshed, 913–17; Cavendish, 129–82. At 4.2.17–30 Griffith,
Katherine's gentleman usher, briefly relates to her Wolsey's last days and death.

[3] Part of this speech, and perhaps its inspiration, derives from Holinshed, 917.

[4] Shakespeare's relatively moderate anti-Catholicism, here as in *King John*, compared to Fletcher's stronger Protestantism (his father, a militant Protestant,
became Bishop of London) may have led the authors to eschew theological debate,
as my colleague Lois Potter suggests, and argues further for Shakespeare's greater
responsibility in the play's design.

ways to reform the church. Wolsey had often promised to remedy abuses, though little ever came of his professed intentions. It remained for Cranmer as Archbishop of Canterbury to bring about the reforms that were viewed as necessary, aided in his efforts by none other than Wolsey's former secretary, Thomas Cromwell.[1]

Church reform was ongoing in the sixteenth century and well into the seventeenth, of course, culminating in the Civil War that led to the execution of Charles I and the rule of another Cromwell. For this reason and doubtless others, Shakespeare was well advised to steer clear of clerical and theological issues, for they could be very dangerous. His highly sympathetic treatment of Katherine and his ambivalence towards Wolsey—certainly when compared with the harsher treatment of him by Tudor historians—may suggest to some that Shakespeare was not altogether partial to many aspects of the Reformation in England. Elsewhere, he satirizes excessive religiosity, as in *Measure for Measure*, and the puritanical Malvolio in *Twelfth Night* is well mocked. On the other hand, Cranmer's treatment at the hands of the extremely orthodox Bishop of Winchester, Stephen Gardiner, the ringleader of the cabal against him in Act 5, shows that Shakespeare could be critical of excess in any form it took.

Appearing as a meek and mild Christian servant to king and country as well as church, Cranmer supplants Wolsey as the triumphant cleric. Shakespeare did not have to remind his audience of Cranmer's later accomplishments—or his fate under Queen Mary. Ending his play as he did, Shakespeare left much to implication and suggestion, avoiding the contentious issues that ignited during Henry's reign and continued burning in his own time, with greater or less heat. Nevertheless, the play ends by pointing to an interval of relative peace under the then ruling monarch, James I, Elizabeth's heir,

> As great in admiration as herself . . .
> Who from the sacred ashes of her honour
> Shall star-like rise . . .
> And so stand fixed.

$$(5.4.42-7)$$

---

[1] See Saccio, 222–4.

This, near the end of his own career and his life, at least was Shakespeare's hope.

One further point regarding Henry VIII, Shakespeare, and the Reformation in England needs to be made. In an essay on 'England and the Continent in the Sixteenth Century', G. R. Elton argues for the native influences on the development of the Anglican Church along with the strong if not always complementary influences from abroad. By showing how 'the English predilection for naturalising foreign imports operated on the reformation', he concludes that 'the protestant Church of England . . . emerged by the end of the century as a distinguishable form of Christianity'.[1] Shakespeare's play, as we have seen, does not delve into the specifics that went to make up that 'distinguishable form of Christianity'. That was not the dramatist's purpose. As his treatment of the sources shows, *King Henry VIII* nevertheless reflects the 'naturalising' tendency in its treatment of events, as much by what the dramatist does not include in his play as by what he does, as the next section of this Introduction will further demonstrate.[2] From an oblique angle, even Katherine's rejection, however sympathetically treated, and the wooing and wedding of Anne indicate the preference for native English over foreign influences, just as Cranmer—far more thoroughly English than Cardinal Wolsey—also does. Only to this extent, I think, can Shakespeare (in this play at least) be said to be seriously concerned with the Reformation, which by the time of his birth was well on its way to becoming what it was at his maturity.

Sources

Any examination of a dramatist's use of his sources must consider not only what was used in the work under consideration, but what was not. In this way understanding the creative process, one of the aims of source study, benefits. Another goal of source study, closely related to literary genetics, is its usefulness in helping the critic interpret a work. Again, not only what the dramatist

[1] In *Reform and Reformation: England and the Continent, c.1500–1750*, ed. Derek Baker (Oxford, 1979), 11. Cf. Saccio, 225–8: the Reformation under Henry VIII was mostly political, not doctrinal, which followed later.

[2] See also Stuart M. Kurland, '*Henry VIII* and James I: Shakespeare and Jacobean Politics', *SSt* 19 (1987), 203–17.

directly adapts for his purposes is important; what he omits may also be significant.

The major sources for Shakespeare's *King Henry VIII* are Raphael Holinshed's *Chronicles of England, Scotland, and Ireland* (second edition, 1587) and John Foxe's *Acts and Monuments* (1563; 1597 edition). Scholars are divided over the relative importance of Edward Hall's *The Union of the Two Noble . . . Families of Lancaster and York* (1550), from which Holinshed borrowed; George Cavendish's *The Life of Cardinal Wolsey* (*c*.1553; first published 1641); John Speed's *History of Great Britain* (1611); and Samuel Rowley's play, *When You See Me, You Know Me* (1603; reprinted 1613). Part of the problem in ascertaining specific debts derives from the fact that Tudor historians borrowed freely from one another, sometimes verbatim, so that one cannot be sure which source the dramatist was actually using at a given moment. But to puzzle over this unduly is to practise mere pedantry. What matters more are the attitudes, ideas, reflections of opinion that the drama may share with its purported sources, and the ways these may have influenced the playwright, directly—or, perhaps more often—indirectly.[1]

A case in point is the depiction of Cardinal Wolsey. Writing when the English Reformation was gathering ever greater momentum, Tudor historians were likely to see this prince of the Roman church in a far more negative way than, say, his gentleman usher George Cavendish, who wrote the *Life and Death of Cardinal Wolsey* while Catholic Queen Mary reigned. The *Life* remained unpublished (doubtless for good reason) until the middle of the next century, but it was well enough known, as copies circulated in manuscript during the latter half of the sixteenth century and the first half of the seventeenth. Did Shakespeare have access to one of these copies? Did Fletcher? That cannot be proved. On the other hand, when *King Henry VIII* appears to reflect Cavendish's description or interpretation of events, it seems worth noting, as this edition does, in the Commentary, where and as appropriate. Thus, regardless of whether a direct borrowing can be demonstrated, one

---

[1] On the complex relationships among the various sources and Shakespeare's play, see Annabel Patterson, '"All Is True": Negotiating the Past in *Henry VIII*', *Elizabethan Theater: Essays in Honor of S. Schoenbaum*, ed. R. B. Parker and S. P. Zitner (Newark, Del., 1996), 147–66.

can see how something other than coincidence may be involved in the dramatic representation. Rather, a common attitude or stance may be operative.[1]

A review of Holinshed's *Chronicle* and of Hall's *Union* from the beginning of Henry VIII's reign up to the birth of Princess Elizabeth reveals immediately the enormous amount of material Shakespeare left out of his history play. Except for the preliminary discussion in 1.1 of events surrounding the famous Field of the Cloth of Gold, which occurred in 1520, one has no sense of Henry's—and therefore England's—deep immersion in foreign affairs in the early decades of the sixteenth century. Wolsey, as Henry's agent, was extremely active in diplomatic enterprises in Europe during the period 1514–29, negotiating treaties with various monarchs, such as Francis I and Charles V, as well as with the pope, who in the Renaissance was a political, military, as well as spiritual power. By omitting most of this activity, Shakespeare kept his focus on events in England, events that would have been presumably of greater familiarity and interest to his audience. Allusions to Wolsey's notorious dealings with the Holy Roman Emperor, Charles, appear (for example 1.1.176–90), but they are subsidiary to the more dramatically significant issues at hand: the enmity between Buckingham and the Cardinal, the hated taxes Wolsey imposed in England (1.2.19–102), and, most important of all, the divorce question that occupies most of Acts 2 and 3. All this was happening during a time when on the Continent far more consequential events were taking place: alliances made and broken between France and England, England and Spain, the pope and France, and so forth.[2]

---

[1] On Cavendish's *Life* and its relation to the chronicles, especially Holinshed and Stow's *Annales* (1592), see Anderson, 132, 135–42. Anderson argues (136) that Cavendish's *Life* is at the heart of the treatment of Wolsey in *King Henry VIII*, and that Stow preserves more faithfully than Holinshed the essential ambiguity of Wolsey's awareness that is found in Cavendish. This ambiguity is then found in Shakespeare's play, but whether from Stow or directly from Cavendish is impossible to determine. Anderson implies that the former is responsible; although she later notes a passage in *King Henry VIII* that seems to come from Cavendish without the mediation of Stow, she remains sceptical that Shakespeare knew Cavendish's work directly (141). See also Patterson, 'Negotiating the Past', 151–3, for further discussion of Cavendish and Stow.

[2] Saccio, 211, notes that in the period 1520–33 covered by the play, 'Shakespeare touches only lightly on the great issues of foreign policy, papal authority, canon law, parliamentary statute, religious reform, and governmental structure that arose from the break' with Rome.

Perhaps the most significant events of all, having a direct bearing on Henry's efforts to obtain an annulment of his marriage to Katherine from the Pope, occurred in 1525: Charles V's conquest of papal Italy, the Sack of Rome, and the capture of Pope Clement VII. With the Pope effectively in the control of the Emperor, who was Katherine's nephew, Henry had little hope of obtaining from him what he most desired, try though he and Wolsey did.[1] But none of this appears in Shakespeare's play. Instead, by inserting a meeting with Anne Boleyn at Wolsey's feast in 1.4, Shakespeare sets up a complicating factor in the divorce that has a great deal to do with his representation of Henry and his motives, but that is quite unhistorical.[2]

Nor does anything appear in the play regarding Anne's sister, Mary, or Elizabeth Blount, with each of whom Henry had an affair some time before he met and fell in love with Anne. Elizabeth actually bore him a son, Henry Fitzroy, but again, none of these personages is so much as mentioned in the drama, as they are nothing to the dramatic purpose; on the contrary, they would be distractions and perhaps dangerous ones. During the period (1527–33) when Henry was trying so hard to have his marriage to Katherine dissolved, Protestantism began making headway in England. Whether it did so directly through Lutheranism, through the older forms of Lollardy, through reaction against clerical abuses, or (most likely) through a combination of all of these forces does not matter: except for an occasional reference, such as Wolsey's negative appraisal of Anne as a 'spleeny Lutheran' (3.2.100), little of this ferment appears until Act 5, in Gardiner's attack on Cranmer as a heretic. Shakespeare's interests were directed mainly elsewhere: to the fall of great English notables (Buckingham and Wolsey) and to Henry's domestic problems involving Katherine and Anne.[3]

---

[1] See Elton, 101–2.

[2] Henry did not meet Anne until several years later (Bullough, 444), though exactly when is not recorded.

[3] 'The reduction in controversial discussion is doubtless due as much to Shakespeare's disinclination for sectarian dispute as because of James I's known dislike of poets who dabbled in state affairs' (Bullough, 442; see also 'Reform of the Church', above). Rowley's *When You See Me, You Know Me*, a possible source or influence (see below), does not eschew sectarian dispute and in fact concludes with a long debate on doctrinal matters between the bishops, Bonner and Gardiner, and Queen Katherine Parr. But Rowley apparently wrote before James ascended the throne and his views became well known.

By comparison with Rowley's *When You See Me, You Know Me*, Shakespeare's play is a model of historical accuracy, notwithstanding its violations of chronology for the sake of dramatic compression. With no discernible dramatic justification, Rowley has Wolsey alive and active during the time when Jane Seymour was queen and giving birth to Prince Edward, though Wolsey died in 1530, and Jane did not become queen until 1536. The dramatist was simply interested, it seems, in bringing episodically into his play as sensational events as he could find. By contrast, Shakespeare alters history for clear dramatic advantage. For example, he has Buckingham absent from the Field of the Cloth of Gold so that he (and we, the audience) may hear Norfolk's glowing account (1.1.14–45). His speech leads to a criticism of Cardinal Wolsey, who orchestrated the event, and the unconscionable amount of riches expended on it. Buckingham's indictment and trial occurred several years before Wolsey's 'commissions', the hated taxation that Katherine brings to Henry's attention in 1.2. But Shakespeare compresses events so that Katherine can plead for Buckingham while at the same time being brought into close opposition to Wolsey, an antagonism that developed further later on.[1] Shakespeare may have borrowed some of Henry's exclamations, notably his famous 'Ha!', from Rowley's play, but might not this have been part of a tradition from which both playwrights borrowed?[2]

A colourful incident that both Holinshed and Hall record regarding Katherine's marriage to Arthur, which had some bearing on Henry's appeal for an annulment, is nowhere mentioned or even alluded to in Shakespeare's play. On the morning after their wedding, Arthur awoke and called for drink, saying 'I have this night been in the midst of Spain, which is a hot region, and that journey maketh me so dry. . . .'[3] The Tudor chroniclers interpret the incident as a clear indication that the marriage had been consummated. To the end Katherine denied that it had, while Henry insisted otherwise. Of course, only three people knew the truth, and one of them was long since dead. The incident is reported near the end of the section on Henry VII, just before the reign of Henry VIII begins, but Shakespeare evidently read widely in the

---

[1] Bullough, 444; Humphreys, 192.

[2] For a fuller discussion of possible debts to Rowley's play, see Bullough, 437–42.

[3] Hall, 494; Holinshed, 789.

chronicles, selecting what suited his purposes, omitting what did not. To cite another example: he apparently recalled an incident early in Henry VIII's reign involving the Bishop of Durham, Thomas Ruthall, who had inadvertently included an inventory of his goods among some papers he sent to the King. Shakespeare adapts this incident to propel Wolsey's downfall, though historically it was Wolsey who discovered his enemy Ruthall's inventory and gleefully showed it to Henry, precipitating the Bishop's ruin.

While no direct topical allusions appear in *King Henry VIII*, many critics believe that its composition was occasioned, or at least prompted, by the elaborate wedding celebrations for the marriage in February 1613 of Princess Elizabeth, daughter of James I and Queen Anne, to Prince Frederick, the Elector Palatine and leader of the Protestant union of German princes.[1] The climax of Act 5, the birth and christening of the daughter (also named Elizabeth) of Henry VIII and his Queen Anne, and the prophecy of a glorious future awaiting her, can be viewed as a high compliment to the seventeenth-century couple. At least six of Shakespeare's plays were performed before the happy pair during the festivities. As *King Henry VIII* is not listed among them, it may have been cancelled at the last minute in favour of a masque on 16 February and staged later at the public theatre, the Globe.[2]

Date, Authorship, and Printing

Everyone familiar with theatre history will remember that it was during a performance of 'the play of Henry VIII' that the Globe

[1] On the importance of this union for the Protestant cause in northern Europe, see William M. Baillie, '*Henry VIII*: A Jacobean History', *SSt* 12 (1979), 251–2. Baillie also draws parallels between Buckingham's sudden arrest and imprisonment and the arrest and imprisonment of Sir Thomas Overbury on 21 April 1613, and between Henry's divorce case and Frances Howard's notorious suit against her husband, the Earl of Essex, in the spring of 1613 for annulment of their marriage (256–9). Kurland, '*Henry VIII* and James I', 204–5, notes the factionalism in Henry VIII's court and James I's.

[2] See Bullough, 437, and cf. Baillie, 'A Jacobean History', 259–60. Considering the multiple court intrigues, the falls and executions of great courtiers, a stealthy royal wedding, and a prominent royal divorce, Baillie doubts that *King Henry VIII* was to be performed at court in February 1613, when he says the play was probably still being written. When it was performed at the Globe in late June, moreover, it was 'a new play' (see Sir Henry Wotton's letter, quoted in 'Date, Authorship, and Printing').

burned down on 29 June 1613. The fire was caused by a discharge of ordnance during the first act when Henry makes a surprise appearance at Cardinal Wolsey's feast. The play was evidently a new one; Sir Henry Wotton refers to it as such in his famous letter to Sir Edmund Bacon a few days later (2 July):

Now . . . I will entertain you at the present with what hath happened this week at the Bank's side. The King's players had a new play, called *All is True*, representing some principal pieces of the reign of Henry 8, which was set forth with many extraordinary circumstances of pomp and majesty, even to the matting of the stage; the Knights of the Order with their Georges and garter, the Guards with their embroidered coats, and the like: sufficient in truth within a while to make greatness very familiar, if not ridiculous. Now King Henry making a masque at the Cardinal Wolsey's house, and certain chambers being shot off at his entry, some of the paper, or other stuff, wherewith one of them was stopped, did light on the thatch, where being thought at first but an idle smoke, and their eyes more attentive to the show, it kindled inwardly, and ran round like a train, consuming within less than an hour the whole house to the very grounds. This was the fatal period of that virtuous fabric, wherein yet nothing did perish but wood and straw, and a few forsaken cloaks; only one man had his breeches set on fire, that would perhaps have broiled him, if he had not by the benefit of a provident wit put it out with bottle ale.[1]

Doubtless more than 'a few forsaken cloaks' were lost in the blaze, among them possibly some of Shakespeare's manuscripts. But Wotton's letter helps date the play quite precisely. His reference to its title as 'All is True', coupled with the several claims made in the Prologue to the 'truth' of the presentation (e.g. Pro.9, 18), has led some scholars to believe that 'All is True' was indeed the play's original title.[2] The Folio editors evidently changed the title to make it consistent with those of the other English history plays.

---

[1] Quoted in E. K. Chambers, *William Shakespeare* (Oxford, 1930), ii. 343–4. For other contemporary accounts, including William Parrat's ballad written the day after the fire with the refrain 'Oh sorrow, pittiful sorrow, and yett all this is true', see E. K. Chambers, *The Elizabethan Stage* (Oxford, 1923), ii. 419–23; also Foakes, 179–81. See *TC* 29–30 for photographic facsimiles of these documents along with two others discovered in the 1980s concerning the Globe fire. Stanley Wells discusses the significance of these documents in *Shakespeare: A Dramatic Life* (1994), 372–6.

[2] It is so named, for example, in the Oxford *Complete Works* (1986). See Wells, *Dramatic Life*, 374–5, on the title, 'All is True', by which he argues the play was probably known to its first audiences.

The play was first printed in the Folio of 1623 at the end of the second section, the 'Histories', where it is called 'The Famous History of the Life of King Henry the Eight' (p. 205, sig. t3). Running titles throughout refer to '*The Life of King Henry the Eight*,' and this, or its shorter form, *Henry VIII*, is the way the play has usually been referred to ever since. Two of Jaggard's compositors, B and I, set the play in type, sharing the work almost equally between them. Compositor B was responsible for t3–t3^v, v2^v, v4–v6^v, x1–x2^v, and Compositor I responsible for t4–t6^v, v1–v2, v3–v3^v, x3–x4^v.[1] Compositor B, we know from Hinman's study and others, was an experienced workman but rather cavalier in his treatment of copy.[2] About Compositor I we know much less; he was apparently a journeyman whom Jaggard employed for a brief stint on the Folio, but since his habits are rather different from those of B—as in his preferences for certain spellings—he can be distinguished from him, a matter of some importance in sorting out the authorship question.

'The play of *Henry VIII*', Allardyce Nicoll remarks, 'is a puzzle, and presumably always will remain so.'[3] The puzzle concerns authorship of the play: Is it Shakespeare's? Shakespeare's alone? Shakespeare in collaboration with another playwright? Many scholars, as Nicoll says, 'pin their faith on Heminges and Condell, refusing to believe that these fellows of Shakespeare would have permitted the text to be included in the collected works had they not been certain it came from his pen'.[4] After all, they had excluded *Pericles* and *The Two Noble Kinsmen*, which we are fairly

[1] Charlton Hinman originally thought this compositor was Compositor C, though he had some doubts. Gary Taylor subsequently demonstrated that it could not have been C and identified him instead as another compositor, I. See Hinman, *The Printing and Proof-reading of the First Folio of Shakespeare* (Oxford, 1963), ii. 213–34; Taylor, 'The Shrinking Compositor A of the First Folio', *SB* 34 (1981), 96–117, esp. 103–6.

[2] See Hinman, i. 10–12.

[3] Foreword to A. C. Partridge, *The Problem of 'Henry VIII' Reopened* (Cambridge, 1949), 5.

[4] Ibid. For a spirited anti-collaborationist argument, see P. Alexander, 'Conjectural History, or Shakespeare's *Henry VIII*', *Essays and Studies*, 16 (1930), 85–120, esp. 99–119, and Foakes, pp. xv–xxviii. In '"Our Whole Life is Like a Play": Collaboration and the Problem of Editing', *Textus*, 9 (1996), 437–60, Gordon McMullan presents many of the theoretical and practical issues that concern editors who accept the collaborationist argument, and uses the example of *King Henry VIII* as his primary illustration.

certain are not entirely and possibly not even mainly by Shakespeare. For many years after publication of the Folio the 'puzzle' wasn't one, although several eighteenth-century critics raised questions about its style in different parts of the play.[1] In 1850, James Spedding's essay 'Who Wrote Shakespeare's *Henry VIII*?' appeared in the *Gentleman's Magazine*, followed shortly thereafter by Samuel Hickson's similarly titled article in *Notes and Queries*.[2] Both writers claimed, independently of each other, that John Fletcher had a hand in the composition, and from that time forward debate has continued.

Spedding's allocations, as amended by Hickson, assigned 1.1–2, 2.3–4, 3.2.1–204, and 5.1 to Shakespeare. The rest of *King Henry VIII* they attributed to Fletcher, including both its Prologue and Epilogue. The arguments favouring Fletcher as co-author centred on certain stylistic analyses, such as the use of end-stopped lines and 'redundant' syllables at the ends of lines, which Spedding found proportionally more characteristic of Fletcher's verse than Shakespeare's. Later scholars used other kinds of internal evidence to make the case, such as the use of contractions[3] and the relative frequencies of *doth* vs. *does*, *hath* vs. *has*, *them* vs. *'em*, *you* vs. *ye*, and *do* as an expletive, i.e. in expressions like 'I do beseech you'. As A. C. Partridge says, 'Where two authors are thought to have been at work on a play . . . little mannerisms of grammatical usage, easily passed over in the weightier aesthetic considerations, are those most likely to betray their several hands.' Accordingly, he tabulated these kinds of data, which confirm Spedding and Hickson's attributions. For example, in 3.2, *do* as an expletive, favoured by Shakespeare throughout his career, turns up twelve times in the first half of the scene, whereas in the rest of the scene it occurs only once, suggesting that this is a scene

[1] R. Roderick may have been the first (in T. Edwards, *Canons of Criticism*, 1758), followed by Farmer, Steevens, and Malone, who believed that some passages were Jonson's interpolations in 1613 in an old play dating back to 1601. See, for example, Malone's 'Preliminary Remarks' to his edition of the play (1790).

[2] Spedding, in *Gentleman's Magazine*, 178 (August–October 1850), 115–24; Hickson, in *Notes and Queries*, 24 August 1850, 198.

[3] See, for example, Willard Farnham, 'Colloquial Contractions in Beaumont, Fletcher, Massinger, and Shakespeare as a Test of Authorship', *PMLA* 31 (1916), 326–58, and cf. *TC*, 101–6. Partridge, *Problem Reopened*, 25, notes that colloquial contractions in the scenes assigned to Shakespeare are 'three times as prolific' as those assigned to Fletcher.

in which both Shakespeare and Fletcher had a hand.[1] Similarly, Shakespeare's preferences for *hath*, *them*, and *you* are especially pronounced in those scenes attributed to him, whereas *has*, *'em*, and *ye* are more frequent in Fletcher's scenes.[2]

Comparisons of these frequencies with Shakespeare's other plays, especially the later ones, are both useful and necessary to demonstrate that the perceived differences in *King Henry VIII* are not a result of Shakespeare's changing tendencies. Examination reveals that they do bear out the differences, as comparisons with Fletcher's plays written by himself alone do also.[3] But in his Arden edition of *Henry VIII*, R. A. Foakes has remarked that despite the 8:1 ratio of *ye* to *you* in scenes assigned to Fletcher, as compared to 4:1 for Shakespeare's, the frequency was not 'Fletcherian enough'. Cyrus Hoy, a Beaumont and Fletcher specialist, concedes the point, but notes what Foakes had overlooked: that Compositor B, who set many of Fletcher's lines, is notorious for altering *ye* in his copy to *you*.[4]

Other seemingly minor aspects of style tell the same story. Anyone collating *Henry VIII* in the 1623 Folio against modern editions will be struck, as I was, by the frequency throughout the play of *y'are* (= you're) and similar contractions (for example, *y'haue*, *th'haue*, *th'are*), modernized in this edition. A tabulation of incidences shows that of the dozen *y'* contractions, 10 are in scenes assigned to Fletcher, and only 2 in Shakespeare's, with the great majority of all instances in lines set by Compositor I. While *y'are* is by no means unknown in Shakespeare's received canon, its frequency is much lower. In the late plays, for example, it appears only once in *The Winter's Tale* and *Cymbeline*, compared with *you're* 5 and 6 times respectively, and not at all in *The Tempest*. The pronominal form *ye* is also rare. Finally, the frequency of parentheses in *King Henry VIII* may be remarked and tabulated according to Shakespeare's shares and Fletcher's, and here again the proportions are revealing. In the Shakespearian scenes, parentheses

[1] Partridge, *Problem Reopened*, 17.   [2] See chart, ibid., 22.

[3] Ibid., 21; also Cyrus Hoy, 'The Shares of Fletcher and His Collaborators in the Beaumont and Fletcher Canon (VII)', *SB* 15 (1962), 71–90.

[4] Hoy, 'Shares of Fletcher', 79. Thomas Clayton's caveat should also be kept in mind, i.e. that use of *ye* and *you* may vary also with dramatic circumstance and characterization. See his review article, 'Internal Evidence and Elizabethan Dramatic Authorship: An Essay in Literary History and Method', *SSt* 4 (1969), 365–74, esp. p. 368.

appear 37 times among a total of 1,167 lines, giving a ratio of once every 31.5 lines; in Fletcher's scenes, they appear 255 times among 1,599 lines, giving a ratio of once every 6.27 lines.[1]

The copy from which Compositors B and I set *King Henry VIII* in the Folio may have something to do with the idiosyncrasies (or the lack of them) upon which we have been focusing, although the proportions I believe speak for themselves quite clearly. Judging from the evidence of stage directions and other data, John Dover Wilson concluded, as W. W. Greg had done, that the copy was a scribal transcript of authorial papers and not a prompt book.[2] The few variations in speech prefixes that occur are 'not of an elaborately "functional" kind', Wilson notes.[3] Probably only one scribe was responsible for the transcription, and he apparently did not impose his own preferences upon pronominal forms or colloquial abbreviations. The punctuation often tends to be faulty, especially by modern standards, and some speech prefixes are wrong or ambiguous (such as the use of *Car.* or *Card.* when both Wolsey and Campeius are present), but otherwise the text is seldom difficult or corrupt.[4] The absence of odd spellings further points to scribal copy rather than authorial papers.

But if we concede that composition was shared, how was this accomplished? Did Shakespeare rough out a plan for the play and assign some scenes to Fletcher and others to himself? Did he draft several scenes first and then leave the rest to his collaborator to fashion?[5] Did Fletcher actually compose fewer scenes than

[1] Gary Taylor attributes the large number of round brackets mainly to the scribe, although he notes Compositor B's tendency to add brackets not found in copy. Taylor does not calculate the differences between the Shakespeare and Fletcher scenes, stating simply that a great number of brackets are set across both authors' stints as well as both compositors' stints (*TC*, 619). In his essay '*Henry VIII* and Fletcher', Marco Mincoff comments on Fletcher's 'parenthetical mode of construction', i.e. 'the way in which the flow is frequently broken by sharp, clear-cut parenthetical comments, which may vary from a word or two like "nay, more" to complete clauses', *SQ* 12 (1961), 243. His method of calculating percentages of Shakespeare's and Fletcher's use of brackets differs from mine and is based on modern texts, but he arrives at the same conclusion.

[2] Wilson, 'The Copy for *Henry VIII*, 1623', in Maxwell, 113; Greg, *The Shakespeare First Folio* (Oxford, 1955), 425; *TC*, 618–19.

[3] Maxwell, 113–15.

[4] See Wilson's lists, Maxwell, 115–17.

[5] This is the theory proposed by Marjorie H. Nicolson in 'The Authorship of Henry the Eighth', *PMLA* 37 (1922), 484–502, but as Humphreys says (53), her argument is unconvincing.

Spedding and Hickson assign him, 'touching up' or interpolating passages or words in lines that Shakespeare originally wrote? We can of course never have definitive answers to these questions, unless information comes to light that is not now available. On the evidence that we do have—again, all of it internal—Hoy argues for a smaller share by Fletcher, who (according to Hoy) revised rather than wrote 2.1–2, the latter part of 3.2, and 4.1–2. This assignment reduces Fletcher's share to only a third of the play rather than fully a half or more.[1] But Jonathan Hope's more recent study refutes Hoy's theory and confirms the assignments made by Spedding and Hickson.[2]

The situation is not the same in *King Henry VIII* as it probably was in another shared play, *The Two Noble Kinsmen*. In the later play, as Lois Potter argues in her Arden edition, the two dramatists, Shakespeare and Fletcher, began writing concurrently, Fletcher constructing the final draft. In several scenes, such as 1.4, 2.2, and 5.1, Fletcher seems to have been working with Shakespearian material, but nothing indicates that Shakespeare worked on Fletcher's. In *King Henry VIII* the influence appears to be reciprocal, although it is just possible that Fletcher may have taken responsibility at the end for 'touching up' and finishing the play as a whole before it was acted and later printed. The reciprocal influence was the more likely if Shakespeare, who had recently purchased his Blackfriars property, was still in London occasionally and available to work with Fletcher on the new play. Then, after the Globe burned down, he may have given up, or sold, his shares in the company and consequently become less active in its affairs.[3]

Apart from linguistic evidence, other kinds also point to shared

[1] Hoy, 'Shares of Fletcher', 79–85. As Hoy says, the weakness in his theory of Fletcher as interpolator in certain scenes and sole author of others is that so many of the scenes in question were set by Compositor B, who could have altered some of the linguistic evidence—and probably did—such as changing *ye* to *you*. See 81–2.

[2] See *The Authorship of Shakespeare's Plays* (Cambridge, 1994), 70–83. Hope believes that Shakespeare and Fletcher wrote and planned the play together rather than that Fletcher finished off a play that Shakespeare began and then abandoned (82).

[3] See Irwin Smith's *Shakespeare's Blackfriars Playhouse* (New York, 1964), 250–2. He notes that while the Gatehouse property is mentioned in Shakespeare's will, the Globe shares are not. After the theatre burned down, sharers were assessed to help rebuild it, but at that moment, having purchased the Gatehouse, Shakespeare may have sold his Globe shares to avoid the assessment and help pay for the Gatehouse. Compare Chambers, *William Shakespeare*, ii. 67–8.

authorship, such as metrical and structural analyses. Marina Tarlin-skaja has analysed the 'stress profiles' of Shakespeare's scenes and Fletcher's, and her findings confirm those of earlier studies and the traditional assignment of scenes.[1] For example, the incidence of unstressed monosyllables, 'a sign of acute run-on lines', is demonstrably higher in Shakespeare's scenes than in Fletcher's, while the percentage of non-masculine endings is much higher in Fletcher's.[2] Rhythmical differences are also revealing: as a study of stress positions shows,[3] plays written solely by Shakespeare tend to be rhythmically much more homogeneous than *King Henry VIII* proves to be.[4]

Critics have sometimes complained that *King Henry VIII* lacks coherence, that its scenes and even the portrayals of major characters are not fully integrated into a well-ordered whole.[5] Humphreys observes that 'the play's successive moods pay curiously little attention to what has gone before', and that the plot 'consists of episodes laid in sequence rather than dynamically' (35). Nicolson remarks on the changes in Katherine's, Wolsey's, and Henry's characters. For example, where Shakespeare drew Katherine much in the vein of his other great heroines—a combination of 'fearlessness, courage, steadfastness, keen judgment'— Fletcher gives us her dying vision;[6] where Shakespeare portrayed Wolsey as proud, vindictive, powerful, and shrewd, Fletcher sentimentalizes his death as he did Buckingham's.[7] Finally, whereas Acts 1 to 4 are chiefly concerned with the 'fall of princes'—the

[1] *Shakespeare's Verse: Iambic Pentameter and the Poet's Idiosyncrasies* (New York, 1987), 127–8, 198–200. Compare R. A. Law's earlier study, which also confirms traditional assignment of scenes: 'The Double Authorship of *Henry VIII*', *Studies in Philology*, 56 (1959), 471–88.

[2] Ibid., 200–1.   [3] Ibid., 128–9.

[4] Mincoff makes the same point. Compare his discussion of metrics in '*Henry VIII* and Fletcher', 245–50.

[5] See, for example, Eugene M. Waith, *The Pattern of Tragicomedy in Beaumont and Fletcher* (New Haven, Conn., 1952), 119: 'Among Shakespeare's history plays *Henry VIII* is conspicuous for its disunity. . . . One substitute for continuity in this play is the impressive amount of pageantry. . . . Whether or not this preponderance of spectacular effect was due to Fletcher, it was a technique with which he was quite familiar, as we know from his other plays.'

[6] See Law's analysis of this scene, as adapted from Holinshed's *Chronicle*, 'Double Authorship', 485.

[7] Nicolson, 'Authorship', 492–7. Cf. Waith, *Pattern*, 121–2, and Robert Ornstein, *A Kingdom for a Stage: The Achievement of Shakespeare's History Plays* (Cambridge, Mass., 1972), 205: 'Instead of character in action, Fletcher provides an artfully choreographed ballet of emotional gestures.'

fortunes of Buckingham, Katherine, and Wolsey—Act 5 performs
a volte-face; it presents 'a doubly "merry" appendix' in the birth
and christening of Elizabeth and the triumph of Cranmer, thereby
destroying 'all vestige of the unity in the drama as a whole'.[1]

These comments represent one way of looking at the play and
support the dual authorship theory. But as I shall argue in the next
section of this introduction, an alternative analysis of structure
and themes demonstrates a coherent pattern in the play without
invalidating the dual authorship theory.

In his review of Samuel Schoenbaum's important study of evidence for authorial attribution, Thomas Clayton comments:
' "Evidence" may establish as mathematical fact the validity of a
geometrical theorem, but neither external nor internal evidence
alone can, in the strictest sense, establish as historical fact the
validity of an assertion, whenever made. . . . We do not accept
everything asserted as "established fact"; but we do accord belief
where we acknowledge various probability.'[2] The work of scholars
summarized here establishes if not 'historical fact', then at least
'various probability'. Although Schoenbaum maintains that
external evidence is primary, he nevertheless recognizes the usefulness of internal evidence, especially where external evidence is
minimal or altogether lacking. Of his 'First Principles', among the
most important for attribution studies is the fourth: 'Textual
analysis logically precedes stylistic analysis'.[3] Both kinds are
important, and as we have seen, both help to establish Fletcher's
role in the composition of *King Henry VIII*.

The Play

Whether because of the authorship question, or because the play is,
like *King John*, eccentric to the two great history cycles Shakespeare
wrote earlier, critics have tended to slight *King Henry VIII*.[4] This is

[1] Law, 'Double Authorship', 486. Like others, Law notes that here as elsewhere
Fletcher depended on the sources in Holinshed and Foxe more than Shakespeare did.

[2] Clayton, 'Internal Evidence', 360.

[3] Schoenbaum, *Internal Evidence and Elizabethan Dramatic Authorship* (Evanston,
Ill., 1966), 172–5.

[4] On the way the authorship question has affected critics, see H. M. Richmond,
'Shakespeare's *Henry VIII*: Romance Redeemed by History', *SSt* 4 (1968), 334–6,
and note: 'The ultimate question for the critic about *Henry VIII* must surely . . . not
be "Who wrote it?" It should be "Is this a good play, and if so, why?" ' (336).

unfortunate, for the play is fascinating in its own right, and as its performance history shows (see below), it can be most impressive on the stage. Many of the standard critical studies of Shakespeare's work fail to include it, preferring to end their discussions with an analysis and evaluation of *The Tempest*, as if it were the author's final work.[1] When critics deign to consider *King Henry VIII*, they often dismiss it as almost an irrelevance. Even so astute a critic as Norman Rabkin, while recognizing that it is 'in many respects a fine play', regards its structure as 'cynically arbitrary', and damns it accordingly. He does not think Shakespeare took his subject seriously (otherwise, it could have been another great chronicle play), but instead he made it into 'a half-hearted and unconvincing piece'.[2]

Rabkin could not be more wrong. The play's structure is far from merely arbitrary and its themes are important. *King Henry VIII* has too often been regarded as a pageant play, designed to provide spectacle and colour for London's crowds at the time of Princess Elizabeth's marriage to the Elector Palatine in 1613. While it does provide these attractions, like Shakespeare's other work its value does not lie chiefly or only there.[3] The play, moreover, can be performed effectively with very little pageantry, as the BBC television production demonstrates (see below). But for all its pomp and splendour, *King Henry VIII* focuses mainly on the use and abuse of power. In this respect, it has links to the earlier histories and to the tragedies as well.

Some previous studies have seen in the presentations of Buckingham, Katherine, and Wolsey a throwback to the *de casibus* tradition of medieval tragedy, as in Chaucer's 'Monk's Tale' or later in *The Mirror of Magistrates*.[4] Without question, the fall of these

---

[1] To cite just two such studies, one British and one American: see Derek Traversi's *An Approach to Shakespeare*, 2 vols. (New York, 1969) and Harold C. Goddard's *The Meaning of Shakespeare*, 2 vols. (Chicago, 1951). Even books devoted entirely to the history plays, such as E. M. W. Tillyard's and Lily Bess Campbell's, exclude *Henry VIII* from consideration. An exception is Elihu Pearlman's more recent study, *William Shakespeare: The History Plays* (New York, 1992), but he dismisses *King Henry VIII* as 'A Play of Spectacle', 173–4.

[2] Norman Rabkin, *Shakespeare and the Common Understanding* (1967), 230–1. Cf. G. K. Hunter, *English Drama 1586–1642: The Age of Shakespeare* (Oxford, 1997), 268, who sees the play as 'a series of brilliant rhetorical moments linked together without being attached to an overriding purpose'.

[3] Cf. Kristian Smidt, *Unconformities in Shakespeare's History Plays* (1982), 146.

[4] See, for example, Frank Kermode, 'What Is Shakespeare's *Henry VIII* About?', *Durham University Journal*, NS 9 (1948), 48–55; reprinted in *Shakespeare: The Histories*, ed. Eugene M. Waith (Englewood Cliffs, NJ, 1965), 168–79. Cf. Pearlman, *The History Plays*, 174–80.

great personages is central, and they are tragic, one way or another. But that is only part of the story. They do not all fall the same way or for the same reason; and in Act 5, when it looks as if another is about to fall, Cranmer is saved by the King.[1]

The key to understanding what *King Henry VIII* is about and the way it is structured is to see how the various episodes relate to each other and build to a climax at the end. Shakespeare begins the dialogue with Buckingham and the other lords discussing the Field of the Cloth of Gold in France. Although historically Buckingham was present on the occasion, here he says he was absent because of an 'ague', giving Norfolk the opportunity to describe the 'view of earthly glory' that he missed. The point of this passage (1.1.14–38) is not the magnificence of the occasion, but its excess and cost. That leads directly into the conflict between Wolsey, the upstart prelate who arranged it, and Buckingham, the nobly descended aristocrat, who despises him. The competition between the two continues until first one and then the other falls by overreaching himself, the besetting fault of many powerful figures even before Marlowe's tragic heroes took the stage decades earlier.

Norfolk's counsel to Buckingham to exercise temperance falls on deaf ears (1.1.124–45); by the end of the scene Buckingham and his son-in-law are under arrest and sent to the Tower. Buckingham knows too much and speaks too freely: dramatically, this is the function of his speeches before his arrest and the explanation for his imprisonment (1.1.157–97). The Cardinal's brief appearance and few lines of dialogue demonstrate his awareness of Buckingham's threat and the means he will use to deal with it; Wolsey shows he can exercise power ruthlessly to gain his ends far better than the high-minded, intemperate Buckingham.

---

[1] Kermode thus sees the play as a late morality and tends to allegorize characters and events. Katherine, Wolsey, and Henry may appear as the 'Good Queen', the 'Ambitious Prelate', 'Mercy', and so forth, but they are not merely allegorical figures and have much more solid dramatic and historical significance. S. C. Sen Gupta, *Shakespeare's Historical Plays* (Oxford, 1964), 165, cites the *de casibus* tradition as lending unity to the play but sees variety in both the characters and their falls. Cf. also Howard Felperin, *Shakespearean Romance* (Princeton, 1972), 199–202, who notes that the falls of Buckingham, Katherine, and Wolsey are 'romantically, rather than tragically, conceived' and different from the falls, for example, of Hastings and Buckingham in *Richard III*. Like Adam in *Paradise Lost*, they achieve a 'Paradise within' as a result of their falls (203). Felperin goes on to demonstrate a connection between *King Henry VIII* and morality drama, especially its wavering or misguided kings (203–7).

The stage directions for the next scene are symbolically very significant, as the King enters 'leaning on Cardinal Wolsey's shoulder'. This is Henry's first appearance on stage,[1] and his dependence upon Wolsey is conspicuous. As the scene unfolds, it is clear that Henry knows little of what is happening in his realm.[2] Unexpectedly, Katherine enters and appeals to Henry on behalf of his subjects, who are being taxed to the point of rebellion. She says they blame not only Wolsey, but also the King (1.2.19–30). With the best and most compassionate intentions, Katherine thus dares to intervene in the dangerous game of power politics, and wins— up to a point. Henry demands that the taxes be withdrawn: that is her victory. Squeezing out of major responsibility for the uproar, Wolsey has his minions spread the word that the relief comes from his (not Katherine's) intercession with the King (106–8): that is his victory.

But not his sole victory. By skilfully manipulating Buckingham's Surveyor to testify against his master, he wins again, this time defeating Katherine. Although she suspects the Surveyor is perfidious, she can only appeal piously to Wolsey for 'charity' (144) and warn the Surveyor of the danger to his soul (174–6). Neither appeal carries any force or weight. Here and in the conflicts that follow, Wolsey shows himself far more capable than the Queen or her supporters. But through it all, the King is present and observant. This is crucial. By the end of the play, he has learned from his erstwhile servant how to play the power game—and win—better than anyone else.[3]

The next two scenes help to reinforce Wolsey's position of power and influence while at the same time building aspects of ambiguity

[1] In some productions, he appears at the beginning, a solitary, thoughtful figure (the BBC TV version), or gloriously resplendent in tableau (the 1996 RSC production), but the directors stage the opening to suit other purposes.

[2] See Kurland, '*Henry VIII* and James I', 206–7, who compares Henry's 'distaste for administration' to James's; both preferred private pleasures, such as their passion for hunting. Yet both maintained the primacy of authority, as Katherine recognizes when she makes her appeal directly to the King in 1.2 and during her trial in 2.4 (Kurland, 212).

[3] Richmond, 'Romance Redeemed', 340, compares Henry's 'hasty and extreme judgment' regarding Buckingham (1.2.119–29) to Henry V's reaction to Scrope's conspiracy (*Henry V* 2.2.91 ff.) and to Othello's misjudgement of Desdemona. By Act 5, according to Richmond, Henry learns how to judge and act more judiciously, tempering mercy with justice (341). He also learns how to act with greater political acumen.

and ambivalence that become increasingly important in the complementary design of this play. The French who had been apostrophized along with the English in the first scene are here satirized along with their English imitators. Wolsey, the evident villain in 1.2, gets praise now for his liberality, shown to excess in the following episode, the feast at York Place.[1] Rearranging history, Shakespeare introduces Anne to Henry at the feast years ahead of their actual meeting. The occasion complicates his motives shortly afterwards when he contemplates his separation and eventual divorce from Katherine and thereby justifies the dramatic compression. Shakespeare alters history also by having Wolsey guess correctly that the mysterious guest is the King.[2] A minor matter, perhaps, but alterations are never insignificant in the dramatist's treatment of source material. The incident underscores the closeness between Henry and Wolsey, who can penetrate through the King's disguise and knows very well how and when to defer to his master.

Shakespeare does not dramatize Buckingham's trial in Act 2, but only describes it to show how ineffectual the nobleman is against the Cardinal's superior power (2.1.1–30, 40–6). As against the praise for Wolsey in 1.3, here is denigration of him by the commons (50–2) in favour of the noble and 'bounteous' Duke.[3] Buckingham's valediction of more than seventy lines is a model of patient resignation, humility, and charity. In winning compassion and sympathy, it nevertheless reminds us that this is a defeat, and not the defeat of any man—the defeat of the most potent nobleman in England. Only Katherine's last speeches surpass Buckingham's moving rhetoric, and she too is defeated—a defeated Queen. The stakes in the power politics of empire are high, none higher, and loser Buckingham pays with his life. That is the point his long valediction—like Wolsey's later—most emphatically makes.[4]

---

[1] See Lee Bliss, 'The Wheel of Fortune and the Maiden Phoenix of Shakespeare's *King Henry the Eighth*', *ELH* 42 (1975), 3–4, for the 'pattern of contradiction' in this act.

[2] See 1.4.82n.

[3] Cf. 1.3.55, where Lovell refers to Wolsey's 'bounteous' mind.

[4] Cf. M. W. Wikander, *The Play of Truth and State: Historical Drama from Shakespeare to Brecht* (Baltimore, 1986), 42: 'Buckingham's challenge to the process of the king's justice is not merely emotional. His definition of truth clearly conflicts with the law's.' Wikander explores the whole notion of 'truth' in the play, signalled by its subtitle, and finds numerous contradictions and inconsistencies. In power politics, truth as a commodity subject to political expediency is precisely what we should expect.

And where is Henry in all this? Not present. He is not with the losers, and never is, although the losers typically invoke his presence, if only to bless him (2.1.89–95, 3.2.415–16, 4.2.164–5).

Hard upon Buckingham's disgrace preparations follow for Katherine's trial, as much a trial of her power against Wolsey's and the King's as of her worthiness to remain Queen. But well before it begins we get a glimpse of Wolsey's overreaching in the letter that the Lord Chamberlain reads (2.2.1–8). Whereas the Cardinal, or the Cardinal's man, may lord it over others, he cannot lord it over Katherine. That battle of wills ends in a draw, which is the beginning of the end for Wolsey. Henry counts on Wolsey to succeed, and when he does not get Katherine to knuckle under, the King loses confidence in him as well as his fellow legate, Campeius.

The dialogue between Suffolk and the Lord Chamberlain in 2.2 explains why Shakespeare introduced Anne earlier in the play:

> LORD CHAMBERLAIN
> It seems the marriage with his brother's wife
> Has crept too near his conscience.
> SUFFOLK   No, his conscience
> Has crept too near another lady.   (2.2.15–17)

While Norfolk blames Wolsey for this, he adds that the 'King will know him one day' (l. 20). So he must: 'He'll never know himself else', Suffolk replies. Knowing oneself is another important theme and relates closely to the knowledge and use of power. For without knowing oneself, one is powerless.[1] Ironically, Wolsey also has further to go on the journey to self-knowledge, and when he arrives there, he is joyful even though defeated (3.2.379).[2] This is another ambivalence Shakespeare weaves into the fabric of his design.

Wolsey of course is not responsible for Henry's qualms of conscience. The divorce was not his idea, and he is unjustly maligned by Norfolk (2.2.18–20, 22–9); yet he must bear responsibility for carrying out his sovereign's will. Henry is not ready to take full charge of affairs himself, though he will do so eventually. For the present, Wolsey is the 'quiet of my wounded conscience . . . a cure fit for a king' (2.2.74–5). Nevertheless, the King has sent Cranmer

---

[1] Richmond, 'Romance Redeemed', 342–3, compares Henry's 'erratic self-defence' in 2.4 to Lear's lack of self-knowledge, and citing 2.2.25–35 he compares Wolsey's 'subtle interventions' regarding the divorce to Iago's effect on Othello.

[2] On Wolsey's self-knowledge, see note to 3.2.379.

abroad to canvass the universities on behalf of his divorce. Wolsey reassures Henry that between them, he and Campeius will conduct a 'just and noble' trial (2.2.91), and he appears optimistic about the results. Before this composite scene ends, while the King talks apart with his new secretary, Gardiner (avowedly a tool of Wolsey's), Campeius asks Wolsey about Dr Pace, Gardiner's predecessor. The dialogue, which otherwise seems superfluous, again shows how ruthless Wolsey can be in the exercise of his power (2.2.121–35).

By contrast to Wolsey's machiavellianism, Anne's behaviour in the next scene is utterly naive. Her professions of concern for Katherine ring sincere,[1] but her insistence that she would not change places with her does not. The Old Lady undercuts her repeatedly and successfully, as Emilia does not with Desdemona (*Othello* 4.3). Of course history supports the Old Lady; but if Anne protests too much, she also reflects an ambivalence that, however tinged with insincerity, fits into the overall pattern of ambivalence or complementarity that the play insistently develops.[2]

The announcement that the King has made Anne the Marchioness of Pembroke (2.3.63) is a prelude to the climactic scene of Act 2, the Blackfriars trial. Anne's rise harbingers Katherine's fall. The thousand pounds a year that Henry gives Anne promises more thousands: 'Honour's train | Is longer than his foreskirt' (98–9). Evidently oblivious to all this (she never mentions Anne, nor do they ever meet[3]), Katherine nonetheless puts on a spirited defence of herself in 2.4. Like Buckingham's, it wins sympathy and compassion, but it does not prevail. Nor does the Cardinals' effort to persuade her against delaying the proceedings. If Katherine errs in blaming Wolsey for what is happening to her (2.4.73–82), she does not miss by much, in so far as Wolsey has been the willing instrument of Henry's wishes. Furthermore, she goes beyond the immediate to the general, reproaching him for his 'arrogancy, spleen, and pride' (108) and for his preoccupation

---

[1] Cf. Smidt, *Unconformities*, 151.

[2] Cf. Anderson, 130: 'Disjunctive truths and ambivalent moral attitudes are not what the play commits but what it studies, perhaps too truly'.

[3] Smidt, *Unconformities*, 150; he remarks that no open conflict between the two women occurs, nor are we led to expect one. Cf. Sen Gupta, *Shakespeare's Historical Plays*, 156, who notes also how Henry's feelings for both women co-exist: 'they do not attract and interpenetrate each other and produce a tragic tension'.

more with personal honour than his 'high profession spiritual' (115). While this attack gains her nothing, it affects the atmosphere of the trial, the audience's attitude, and doubtless Henry's, who in the next act finds tangible evidence of Katherine's truth.

When Katherine abruptly exits from the trial, retaining her dignity if not much else, she wins a heartfelt tribute from Henry, the man about to divorce her (130–40). It is by no means insincere; again, it is a reflection of the ambivalence prevalent in the play and, historically as well as dramatically, consistent with what Henry truly feels. Wolsey's appeal for exoneration from the charges Katherine has laid against him gives the King an opportunity to explain why he is proceeding as he is (164–227). He sounds convincing; but only a few moments before in actual playing time we heard how he bestowed title and riches upon Anne. The juxtaposition is of course deliberate, not so much to undercut Henry's position as to indicate its complexity and his own ambivalence.[1] By the time he finishes, we are almost persuaded that he means what he says:

> Prove but our marriage lawful, . . .
> . . . we are contented
> To wear our mortal state to come with her,
> Katherine, our queen, before the primest creature
> That's paragoned o'th' world.   (2.4.223–7)

But on reflection we know that he really does not want this proof. He wants Anne, and will have her.

By the end of the scene that much is clear. Wolsey is all but finished, though he does not know it: 'I may perceive', Henry says,

> These cardinals trifle with me. I abhor
> This dilatory sloth and tricks of Rome.
>   (2.4.232–4)

He is impatient for Cranmer's return with the proof he needs—that his marriage to Katherine is unlawful and he is free to marry Anne. He has begun to know himself and those around him and to take charge at last.

---

[1] On Henry's ambivalent motives, see Bliss, 'Wheel of Fortune', 7, who argues that 'Henry is more complicated that he would perhaps like to appear'. Cf. Smidt, *Unconformities*, 150: the ordering of scenes suggests Henry's 'double motive' for the divorce.

He therefore sends the Cardinals in 2.4 using bribes as well as threats to induce Katherine to accept a divorce (3.1.92–6). Outraged, she refuses and continues the dressing down she began at her trial along with a renewed defence of her position (97–136). Henry's knowledge of others has not yet extended so far as to understand his own wife. Although at the end of the scene she yields to Wolsey's blandishments and consents to listen to their counsels, nothing evidently results from their unreported conversation.

Katherine's defeat at her trial signals Wolsey's, just as Buckingham's signalled hers. But whereas Buckingham and Katherine feel their innocence deeply and assert it to the end,[1] Wolsey at length sees the folly of his ambition and repents. The perception does not come easily, but it does come. The cabal of the nobility that opens 3.2 actually has little to do with his fall, except dramatically to prepare for it. What fuels the nobles' growing antagonism is the knowledge that Henry has evidence against Wolsey that will undo him (3.2.20–40). We also learn—before Wolsey—that Henry has already married Anne and has given order for her coronation (41–6). Moreover, Cranmer has 'returned in his opinions', having satisfied Henry for his divorce, and is made Archbishop of Canterbury (64–5, 73–4). Henry has indeed taken charge of his own affairs and no longer depends on Wolsey, whom he now knows— and knows he cannot trust.

When Wolsey enters and meditates on whom the King should marry—the French King's sister, not Anne Boleyn—he unwittingly becomes a object of derision. Henry soon enlightens him, toying with him as he does so, and as he does so, Wolsey becomes alarmed and tries to deflect Henry from his predetermined purpose. Although there is much truth in what Wolsey claims he has done on the King's behalf (170–5, 191–200), it is not enough to counter the good he has done for himself. For that he is doomed. Briefly he thinks he can finesse the situation—until he reads the second paper Henry has given him (210–23). Then he knows certainly that it is all over. He has touched the highest point of all his greatness, he says, and from that meridian of his glory he hastes now to his setting (224–6).

---

[1] Bliss says that it is impossible to know any political or moral truth about Buckingham, though unlike almost everyone else, Katherine remains untouched by ambiguity ('Wheel of Fortune', 6, 10). Yet the question of her first marriage and its consummation is never resolved.

2. King Henry VIII giving Cardinal Wolsey a paper. (From Rowe's edition of 1709.)

Symbolic of the 'bright exhalation' of his fall, Wolsey at first fiercely opposes the lords who come for the Great Seal. But they are too much for him, listing his offences—the 'articles' collected from his life (294–5)—now in the King's hands. After his profession of innocence (301–3) and his defiance of their 'objections' (307–9), Wolsey stands silently as the lords itemize his misdeeds—until the Lord Chamberlain intervenes, imploring moderation. The confrontation ends with the demand that the Cardinal forfeit all his worldly possessions to the King. He has by now been thoroughly humbled and has nothing more to say as the lords scornfully depart.

Wolsey's farewell—not to the lords, but to his greatness—shows that he has at last come to know himself and his folly. He has been like 'little wanton boys' who swim on bladders far beyond their depth and now finds his ambition break under him, leaving him 'Weary and old with service to the mercy | Of a rude stream' (364–5). His is the old story of someone who 'hangs on princes' favours', though as churchman he recognizes that he should have known better.[1] Seeing clearly what he is and what he has been, he can honestly say to Cromwell that he is well and 'Never so truly happy', for the King has cured him of his ambition. Knowing himself, he is now at peace (377–81).

Despite his fall, Wolsey is still interested in the 'news abroad' (the Old Adam does not easily or quickly vanish).[2] Cromwell tells him that Sir Thomas More is now Lord Chancellor, that Cranmer has returned and is Archbishop of Canterbury, and that Henry and Anne have long been married in secret and she is about to be crowned (406–7). Wolsey is probably wrong in thinking that Anne was the 'weight' that pulled him down, though he is right that Henry has now gone beyond him (408–9). In exhorting Cromwell to 'Seek the King' (415), Wolsey still involves himself in power politics, but no longer for his own benefit. He knows where Cromwell's best advantage lies, and to his credit he has already put in a good word with Henry. If Wolsey was 'Lofty and sour to them that loved him not', as Griffith later says, yet to those who sought him out he was 'sweet as summer' (4.2.53–4), as this scene shows. It also shows what Griffith further says:

> His overthrow heaped happiness upon him;
> For then, and not till then, he felt himself
> And found the blessedness of being little.
>
> (4.2.64–6)

The mixed view we have of Wolsey both here and later in 4.2, as Katherine and Griffith speak of him, is the strongest indication that Shakespeare was not interested in emphasizing one side or another of his character but in revealing both, the 'mingled yarn'—good and ill together—that comprises the 'web' of human life.[3] Both the length and the centrality of 3.2 indicate the importance of Wolsey's moral regeneration, as Lee Bliss says,[4] and anticipate the

[1] Cf. Psalm 146: 3 (Geneva): 'Put not your trust in princes, nor in the son of man, for there is none help in him', and Psalm 118: 9: 'It is better to trust in the Lord than to have confidence in princes'. Wolsey's words echo these verses.

[2] Anderson notes the 'ambiguity, the *half*-heartedness', of Wolsey's previous renunciation. Although his last long speech in the scene is 'increasingly plain and "honest" ', it does not fully resolve the ambiguity of his awareness (pp. 150–1).

[3] *All's Well That Ends Well*, 4.3.74–5. Cf. Anderson, 151, on the 'epitaph to Wolsey's ambiguity' in the 'twin characterizations, one critical and one laudatory' in 4.2.

[4] 'Wheel of Fortune', 12.

movement toward political transcendence in Katherine's last scene. It also serves as a prologue to Anne's coronation: the gentlemen's reminiscence of Buckingham's fall enhances the juxtaposition of joy and sorrow (4.1.5–6). Inasmuch as 3.2 and 4.2 frame the coronation with expressions of disillusionment and rejection, they put into significant perspective the pomp and glory of monarchs and further encourage an ambivalent attitude.

Though his presence is invoked by others talking about him, Henry does not appear in Act 4. As elsewhere in Shakespeare's plays—*Richard II*, *Romeo and Juliet*, and *Hamlet*, for example—when the protagonist remains off-stage for a considerable time, his absence prefigures a change. Henry's next appearance, at 5.1.56, shows a difference, as his character has fully evolved.[1] Throughout this act, he is absolutely in charge of everything that happens, no longer dependent upon anyone for advice or counsel or acting in his place. He does not merely foil Gardiner's plot to undo Cranmer; in the process he demonstrates a consummate ability to engage with others in power politics and win at the odds. In the midst of it all, he is also preoccupied with the difficult labour of his queen and his hope for a viable male heir.

Aware of what the lords are planning against Cranmer, Henry goes along with them for a while. In the interim he lectures Cranmer on the ways of the world, in particular the ways of the political world in which the Archbishop is, willy-nilly, a player. Astonished at the man's innocence, Henry warns Cranmer how dangerous his 'state' stands; how powerful and numerous his enemies are; and how 'not ever | The justice and truth o'th' question carries | The dew o'th' verdict with it' (5.1.130–2). These words may recall Buckingham's fate, especially as Henry goes on to warn Cranmer about 'corrupt minds' that may suborn knaves to swear against him. 'Such things have been done', he says, possibly alluding consciously or otherwise to the Surveyor's testimony, although his more direct allusion is to Christ's indictment and execution (134–9). At the end, he reassures his friend and 'brother' (107) that he will not allow these enemies to prevail, giving Cranmer his ring as earnest of his protection.

---

[1] Cf. Anderson, 135: 'If Henry grows in stature, we do not see it happen. The changes he undergoes are credible as *facts* on stage, but their true meaning is ambivalence'.

And protect him he does. Outraged at the humiliation to which Gardiner and the others of the Council subject Cranmer, Henry first gives them enough rope, figuratively, to hang themselves. But he is nonetheless astonished at their behaviour (5.2.25–31). After they finally summon Cranmer to the Council chamber, they accuse him of heresy, although (in keeping with the dramatist's evident intention to eschew theological controversy) the forms of his heresy are not specified. Cranmer's eloquent defence avails him nothing, nor does his demand to face his accusers (66–82). At this point he catches on to what is happening and starts responding with calculated irony, particularly against his chief antagonist, Gardiner—again to no avail. When Cromwell presumes to intervene on his behalf, he too becomes the target of Gardiner's accusations, until the Lord Chancellor puts an end to the quarrels.

When the Councillors, refusing mercy, commit Cranmer to the Tower, he shows them the King's ring, and their whole attitude alters abruptly. A few moments later Henry takes command of the situation, scolding the lords for their behaviour and restoring Cranmer to his position of honour at the table. He reads the Councillors a lesson in humility and in the proper service of their sovereign. Through it all Henry shows them—and us—that he is now not only a king who reigns, but a king who rules. He is himself at last.[1]

The christening scene that ends the play is the final occasion for pageantry and display, but Cranmer's prophecy is its chief dramatic justification. Lee Bliss and Alexander Leggatt have shown how his utopian or ideal vision is a fitting conclusion, recounting the rise and fall pattern we have been observing and unifying the play by the shaping power of 'an art that coerces reality' and thereby helps us to understand it more closely.[2] Or, as Bliss says:

Shakespeare offers, in the form of an ideal, a solution to the political world's sickness and corruption and an escape from the endless repeti-

---

[1] Cf. Saccio, 211; Sen Gupta, *Shakespeare's Historical Plays*, 166; and Alexander Leggatt, '*Henry VIII* and the Ideal England', *SS* 38 (1985), 137: 'The play as a whole shows the emergence of Henry as the clear centre of authority in his kingdom, and the frustration of Wolsey's attempt to usurp that position for himself'. Cf. also Camille Wells Slights, 'The Politics of Conscience in *All Is True* (or *Henry VIII*)', *SS* 43 (1990), 59: 'Henry appears progressively more active and responsible'. Foakes, too (p. lxiii), notes Henry's 'growth in stature', his 'emergence into authority', often neglected in performance. For a contrary view, see Robert Ornstein, *A Kingdom for a Stage*, 215.

[2] Leggatt, 143.

tions of history. His paean to Elizabeth and James I cannot be confined to literally 'true' predictions of their actual reigns (already belied by the sublunar world of the original audience), or designed merely to feel nostalgic memories of Elizabeth and satisfy the reigning monarch's taste for flattery. Rather, this praise fulfills the didactic function of panegyric in the Renaissance: idealized portraits which heighten the subject's exemplary traits in order to incite emulation.[1]

What is the 'solution', the 'ideal' that Shakespeare offers in Cranmer's speech? It is summed up in the praise of Elizabeth:

> Truth shall nurse her,
> Holy and heavenly thoughts still counsel her.
> She shall be loved and feared. Her own shall bless her;
> Her foes shake like a field of beaten corn,
> And hang their heads with sorrow. Good grows with her.
> In her days every man shall eat in safety
> Under his own vine what he plants and sing
> The merry songs of peace to all his neighbours.
> God shall be truly known, and those about her
> From her shall read the perfect ways of honour
> And by those claim their greatness, not by blood.
>
> (5.4.28–38)

As Bliss says, we cannot take this as the literal 'truth', despite the play's alternative (or original) title 'All is True', nor was it intended as such. It is more an exhortation to the reigning monarch, James I (we recall that the play may have been designed for performance at court), a mirror held up to him of what a great king should be. Nor does Shakespeare sentimentalize this ideal: just as Elizabeth is both loved and *feared*, James too will have 'Peace, plenty, love, truth, *terror*' serve him (47–9; emphasis added). Moreover, through this account of the golden age the rhythms of time still beat.[2] Elizabeth must die—she must—Cranmer reiterates (59–60), though from her ashes will rise an heir 'As great in admiration as herself' (40–2). In this way 'humanity's endless, profitless cycle of rise and fall can be translated into the more miraculous image of the death and rebirth of "the maiden phoenix"'.[3]

---

[1] Bliss, 'Wheel of Fortune', 20. Cf. Felperin, *Shakespearean Romance*, 209–10, who therefore links the play with romance rather than history.

[2] Leggatt, 'Ideal England', 142.   [3] Bliss, 'Wheel of Fortune', 23.

'O Lord Archbishop', Henry begins his last speech,

> Thou hast made me now a man. Never before
> This happy child did I get anything.

$$(5.4.64-5)$$

True enough, but Henry is made a man more by his own growth and maturity than through the Archbishop's 'oracle', comforting as it may be. He is by no means the ideal ruler that Cranmer envisions, and may be little more than 'a thoroughly political, self-aggrandizing monarch'.[1] But he has become a successful and powerful king, and in the context that Shakespeare presents, that is something. Nothing further about a male heir is mentioned, the ostensible cause for the divorce, his marriage to Anne, and the break with Rome. Nor need it be. Shakespeare has history on his side, and through Cranmer's vision of the future he foretells a future that for this audience is already the past. But another future, already present, is also there and being formed, though Shakespeare like some others in his audience and among his colleagues will not live to see it completely unfold.

The Language of 'King Henry VIII'

Alfred, Lord Tennyson had an uncommonly good ear for verse, and it was he who suggested to Spedding that more than one hand was detectable in *King Henry VIII*. Spedding's tests, carried forward by others, support the hypothesis (see 'Authorship', above), but as Stanley Wells has argued, 'the authors worked closely enough together to achieve at least a superficial unity of tone for most of the play'.[2] Except for technical aspects of grammar and versification, which help distinguish the shares attributed to each

---

[1] Frank S. Cespedes, '"*We are one in fortunes*": The Sense of History in *Henry VIII*', *English Literary Renaissance*, 10 (1980), 414. Claiming that as early as 1.2 Henry decides for himself what is to be done, Cespedes argues that this fact 'negates any sense of [his] "development" or "education" which culminates in his rejection of Wolsey' (422). But his argument overlooks much else in 1.2 as well as in the rest of the play. Intent on seeing the drama as a veiled critique of the reign of James I, Stuart Kurland similarly concludes that '*Henry VIII* does not portray a monarch who excites admiration or inspires emulation', though he admits the 'occasional fine sentiments' that Henry professes ('*Henry VIII* and James I', 214).

[2] *Shakespeare: A Dramatic Life*, 381.

author, this overall unity of tone enables us here as elsewhere to refer to the language of the play as 'Shakespeare's'.

Indeed, some of the qualities of verse usually associated with Fletcher are also characteristic of Shakespeare's late plays. Maurice Hunt notes, for example, that the 'juxtaposition of limpid, sweet verse with rough, elliptical, often metaphorically opaque poetry', found in Fletcher's work and in Buckingham's valedictory scene (2.1), may also be found in *Cymbeline* and *The Tempest*. He compares Prospero's farewell to his art (5.1.33–87), which similarly breaks into two parts: the first 'quaint, nonelliptical', the second 'elliptical, stirred, writing with energy'.[1] The same sort of juxtaposition occurs later during Katherine's trial (2.4). Her first speeches, filled with pathos and rhythmically smooth, alter noticeably when Wolsey tells her that members of the consistory will speak for her, as her 'drops of tears | . . . turn to sparks of fire' (70–1).[2]

Two basic styles pervade the play, partly suggested by the juxtapositions just described. The first is the formal 'high' style appropriate to the court and its courtiers; the other is the more informal conversational style, also used by courtiers but on less ceremonious occasions. Shakespeare offers an example of the former when early in 1.1 Norfolk describes the meeting of the Kings of France and England at the Field of the Cloth of Gold to Buckingham, who was absent on that occasion:

> Then you lost
> The view of earthly glory. Men might say
> Till this time pomp was single, but now married   15
> To one above itself. Each following day
> Became the next day's master, till the last
> Made former wonders its. Today the French,
> All clinquant, all in gold, like heathen gods
> Shone down the English; and tomorrow they   20
> Made Britain India. Every man that stood
> Showed like a mine. Their dwarfish pages were
> As cherubins all gilt; the madams, too,
> Not used to toil, did almost sweat to bear
> The pride upon them, that their very labour   25

---

[1] *Shakespeare's Labored Art: Stir, Work, and the Late Plays* (New York, 1995), 203.

[2] Ibid., 204–5.

Was to them as a painting. Now this masque
Was cried incomparable, and th'ensuing night
Made it a fool and beggar. The two kings
Equal in lustre, were now best, now worst,
As presence did present them. Him in eye   30
Still him in praise, and being present both,
'Twas said they saw but one, and no discerner
Durst wag his tongue in censure. When these suns—
For so they phrase 'em—by their heralds challenged
The noble spirits to arms, they did perform   35
Beyond thought's compass, that former fabulous story
Being now seen possible enough, got credit
That *Bevis* was believed.

Norfolk weaves a description that repeatedly vies with itself, just as
the French and English vied with each other on the field. Inter-
woven within the description are metaphors and personifications
that require careful attention. At ll. 15–16 pomp becomes a single
person suddenly 'married' to a superior being so as to convey not
only union but elevation. The next lines continue the metaphor
and the paragraphing technique, ending with the terminal
position of, and thus the unusual stress on, 'its'. Norfolk then
becomes increasingly specific: the French, like 'heathen gods' in
their golden armour, outshone the English—until the next day,
when Britain became 'India' and showed 'like a mine'. Their
pages were golden cherubins; their ladies, overladen with costly
attire and cosmetics, blushed with their exertions. Each night's
revelry was declared unsurpassable, until the next night's made
the previous one seem paltry and foolish. And so the description,
to the ear as literally to the eye, moves forward and backward, up
to the climax, which argues the incredible credible.[1]

The speech is typical of Shakespeare's late style as seen in his
romances—much more so than the 'high' style of his earlier history plays—and appropriately in the context of the opening of 1.1.
But the rich and ceremonial rhetoric soon gives way to colloquial
condemnation—the blunter style of the nobles' animadversions
against Wolsey—as in Abergavenny's lines:

[1] Hunt (ibid., 200) argues that by his choice of diction Shakespeare implicitly
criticizes the opulence that Norfolk ostensibly celebrates. He cites the 'heathen
gods', the 'dwarfish pages', and the ladies unused to toil as examples of the way the
author undercuts the tenor of the piece.

> I cannot tell
> What heaven hath given him: let some graver eye
> Pierce into that; but I can see his pride
> Peep through each part of him. Whence has he that?
> If not from hell, the devil is a niggard
> Or has given all before, and he begins
> A new hell in himself.　　　　　(1.1.66–72)

The colloquialisms—'the devil is a niggard', 'Peep through each part of him'—bring the high-flown language Norfolk has used previously crashing down.

The image of the ladies labouring and sweating under their cumbersome, expensive attire conveys the idea of earthly pomp as a heavy burden that ambitious mortals must bear. The imagery recurs later in the play, as when the Old Lady teases Anne with Henry's expectations: 'Have you limbs | To bear that load of title?' she asks, referring to the possibility of Anne's becoming queen (2.3.38–9).[1] In the next act, Wolsey acknowledges the numerous favours that Henry has loaded upon him, along with the duties to the state that he has also borne (3.2.145–80). Only afterwards does he realize his folly, but he misattributes the 'weight' that pulled him down to Anne's influence with Henry (3.2.408). Nevertheless, the relief he feels after the King's dismissal is great, as he tells Cromwell:

> The King has cured me.
> I humbly thank his grace, and from these shoulders—
> These ruined pillars—out of pity taken
> A load would sink a navy: too much honour.
> O, 'tis a burden, Cromwell, 'tis a burden
> Too heavy for a man that hopes for heaven.
> 　　　　　　　　　(3.2.381–6)

The overload of honour, a major theme in the play, is throughout represented by weighty burdens.[2] Although Henry heaps honour upon Cranmer by making him Archbishop of Canterbury, the cleric shows a contrasting ability to bear them. The good he stands on, he tells Henry in Act 5, is his 'truth and honesty' (5.1.123), and his labour, he tells his accusers, 'Was ever to do well' (5.2.71).

---

[1] Hunt, *Shakespeare's Labored Art*, 201.

[2] Caroline Spurgeon, *Shakespeare's Imagery and What It Tells Us* (Cambridge, 1935), 255.

Since Shakespeare had developed the imagery, or conceit, of the body politic in one of his last tragedies, *Coriolanus*,[1] he does not repeat it in *King Henry VIII*. But body imagery pervades the play, which is clearly concerned with the health and welfare of the state and the ability of its ruler to govern it well.[2] Similarly, tempest, or storm, imagery, which appears frequently in the late plays, occurs in *King Henry VIII*, though more subtly. No actual tempest rages, such as we find in *Pericles* or *The Tempest*, but storms of doubt afflict Henry, as he ponders the validity of his marriage to Katherine. He tells the members of the court at Blackfriars after Katherine leaves the trial, referring to the concerns the Bishop of Bayonne had raised:

> This respite shook
> The bosom of my conscience, entered me,
> Yea, with a spitting power, and made to tremble
> The region of my breast, which forced such way
> That many mazed considerings did throng
> And pressed in with this caution. (2.4.178–83)

Thus shaken, Henry wrestled with the problem, considering the failure of his marriage to produce any viable male offspring as the punishment of heaven. From there he pondered the danger to his kingdom, a danger he found overwhelming:

> Thus hulling in
> The wild sea of my conscience, I did steer
> Toward this remedy, whereupon we are
> Now present here together—that's to say
> I meant to rectify my conscience, which
> I then did feel full sick, and yet not well,
> By all the reverend fathers of the land
> And doctors learned. (2.4.196–203)

If Henry's metaphor is confused—a hulled ship cannot, by definition, be steered—it may testify to his sorely conflicted thoughts. The storms of doubt he entertains, however, are but the forerunners, as his audience well knew, of the storms of state that followed later, once the Reformation in England began to make its way through the realm.

A storm of another sort, though subtly related to this one,

---

[1] See 1.1.94–156.   [2] See Spurgeon, 253–8.

occurs off-stage in 4.1, as described by the Third Gentleman. This
is the commotion caused by Anne's beauty, when she stops to rest
during her coronation procession:

> such a noise arose
> As the shrouds make at sea in a stiff tempest,
> As loud and to as many tunes. Hats, cloaks—
> Doublets, I think—flew up, and had their faces
> Been loose, this day they had been lost. Such joy
> I never saw before. Great-bellied women
> That had not half a week to go, like rams
> In the old time of war would shake the press
> And make 'em reel before 'em. No man living
> Could say 'This is my wife' there, all were woven
> So strangely in one piece.   (4.1.73–83)

This storm anticipates the commotion that the christening causes
in 5.3,[1] when the Porter and his Man have all they can do to control the mob pressing to come within the gates. Except for the Old
Lady's wit, this is the only comic episode in the play, though of a
low order, to be sure. Both 4.1 and 5.3 are scenes of great joy; as
the Third Gentleman remarks, Anne's presence weaves the crowd
into one piece, performing a royal version of woman's traditional
work—gathering diverse threads into a unified national garment.
The homonym *piece/peace* at line 83 may allude to the social harmony Shakespeare's audience liked to imagine was the legacy of
Anne Boleyn's daughter, which Cranmer prophesies at the end of
the play.[2]

Commentators are fond of showing how in some places the
poetry of *King Henry VIII* closely follows the text of the sources. To
cite just one example, compare the following passage from
Foxe's *Acts and Monuments* with the relevant lines in the play
(5.2.169–80):

Ah my Lords, I thought I had had wiser men of my council than I now find
you. What discretion was this in you, thus to make the Primate of the
realm, and one of you in office, to wait at the council chamber door
amongst serving men? You might have considered that he was a councillor as well as you, and you had no such commission of me so to handle

---

[1] The reference to the 'great-bellied women' at l. 78 may allude to the historical
fact that Anne was already several months pregnant at her coronation.

[2] See Hunt, *Shakespeare's Labored Art*, 215–16.

him. I was content that you should try him as a councillor, and not as a mean subject. But now I well perceive that things be done against him maliciously, and if some of you might have had your minds, you would have tried him to the uttermost. (1694)

Close as the lines in the play are to this excerpt, elsewhere they reveal a freer hand in adaptation, as at 5.1.96–117. Shakespeare was no slavish follower of his sources.

A more important aspect of the language in *King Henry VIII* is the frequent allusions to Scripture. While many go unnoticed by modern audiences, Shakespeare's playgoers would have grasped most, if not all. The allusiveness is by no means unique to this play; it is found throughout the canon and, as Naseeb Shaheen comments (196), it is remarkably present in scenes attributed to either Shakespeare or Fletcher—another indication of the play's unity of tone. In a drama that involves a number of important clerics—Wolsey, Gardiner, Cranmer—it is hardly surprising that Scripture should be frequently referred to, but as in Shakespeare's other plays, other characters allude to Scripture as well. Even minor comic characters, like the Porter and his Man, can allude to biblical events and theological concepts.[1] Many references are to the Psalms and the Gospels, like Katherine's allusion to the lily of the fields:

> Like the lily,
> That once was mistress of the field and flourished,
> I'll hang my head and perish.   (3.1.150–2)[2]

The function of these references is to invoke a wider dimension of experience, usually one that parallels that of the character making the allusion. For example, as he counsels Cromwell, Wolsey compares his fall to Lucifer's:

> Mark but my fall, and that that ruined me.
> Cromwell, I charge thee, fling away ambition.
> By that sin fell the angels.   (3.2.440–2)[3]

Similarly, Cranmer alludes to Luke 22: 31 when Henry informs him of the Council's charges against him:

> I humbly thank your highness,
> And am right glad to catch this good occasion

---

[1] See 5.3.21, 61, and Commentary.
[2] Shaheen cites Matthew 6: 30 and Psalm 103: 15–16 (see Commentary).
[3] See Shaheen, 206–7, and Commentary.

> Most throughly to be winnowed, where my chaff
> And corn shall fly asunder.   (5.1.109–12)

But Henry, too, well-schooled in religion, can also refer to Scripture and draw a pointed parallel between Cranmer's position and Jesus' later in their dialogue:

> Ween you of better luck,
> I mean in perjured witness, than your master,
> Whose minister you are, whiles here he lived
> Upon this naughty earth?   (5.1.136–9)

Finally, in the christening scene, Cranmer looks forward to a time of peace and plenty in the reign of Elizabeth, drawing a comparison between England under her rule and the kingdoms of Judah and Israel in biblical times:

> In her days every man shall eat in safety
> Under his own vine what he plants and sing
> The merry songs of peace to all his neighbours.
> (5.4.33–5)

'King Henry VIII' in Performance

After the disastrous fire of 29 June 1613 (see p. 17), the Globe was speedily rebuilt and completed by 30 June 1614. No record of another performance of *King Henry VIII* exists, however, until 1628. Shortly before his assassination in that year, George Villiers, Duke of Buckingham (b. 1592), went to the Globe to see this play, 'bespoken of purpose by himselfe'. Although he stayed only until the Duke's farewell speech before his execution, he went again a few days later, and again left after Buckingham's final speeches.[1]

Restoration and Eighteenth-century Productions. The next record of performance does not appear until after the Restoration of 1660 and the reopening of the theatres, when it was assigned to Sir William Davenant as one of a number of plays by Shakespeare that

---

[1] G. E. Bentley, *The Jacobean and Caroline Stage*, 7 vols. (Oxford, 1941–68), i. (1941) 22–3, 128. The information comes from a newsletter dated August 1628. The play was performed on 29 July. Bentley misdates the assassination 23 August. A favourite of both James I and Charles I, Buckingham had become immensely unpopular with Parliament for his mismanagement of foreign affairs and particularly the wars with Spain and France in the 1620s.

he was licensed to produce at his theatre in Lincoln's Inn Fields. John Downes writes of the play as performed in mid-December 1663:

This play, by order of Sir William Davenant, was all new clothed in proper habits: the King's was new, all the Lords, the Cardinals, the Bishops, the Doctors, Proctors, Lawyers, Tip-staves, new scenes: The part of the King was so right and justly done by Mr. Betterton, he being Instructed in it by Sir William, who had it from old Mr. Lowen, that had his instructions from Mr. Shakespeare himself, that I dare and will aver, none can, or will come near him in this Age, in the performance of that part: Mr. Harris's, performance of Cardinal Wolsey, was little Inferior to that, he doing it with such just state, port and mein, that I dare affirm, none hitherto has equall'd him; . . . Every part by the great care of Sir William, being exactly perform'd; it being all new clothed and new scenes; it continued acting 15 days together with general applause.[1]

Worth noting in Downes's account (which gives the cast names for the more important roles) is not only the repeated reference to new costumes, but also to the tradition of acting handed down from the King's Men and from Shakespeare himself through John Lowen (or Lowin) a member of that company.[2] Pepys saw a performance and did not much care for it (he could be a severe critic),[3] but to judge from an allusion to it in George Villiers's *The Rehearsal* (1672), the production was magnificent and became a theatrical tradition.[4] When Pepys saw it again in December 1668, he was pleased 'better than I ever expected, with the history and shows of it'.[5]

The revival of the public theatres after the Restoration saw not only the emergence of actresses instead of boys performing women's roles, but also some advances in staging, such as the advent of movable scenery, which became more elaborate as technology improved over the next two centuries. 'Theatre is, and certainly in the eighteenth century was, a business', George Winchester Stone, Jr., reminds us in an insightful essay on 'The Making of the Repertory' in the Augustan and High Georgian

---

[1] John Downes, *Roscius Anglicanus*, ed. Montague Summers (1929; repr. New York, 1968), 24.

[2] Lowen may have played the title role in *King Henry VIII* after Burbage died in the decades before the theatres were closed. See E. K. Chambers, *The Elizabethan Stage* (Oxford, 1923), ii. 328–9, and Bentley, ii. 499–508.

[3] Cited by Odell, i. 37–8.   [4] Summers's note, 183.

[5] Odell, i. 179.

periods, which were dominated by Colley Cibber and David Garrick, respectively.[1] Interestingly, audiences seem to have preferred old plays to new ones, although revivals often involved innovations of various kinds—utterly different from today's motion picture revivals or television reruns.

Using the Index to *The London Stage: 1660–1800* (ed. Ben Ross Schneider, Jr.) as a basis for his calculations, Stone has tabulated by number of performances the most popular plays during the two periods he has examined. While comedies far outstripped tragedies (and other serious drama, such as tragicomedies and histories, which he groups with them) in popularity in both periods, interest in the latter was not insignificant. In the Augustan period, Farquhar's *The Recruiting Officer* was the most frequently performed play (with 164 performances), followed by *Hamlet* (with 151). Among other Shakespearian plays included among the eighteen mainpieces with more than a hundred performances, Stone lists *Macbeth* (132), *Julius Caesar* (105), and the operatic *Tempest* (102). Among the twenty-three pieces that enjoyed more than seventy performances, he lists *King Lear* (87), *1 Henry IV* (85), *The Merry Wives of Windsor* (74), and *King Henry VIII* (72).[2] In the High Georgian period, performances of all plays generally increased, though tastes did not alter very much. Gay's *The Beggar's Opera* was by far the most popular (395 performances), with Shakespeare's *Romeo and Juliet* (335) not far behind. *King Henry VIII* improved slightly with 82 performances. We should bear in mind that the texts of these plays, not excepting *King Henry VIII*,[3] frequently departed from those found in the Folio of 1623, most notoriously in the example of *King Lear*, which was heavily rewritten by Nahum Tate and held the stage, in one form or another, from 1681 well into the nineteenth century.

[1] In *The London Theatre World: 1660–1800*, ed. Robert D. Hume (Carbondale, Ill., 1980), 181.

[2] Ibid., 197.

[3] Davies laments the omission of 3.1, for example, in the representation, because it was regarded as 'tedious and unnecessary', though as he says it 'farther displays Queen Katherine's temper and disposition, and contains many characteristical features of that unhappy lady'. See Thomas Davies, *Dramatic Miscellanies*, 3 vols. (1784), i. 391, and cf. Hogan, i. 204, for excisions in the 1734 text used for productions beginning in 1705, where all of 4.1 was omitted except for the 'dumb show' of the Coronation. For later adaptations and their excisions based on the 1762 and later texts used for productions, where again most of 4.1 and much else is cut, see Hogan, ii. 294.

Acting styles also underwent change during the eighteenth century. Betterton's own style changed over his fifty-year career on the stage, but at his most mature his acting was marked 'by restraint, dignity, and subdued fervor, varied as necessary by a passionate forcefulness'. He 'acted much with his eyes' and practised before a mirror.[1] Coming after him, James Quin, who played Henry VIII often between 1726 and 1751,[2] developed a more exaggerated style, which gradually took over in the middle years of the century, until Charles Macklin and David Garrick appeared and could persuade some actors to abandon their excesses in favour of a more natural representation.[3] By the time of Garrick's retirement in 1776, John Philip Kemble had become a leading actor whose style was 'neoclassical in its accent on dignity, on carefully planned and minimal action, on rhetorical speech, on claptraps and addresses to the audience'.[4] Throughout the century formal oratory and acting were linked, so that Edmund Burke, for example, could praise Garrick as 'a great master of eloquence' who had taught him, as he had taught others, the elements of rhetoric.[5] Influencing the acting styles by this time and into the next century also were the much larger theatres that required actors to project into vast spaces—a problem that they often find today in such theatres as the Royal Shakespeare Theatre in Stratford-upon-Avon and the Royal National Theatre's Olivier stage.

Queen Katherine's role as portrayed by eighteenth-century actresses won high praise. Davies comments on Mary Porter, who enacted the role from 1722 to 1733, and Hannah Pritchard, who played her from 1744 to 1761:

Mrs. Pritchard's Queen Katherine has been much approved, and especially in the scene of the trial. She certainly was in behaviour easy, and in speaking natural and familiar; but the situation of the character required more force in utterance and dignity in action. Mrs. Porter's manner was elevated to the rank of the great person she represented. Her kneeling to the King was the effect of majesty in distress and humbled royalty; it was

---

[1] Philip H. Highfill, Jr., 'Performers and Performing', in Hume, *London Theatre World*, 163.

[2] See Hogan, i. 204–17; ii. 295.

[3] Highfill, 'Performers', 163–6.

[4] Alan Downer, 'Nature to Advantage Dressed: Eighteenth Century Acting', *PMLA* 58 (1943), 1021.

[5] Highfill, 'Performers', 166–7.

3. Sarah Siddons as Queen Katherine during her trial (2.4). John Philip Kemble as Cardinal Wolsey, Stephen Kemble as Henry VIII, and Charles Knyvet as Cardinal Campeius. (From Harlow's painting in the Garrick Club, London.)

indeed highly affecting; the suppression of her tears when she reproached the Cardinal, bespoke a tumultuous conflict in her mind, before she burst into the manifestation of indignity, she felt in being obliged to answer so unworthy an interrogator. (i. 385)

In the next generation John Philip Kemble revived the play in 1788 after a twenty-year lapse, casting his sister, Sarah Siddons, in the role on Dr Johnson's recommendation. She was magnificent. She so terrified the Duke of Buckingham's Surveyor when she confronted him, for example, that the actor declared that he would never again face her before the footlights. But she effectively modulated her authoritarian aspect by 4.2, when Katherine appears for the last time near death, and played the scene 'with a realism that broke all the rules of "splendid, formal" acting'.[1]

Indeed, Mrs Siddons is responsible for a revolution in the representation of *King Henry VIII*, restoring the balance among principal characters that earlier eighteenth-century productions had lost in their emphasis upon the male leads and, even more, the spectacle

---

[1] Speaight, 41; cf. Richmond, 47, 51. Curiously, as J. W. Cole notes in commenting on Katherine's role, Kemble omitted 3.1. Cole suspects that Kemble did this because it interfered with his Wolsey and excised it from jealousy; Cole blames his sister's complacency for permitting the cut. See Cole, *The Life and Times of Charles Kean, F.S.A.*, 2 vols. (1859), ii. 148.

provided by the pageant scenes. Hugh Richmond argues for her even greater accomplishment, stressing the 'feminist' interpretation that has continued to the present day. 'In the course of defining her own role', he says, Mrs Siddons 'required of her fellow actors a shift in performance style towards the less "macho" mode of interpreting Henry which remains identifiable in many twentieth-century productions of the play'.[1] Katherine became her favourite part, rivalling the success she achieved in the far different role of Lady Macbeth. Her interpretation is best characterized by a naturalness of manner, and she is credited far more than her brother with the play's direction, which included her reforming influence against the extravagant costumes and coiffures of the day in favour of simpler fashions.[2] Her enactment of Katherine not only earned high praise, but by the middle of the next century it had influenced critical interpretation regarding the importance of the role.

Charles Kean and the Nineteenth Century. That century is well known for the historical authenticity it brought, or tried to bring, to Shakespearian representation, as in the productions directed by Charles Kean. Earlier, though Henry and Wolsey might be costumed according to portraits by Holbein and others, the courtiers assumed the dress of their time, as they did at the Globe (see Fig. 2, above). But a growing antiquarian interest led to staging more carefully reflecting the actual historical period, whenever possible. Increases in technology also led to more elaborate scenic displays, and large numbers of supers crowded the huge stages on which plays were now performed. To accommodate time required for the elaborate scene changes, texts were severely cut, even as actor-managers, like Macready, restored as far as possible Shakespeare's texts from the revisions and 'improvements' foisted upon them previously. *King Henry VIII* was no exception.[3]

Charles Kean's highly successful production that ran for nearly one hundred consecutive nights, beginning 16 May 1855, is just one outstanding example of this nineteenth-century dramaturgy.

---

[1] Richmond, 42.

[2] Ibid., 48, citing James Boaden, *Memoirs of Mrs Siddons* (1827), 237.

[3] See Richmond, 55. Although *Henry VIII* was cut, often severely in the later acts, its structure was not otherwise altered, as in the redactions of *Richard III*, *Romeo and Juliet*, and *King Lear*.

Kean himself played Wolsey and his wife, Ellen Tree, who had played Anne in Kemble's production, played Katherine, admirably following the example set by Mrs Siddons.[1] Presented with a wealth of scenery, costumes, and effects, Kean's *King Henry VIII* inaugurated a 'rapid succession of Shakespearean revivals that brought to the theatre uninterrupted acclaim and prosperity'.[2] But while historical authenticity was a goal,[3] fidelity to the text was not or perhaps could not be. Severe cuts had to be made—in the text, but not in personnel. Although the play requires twenty to twenty-five supers, an unusually large number, for the processional scenes, Kean and his followers multiplied these many times over. In Odell's view, little more than a skeleton of the original was presented—'all that is dramatically feasible'—that is, the scenes that bear on the tragedy of the King, the Queen, and Wolsey. 'They are diminished greatly in substance, but the spirit remains.'[4] Perhaps the most notable inclusion was the enactment of Queen Katherine's vision in 4.2, which had not been staged for a century or more.[5] Kean retained the christening of Princess Elizabeth in the last act, but not much else, arguing that 'Any further addition would extend the presentation beyond reasonable limits'.[6] In Act 5 Kean nevertheless introduced his favourite device of a moving panorama of London as it appeared in the reign of Henry VIII.[7] Ellen Terry, who

[1] See Cole, *Charles Kean*, ii. 149–50. Cole claims that 'in simple pathos, in natural bursts of indignation when urged beyond patience, in the gentle, unartificial, and purely woman-like features of the character' she surpassed her predecessor.

[2] Odell, ii. 289.

[3] See Kean's Preface to his edition in the facsimile reprint published by Cornmarket Press (1970). He generally follows Cavendish, whom he regards as reliable in his descriptions of many events, such as the feast in 1.4. Extensive 'Historical Notes' follow each act in addition to the footnotes in the text.

[4] Odell, ii. 290.

[5] Odell, ii. 336. Odell includes a sketch from the *Illustrated London News*, which he says gives 'but a faint impression of this scene', graphic though it is. Another restoration is that of 3.1, omitted in earlier productions.

[6] Cited by Odell, ibid., from Kean's Preface, p. viii. My collation shows that Kean cut 5.1.1–55, 56, 61–72a, 74b–76a, 84–5, 89, 95b–97, 102b–109a, 112b–114a, 121b–122a, 126b–143a, 145b–153a, [5.2.194–201 interpolated here], 154b–158a, 165b–166a, 167b–169a, [5.2.212–13 interpolated here]; all of 5.2–3, replaced by the 'Moving Panorama'; 5.4.12–14a, 21, 23b–25a, 32b–54a, 64–5, 68b–72; entire Epilogue. This illustrates one way that *King Henry VIII* was adapted for the nineteenth-century stage.

[7] The panorama, copied from a drawing made by Van Den Wynyerde in 1543, replaced 5.2–3. Odell describes it, ii. 338; see also 332–9 for more details of this production.

made her debut in a revival in 1858 at the age of six as one of the angels in the Vision Scene, vividly recalled the production at the Princess's Theatre and gave it superlative accolades for the beauty of the representation and the care given to every detail. The press reviews of the time were equally enthusiastic.[1]

Kean's production of *King Henry VIII* may epitomize the grandest among nineteenth-century productions, surpassed in splendour only by Henry Irving's at the Lyceum Theatre in 1892. Irving played Wolsey, one of his best roles, and Ellen Terry Katherine. Forbes-Robertson was Buckingham and William Terriss the King. It was Irving's last really successful Shakespeare revival, running (with a summer intermission) for 203 performances, and some claim that it was his greatest theatrical achievement.[2] He kept most of the first three acts intact, but severely cut the rest, especially all the matter concerning the conspiracy against Cranmer.[3] Lavish as the production was and immensely popular, it lost money.[4] Justifying his extravagance, his grandson writes that Irving was imbued 'with the infectious pomp of Wolsey' and 'assumed his habit of princely liberality'.[5] Indeed, he so immersed himself in the role that he seemed a reincarnation of the man who once controlled the destinies of England during one of its most momentous epochs. But his greatest gift was in portraying the two sides of Wolsey, the good and the bad, this dual state of mind accounting for some of Irving's 'subtlest and most finished touches'.[6]

King Henry VIII also enjoyed success elsewhere than the London stage. The play was not unknown in the provinces or abroad, especially America.[7] At the Park Theatre in New York, which opened in 1798, the productions of *As You Like It*, *Hamlet*, and *Henry VIII* were said to have surpassed for elegance and effect anything

[1] Odell, ii. 337.   [2] Ibid., ii. 387.

[3] Ibid., ii. 403–4. For detailed descriptions of Acts 1 to 3, see 444–5. Irving retained 4.2 including the Vision, but cut all of 5.1–3.

[4] Austin Brereton, *The Life of Henry Irving*, 2 vols. (1908), ii. 167–8; cited by Odell, ii. 445–6.

[5] Laurence Irving, *Henry Irving: The Actor and His World* (New York, 1952), 541.

[6] Brereton, *Irving*, ii. 168–9. Cf. William Winter, *Shakespeare on the Stage* (New York, 1911), 545–8.

[7] See Sybil Rosenfeld, *Strolling Plays & Drama in the Provinces, 1660–1765* (Cambridge, 1939), for example, for performances in Yorkshire, 141, 164; in Bath, 200–1, 203.

ever seen before on those shores.[1] Early in the next century the impresario Stephen Price brought George Frederick Cooke to America to play Shakespearian and other roles. Among them was Henry VIII, which he played in 1811 at the Park.[2] Charles Kemble and his daughter, Fanny, performed at the same theatre on 29 April 1834. The occasion is noteworthy not only for Fanny's comparative youth as Katherine—she was only twenty-three—but for the introduction of Handel's song, 'Angels Ever Bright and Fair', sung by Emma Wheatley during the Vision Scene.[3] In midcentury, playing opposite Charles Macready in England, Charlotte Cushman, the great American actress, first assayed the role of Queen Katherine. It soon became one of her most notable triumphs, both in London and in New York, rivalling her success (like Sarah Siddons's before her) as Lady Macbeth. Of her performance, William Winter has the highest praise:

Charlotte Cushman as Queen Katherine was the consummate image of sovereignty and noble womanhood, austere yet sweetly patient, in circumstances of cruel injustice and bitter affliction. Her identification with the essential nature of the injured Queen was so complete that it made the spectators of the performance forget the stage and feel that they were looking upon a pathetic experience of actual life. . . . Only a woman of the loftiest spirit could thus have interpreted and made actual Shakespeare's beautiful conception.[4]

The Twentieth Century. The triumphs as well as the excesses of nineteenth-century productions of *King Henry VIII* culminated in Herbert Beerbohm Tree's staging at His Majesty's Theatre in 1910. Producing the play seems to have become a process of outdoing whatever extravagance, usually in the name of historical authenticity, theatrical illusionism had hitherto achieved. As

[1] Speaight, 71. Cf. Winter, *Shakespeare on the Stage*, 537–40. The first performance at the Park was 13 May 1799, acted as a benefit for Mrs Barrett, who played Katherine opposite her husband, Giles Leonard Barrett, as Wolsey. According to Winter (537), *King Henry VIII* was not at any time especially popular in America, a comment that remains accurate to this day.

[2] Charles Shattuck, *Shakespeare on the American Stage*, 2 vols. (Washington, DC, 1976, 1987), i. 31, 35; also Winter, *Shakespeare on the Stage*, 538.

[3] Winter, *Shakespeare on the Stage*, 538–9. Wheatley herself played Katherine four years later at the National Theatre in New York at the age of sixteen.

[4] Ibid., 554. Following Fanny Kemble, Cushman also used Handel's song in the Vision Scene, sung off-stage (557). Cf. Speaight, 78–9, who says she also won acclaim playing Wolsey.

Richmond notes, when Tree revived his production in New York six years later, he shipped 135 pieces of furniture and over 375 costumes, shared by a cast of about 172. He was determined above all 'to give an absolute reproduction of the Renaissance' and accordingly 'ransacked every authority and obtained the most astonishing exactitude'.[1] Tree himself played Wolsey both in London and New York and, like Irving, made it the dominant role, designed to match Katherine's in psychological interest and, moreover, to reveal the kinds of 'ambivalence and unpredictability of temperament' for which the text gives ample warrant.[2] But however historically authentic the staging may have been, textually it was anything but. Tree cut nearly half the lines, including all of the last act; moreover, in Act 4 he reversed the order of scenes, presenting Anne's coronation after Katherine's death vision. While this alteration may have afforded an upbeat conclusion replacing that of the christening, by juxtaposition the coronation thus also became Katherine's second death vision, anticipating Anne's fall as well as her own.[3]

Tree's other innovations—his use of Wolsey's Jester for the Prologue and as a choric figure later, the representation of Anne as 'outrageous flirt', the use of a modified apron stage designed by William Poel—deserve more attention than can be given here.[4] Their influence on twentieth-century productions and theatre architecture may be debated. In any event, reaction eventually set in through scaled down productions, occasioned as much by the economics of theatrical presentation as by a desire to return to the original script. One interesting influence, however, cannot be gainsaid, and paradoxically it concerns a different medium—film. In cooperation with W. G. Barker, Tree filmed five scenes of his production in 1911, and according to film historians, although the film—silent, of course—lasted only about twenty-five minutes (the normal length for such features then), it paved the way not only for

[1] Richmond, 57, quoting from Tree's press conference on 26 July 1910.

[2] Ibid., 59.

[3] Richmond, 61; Cary Mazer, *Shakespeare Refashioned: Elizabethan Plays on Edwardian Stages* (Ann Arbor, Mich., 1981), 29. Despite the cuts, performances ran to over three hours (Richmond, 66). See also Barbara Hodgdon, *The End Crowns All: Closure and Contradiction in Shakespeare's History* (Princeton, 1991), 217–18.

[4] See Richmond, 61–73, and Tree's book, *Henry VIII and his Court* (1910), which his biographer, Madeleine Bingham, discusses in '*The Great Lover*' (New York, 1979), 191–6.

other cinematic renditions of the reign of Henry VIII (for example, Charles Laughton in *The Life and Times of Henry VIII*), but also for the 'historical film spectacular', of which it became the progenitor.[1]

Among the most important twentieth-century productions of *King Henry VIII* undoubtedly are those directed by Tyrone Guthrie at Stratford-upon-Avon in 1949 (revived in 1950 and again in the coronation year, 1953), Trevor Nunn's for the Royal Shakespeare Company (1969), Kevin Billington's for the BBC TV Shakespeare series (1978), Howard Davies's also for the RSC (1983), and Gregory Doran's for the RSC at the Swan Theatre (1996). Richmond gives full accounts and analyses of all of these except the last, produced after his book was published.[2] Guthrie, who first directed the play in 1933 at Sadler's Wells, wins credit for restoring the play's waning popularity with his 1949 production by maintaining in it a very high energy level replacing the florid historicism of Charles Kean, Irving, Tree, and their followers. He presented a nearly complete text, and minor characters received more directorial attention than ever, evoking a social dimension that stressed human relationships over the physical texture of a culture.[3] Anthony Quayle played the vigorous Henry of the Holbein portraits, whereas Diana Wynyard, perceptibly older than Quayle, was deliberately cast as Katherine. In this production, as in Betterton's, Henry was the dominant and unifying figure. The single, permanent set behind a large apron stage with no curtains or scene changes was another throwback to earlier designs, integrating the Elizabethan platform stage with the modern proscenium tradition.[4]

---

[1] Richmond, 69–71.

[2] In his Appendix A, 146–7, Richmond lists over thirty major productions of the play, giving dates, directors, and principals; and in Appendix B, 147–50, he lists the casts of productions he discusses in detail. See also *Shakespeare around the Globe*, ed. S. L. Leiter *et al.* (1986), 245–55.

[3] Richmond, 75. See also Muriel St Clare Byrne's review in *SS* 3 (1950), 120–9, from which Richmond quotes substantially, and Ralph Berry, '"My Learned and Well-Beloved Servant Cranmer": Guthrie's *Henry VIII*', in *Shakespearean Illuminations*, ed. Jay L. Halio and Hugh Richmond (Newark, Del., 1998), 309–16.

[4] Richmond, 77–8. Margeson (NCS, 53) regards the single, carefully constructed stage set permitting rapid and fluid movement as Guthrie's most important contribution to the play's stage history. It was continued in Michael Benthall's production for the Old Vic in 1958, with John Gielgud as Wolsey, Dame Edith Evans as Katherine, and Harry Andrews as Henry VIII. Unfortunately, clumsy use of back curtains and blackouts marred the staging of the otherwise impressive production: see Roy Walker, 'The Whirligig of Time: A Review of Recent Productions', *SS* 12 (1959), 122–6. Walker suggests that Gielgud should have doubled as both Wolsey and

4. Donald Sinden as King Henry, Peggy Ashcroft as Queen Katherine, and Brewster Mason as Wolsey in the Royal Shakespeare Company's production (1969), directed by Trevor Nunn.

Reaction breeds reaction; and directors of Shakespearian drama perennially seek to 'make it new'. The justification for this is not merely to give a fresh look to productions, but to find new insights and meaning in the plays. If Guthrie's productions were reactions against the excesses of his predecessors, then Trevor Nunn's was a reaction against Guthrie's. Where Guthrie's delighted in bustle, humour, spectacular costumes, and innovative staging, Nunn's went to the opposite extreme of sombre and austere stage sets and Brechtian effects, such as the use of pop-up placards bearing modernistic news-reports of the plot (dropped in the 1970 London revival at the Aldwych Theatre). Characterized by such stage 'minimalism', the production focused intensely on the actors' representation of their roles and the development of their psychological complexity.[1]

Cranmer. Doubling, he says, would have eliminated the imbalance of many performances (where a lesser actor usually enacts Cranmer) and have illuminated the whole pattern of the play, showing the development of the Church into the Reformation.

[1] Richmond, 92–5.

Donald Sinden as King Henry was again the main figure, more conspicuously so without the stage business and attention to minor characters Guthrie had introduced. Instead of the Wolsey–Henry conflict, turmoil was centred within the King himself; and dropping both Prologue and Epilogue, Nunn had the King open and close the play, a solitary figure whose silence nevertheless spoke volumes.[1] Peggy Ashcroft's Katherine was another superb achievement, reviving qualities that Mrs Siddons had long ago brought to the role. The quick intelligence she exhibited in penetrating to others' motives was immediately apparent, even as she refused to compromise her own conduct with Henry, whom she loves, or Wolsey, whom she despises. Ashcroft so entered the role that she often brought additional lines to rehearsals from transcripts of Katherine's trial or from the Queen's letters and tried to put them into the text, causing confrontations with her director.[2] In performance, she was 'sharp, precise and revealing the humanity under the surface regality', offering a three-dimensional portrait that showed Katherine's 'resilient toughness as well as the vulnerability of isolation'.[3]

The biggest and most gratifying surprise of the first season of the BBC TV series, 'The Shakespeare Plays', was undoubtedly *King Henry VIII*, directed by Kevin Billington and filmed on location at Leeds Castle, Hever Castle, and Penshurst in 1978–9.[4] Not as well known as others among the first presentations—*Romeo and Juliet*, *Julius Caesar*, *As You Like It*, *Measure for Measure*, and *Richard II*— it was (along with the last two named) the best received, showing what television could do in adapting Shakespeare to the small screen. Filming on location helped convey the solid reality Billington wanted, and in the process it solved some problems encountered in theatres, such as the arrival of the masquers at York Place or the representation of Katherine's Vision.[5] The greatest

---

[1] See Sinden's account of the ending especially, cited by Richmond, 96–7.

[2] See Michael Billington, *Peggy Ashcroft* (1988), 224.

[3] Ibid., 226.

[4] Susan Willis, *The BBC Shakespeare Plays* (1991), 188. As the BBC edition of the play points out, all three places were closely associated with Tudor history and especially Henry VIII. See Richmond, 109.

[5] In the television film, the King and others arrive by barge, obviating the need for drum and trumpet sounding off-stage (Willis, ibid.). The Vision makes use of simultaneous exposures to convey the dreamlike event; and in the christening scene the baby was a real, gurgling infant.

advantage of television, one that it shares with cinema generally, is of course the use of close-ups, enabling the viewer to see facial expressions and other details both clearly and precisely, although it also shares the disadvantage of selecting what is to be seen. Billington may have exploited close-ups to the extent that many scenes simply present 'talking heads', but the clear articulation of speeches thus achieved benefits modern viewers unfamiliar with Shakespeare's language.[1] John Stride played Henry VIII as a vigorous young man gradually taking full charge of his realm. Claire Bloom's Katherine was handsome, dignified, and stately. She broke out with flashes of anger against Wolsey and won sympathy in her last scene as, now showing age and illness, she neared death.[2] By contrast, Barbara Kellerman's Anne appeared as a silly young woman, flattered by the King's attentions, hardly knowing what awaited her.[3] In deference to the small screen (and small budget), Billington avoided presenting large crowds and long processions (5.3 was cut entirely), keeping the attention mainly on dialogue and the presentation of character—an extreme antithesis to Victorian spectacle.

The last two RSC productions of *King Henry VIII* in the twentieth century could not have differed more from each other. Howard Davies's main stage presentation in 1983, with Richard Griffiths as the King and Gemma Jones as Katherine, mixed elaborate historical costumes with Brechtian devices, such as cut-out images sliding across the stage on metal grids and a Kurt Weill band on the side of the stage in plain view of the audience. Gregory Doran's production in the Swan Theatre in 1996–7, with Paul Jesson as Henry and Jane Lapotaire as Katherine, was more conventional, scaled down, but still elaborate in costuming and scenic effects. Davies's production evidently had an agenda: to show that *King Henry VIII* is in fact 'a very modern play, dealing with taxes, unemployment and social divisions', as the director himself said; beneath the ceremonial state robes he saw a bureaucratic society in which differing inter-

[1] Cf. Timothy West's comments, cited by Willis, 221, and Richmond, 119. West played Wolsey.

[2] Billington interpolates a brief scene after 4.2 showing her laid out in death. Earlier, he briefly interpolated Henry VIII and Francis I together celebrating their concord before the dialogue of 1.1 begins.

[3] Cf. Richmond, 115, who notes that all the women's parts were diminished except Katherine's, and that Anne displayed an emotional 'flatness' which misrepresents the historical figure.

5. Queen Katherine's Vision (4.2). Gemma Jones as Katherine in the Royal Shakespeare Company's production directed by Howard Davies (1983).

ests conflicted vigorously, as in 1.2, over taxation and personalities.[1] The political ruthlessness was genuinely modern; or was it? As Richmond argues, Davies achieved 'a lively contemporary synthesis' of almost all the precedents found in Henry's court and in today's world of politics, including not only the ruthlessness but also a growing dependency on centralized, bureaucratic government, with a powerful despot at its head.[2]

Doran's production blazoned 'All is True' both in the programme title and in huge letters against the Swan's rear stage wall, 'not so much to heighten the play's documentary reality as to make you aware how everyone bends the idea of truth to his own purposes'.[3] To this extent, Doran also had a political agenda, though not as evident as Davies's: truth is a malleable political weapon rather than a fixed commodity. Paul Jesson's portrayal of Henry seemed to emphasize the point; he took the role at face value, showing no qualms about self-contradiction and conveying the idea that consistency is merely a literary invention of which real people, and especially kings, have no need.[4] Cutting across

[1] Roger Warren, 'Shakespeare in England, 1983', *SQ* 34 (1983), 453.

[2] Richmond, 124, 134. Cf. Hodgdon, *End Crowns All*, 220.

[3] Michael Billington, 'A Strong Case for the Simple Truth', *The Guardian*, 28 November 1996.

[4] Irving Wardle, 'Royal, Gaudy Fate', *Sunday Telegraph*, 1 December 1996.

6. Pre-Prologue tableau: Paul Jesson as King Henry, Jane Lapotaire as Queen Katherine, members of the Royal Shakespeare Company in the Swan Theatre (1996), directed by Gregory Doran.

this point of view is that which Katherine represents, beautifully and forcefully enacted by Jane Lapotaire. Refusing to compromise her principles right to the end, and suffering for them, this Katherine emerged as the real star of the production, winning from the audience the highest acclaim. The production also showed that even in so small a house as the Swan spectacular effects are possible, as when at the start two majestic doors swung open to permit a 'blinding golden tableau, trucked forward to spill into fanfared processions through the audience'.[1]

Meanwhile, in America, just after World War II, Margaret Webster staged the play in New York with Victor Jory as Henry, Eva Le Gallienne as Katherine, and Walter Hampden as Wolsey.[2] Years afterward, to conclude the New York Shakespeare Festival's 'Shakespeare Marathon' (1987–97), a multi-ethnic production in Central Park's Delacorte Theatre, directed by Mary Zimmerman, was staged. It made good use of the wide, open-air stage and some excellently trained actors. But *King Henry VIII* has not found many other revivals in this century in America or, indeed, anywhere else outside Britain.

[1] Irving Wardle.

[2] Speaight, 241. See also *Shakespeare around the Globe*, 247–8; American regional productions are discussed on 245–6.

The recent stage history of *King Henry VIII*, however, demonstrates that the play has been unjustly neglected. Besides several major roles that remain attractive to leading actors, the inherent political interest, as Davies's production and others' have shown, is more than ever worth exploring. Every age is political, of course; but at a time when media seem to control the presentation of information, if not also its flow, and the availability of information has become essential to both the governed and the governing, Shakespeare's drama has particular relevance. What Henry knows or does not know, the means he uses to discover or confirm the truth, and finally the action he takes based on that truth, have an immediacy comparable to that of our morning newspaper or the evening telecast. Is consistency merely a literary invention? Need we heed the vagaries of others' actions—and our own? These are but some of the issues that *King Henry VIII* in performance explores. If Shakespeare's play does not provide neat, simple answers, it nevertheless demands that we confront the questions.

EDITORIAL PROCEDURES

THIS edition provides a modern-spelling text following the principles set forth by Stanley Wells in 'Modernizing Shakespeare's Spelling' in Wells and Taylor, *Modernizing Shakespeare's Spelling, with Three Studies in the Text of 'Henry V'* (1979) and the procedures used in previous volumes in this series. I have modernized spelling and punctuation without annotation, unless they affect meaning, in which case I list alterations in the Collation with appropriate indications of provenance and any significant variant readings from other editions. I have also modernized quotations from other early texts, such as Cavendish's *Life and Death of Cardinal Wolsey* and the chronicles by Hall and Holinshed, that may appear in the Introduction and Commentary. Unstressed past participles appear as 'ed' and stressed ending as 'èd'. Speech headings have been normalized silently. Act and scene divisions follow the Folio, unless otherwise noted.

I have added or expanded stage directions as necessary to clarify the action. All 'asides' or directions to speak 'to' a particular person are the responsibility of this edition and have not been noted in the Collation unless editors disagree about them. Similarly, minor alterations, such as changing 'the Cardinal' to 'Cardinal Wolsey' at 1.2.0.1, have been silently normalized. More significant editorial changes in the stage directions from the text are noted in the Collation, again with provenance and other editors' alternatives. Altered stage directions that seem probable but not certain are enclosed within broken brackets (⌈ ⌉). Lineation has been regularized and noted in the Collation with provenance when it differs from the Folio lineation.

The question of authorial responsibility for scenes and parts of scenes is dealt with in the Introduction under 'Date, Authorship, and Printing' but is not otherwise indicated in the text or the notes where, for convenience' sake, the author is simply referred to as 'Shakespeare' (see Preface).

Abbreviations and References

Line numbers and references to other Shakespeare plays are from *The Complete Works*, ed. Stanley Wells, Gary Taylor, *et al*. (Oxford,

1986). Titles normally appear in modern spelling. F1 is only specified when the First Folio needs to be distinguished from later folio editions. References to *King Lear* are to the Folio-based version (*The Tragedy of King Lear*) unless Q *Lear* is specified. References to Elizabethan proverbs are to Morris Tilley's *Dictionary*, as supplemented by Robert Dent. Biblical references are to the Geneva Bible, unless otherwise noted. London is the place of publication except when otherwise specified. Material from Hall and Holinshed may also usually be found in Bullough.

EDITIONS OF SHAKESPEARE

F	The First Folio, 1623
F2	The Second Folio, 1632
F3	The Third Folio, 1663
F4	The Fourth Folio, 1685
Boswell	James Boswell, *Plays and Poems*, 21 vols. (1821), vol. 19
Cambridge	W. G. Clark and W. A. Wright, *Works*, Cambridge Shakespeare, 9 vols. (Cambridge, 1863–6), vol. 5
Cambridge 1892	William Aldis Wright, *Works*, 9 vols. (Cambridge, 1891–3), vol. 5 (1892)
Capell	Edward Capell, *Comedies, Histories, and Tragedies*, 10 vols. (1767–8), vol. 7
Collier	John Payne Collier, *Works*, 8 vols. (1842–4)
Collier 1853	John Payne Collier, *Plays* (1853)
Dyce	Alexander Dyce, *Works*, 6 vols. (1857)
Dyce 1866	Alexander Dyce, *Works*, 9 vols. (1864–7), vol. 5 (1866)
Foakes	R. A. Foakes, *King Henry VIII*, Arden Shakespeare (1957)
Globe	W. G. Clark and W. A. Wright, *The Globe Shakespeare* (1864)
Halliwell	James O. Halliwell[-Phillipps], *Works*, 16 vols. (1856), vol. 12
Hanmer	Thomas Hanmer, *Works*, 6 vols. (Oxford, 1743–4), vol. 4
Humphreys	A. R. Humphreys, *King Henry VIII*, New Penguin Shakespeare (1971)
Johnson	Samuel Johnson, *Plays*, 8 vols. (1765), vol. 5
Malone	Edmond Malone, *Plays and Poems*, 10 vols. (1790), vol. 7
Maxwell	J. C. Maxwell, *King Henry VIII*, New Shakespeare (Cambridge, 1962)

NCS	John Margeson, *King Henry VIII*, New Cambridge Shakespeare (Cambridge, 1990)
Oxford	Stanley Wells and Gary Taylor, with John Jowett and William Montgomery, *Works* (Oxford, 1986)
Pooler	C. Knox Pooler, *The Famous History of the Life of King Henry VIII*, Arden Shakespeare (1915)
Pope	Alexander Pope, *Works*, 6 vols. (1723–5), vol. 4 (1723)
Pope 1728	Alexander Pope, *Works*, 10 vols. (1728), vol. 6
Rann	Joseph Rann, *Dramatic Works*, 6 vols. (Oxford, 1786–94)
Riverside	G. B. Evans (Textual Editor), *Riverside Shakespeare*, second edition (1997)
Rowe	Nicholas Rowe, *Works*, 6 vols. (1709), vol. 4
Rowe 1709	Nicholas Rowe, *Works*, second edition, 6 vols. (1709), vol. 4
Rowe 1714	Nicholas Rowe, *Works*, 8 vols. (1714)
Staunton	H. Staunton, *Plays*, 3 vols. (1858–60)
Steevens	Samuel Johnson and George Steevens, *Plays*, 10 vols. (1773), vol. 7
Theobald	Lewis Theobald, *Works*, 7 vols. (1733), vol. 5
Theobald 1740	Lewis Theobald, *Works*, 8 vols. (1740), vol. 5
Warburton	William Warburton, *Works*, 8 vols. (1747), vol. 5
Wright	W. A. Wright, *King Henry the Eighth*, in *Shakespeare: Select Plays* (1895)
Yale	John M. Berdan and C. F. Tucker Brooke, *The Life of King Henry VIII*, Yale Shakespeare (1925)

OTHER ABBREVIATIONS

Abbott	E. A. Abbott, *A Shakespearian Grammar*, second edition (1870)
Anderson	Judith H. Anderson, *Biographical Truth* (1984)
Bullough	Geoffrey Bullough, *Narrative and Dramatic Sources of Shakespeare*, 8 vols. (1957–75), vol. 4 (1962)
Cavendish	George Cavendish, *The Life and Death of Cardinal Wolsey*, ed. Richard Sylvester (Oxford, 1959)
Cercignani	Fausto Cercignani, *Shakespeare's Works and Elizabethan Pronunciation* (Oxford, 1981)
Dent	R. W. Dent, *Shakespeare's Proverbial Language: An Index* (1981)

Elton	G. R. Elton, *Reform and Reformation: England, 1509–1558* (Cambridge, Mass., 1977)
Foxe	John Foxe, *The Acts and Monuments of Martyrs*, 3 vols., pages numbered consecutively (1596)
Gurr	Andrew Gurr, *The Shakespearean Stage* (Cambridge, 1970)
Hall	Edward Hall, *The Union of the Two Noble and Illustre Famelies of Lancaster and York* (1548; repr. 1809)
Hogan	Charles Beecher Hogan, *Shakespeare in the Theatre, 1701–1800*, 2 vols. (Oxford, 1952)
Holinshed	Raphael Holinshed, *The Chronicles of England*, second edition (1587)
Hosley	Richard Hosley, *Shakespeare's Holinshed* (New York, 1968)
Kökeritz	Helge Kökeritz, *Shakespeare's Pronunciation* (1953)
N&Q	*Notes and Queries*
Odell	George C. D. Odell, *Shakespeare from Betterton to Irving*, 2 vols. (New York, 1920)
OED	*Oxford English Dictionary*, second edition (Oxford, 1989)
Onions	C. T. Onions, *A Shakespeare Glossary*, enlarged and revised by Robert D. Eagleson (Oxford, 1986)
Rex	Richard Rex, *Henry VIII and the English Reformation* (New York, 1993)
Richmond	Hugh M. Richmond, *Shakespeare in Performance: King Henry VIII* (Manchester, 1994)
Ridley	Jasper Ridley, *Henry VIII* (1984)
Rowley	Samuel Rowley, *When You See Me, You Know Me*, Students' Facsimile Edition (1913)
Saccio	Peter Saccio, *Shakespeare's English Kings: History, Chronicle, and Drama* (New York, 1977)
SB	*Studies in Bibliography*
Scarisbrick	J. J. Scarisbrick, *Henry VIII* (1968)
Schmidt	Alexander Schmidt, *A Shakespeare Lexicon*, fourth edition (revised by G. Sarrazin), 2 vols. (Berlin and Leipzig, 1923)
Shaheen	Naseeb Shaheen, *Biblical References in Shakespeare's History Plays* (Newark, Del., 1989)
Sisson	C. J. Sisson, *New Readings in Shakespeare*, 2 vols. (Cambridge, 1956)
Solt	Leo F. Solt, *Church and State in Early Modern England, 1509–1640* (Oxford, 1990)

Speaight	Robert Speaight, *Shakespeare on the Stage* (Boston, 1973)
SQ	*Shakespeare Quarterly*
SS	*Shakespeare Survey*
SSt	*Shakespeare Studies*
TC	Stanley Wells and Gary Taylor, with John Jowett and William Montgomery, *William Shakespeare: A Textual Companion* (Oxford, 1987)
Tilley	Morris Palmer Tilley, *A Dictionary of the Proverbs in England in the Sixteenth and Seventeenth Centuries* (Ann Arbor, Mich., 1950)

in which both Shakespeare and Fletcher ha[...]
Shakespeare's preferences for hath, d[...]
pronounced in those case[...]

King Henry VIII, or All is True

THE PERSONS OF THE PLAY

PROLOGUE

EPILOGUE

KING HENRY VIII

QUEEN KATHERINE, later KATHERINE, Princess Dowager

ANNE Boleyn, later Queen ANNE

Duke of BUCKINGHAM

Lord ABERGAVENNY ⎫
⎬ his sons-in-law
Earl of SURREY ⎭

Duke of NORFOLK

Old Duchess of Norfolk

Duke of SUFFOLK

LORD CHAMBERLAIN

LORD CHANCELLOR

Lord SANDS (William Sands)

Lord CAPUTIUS

Sir Thomas LOVELL

Sir Anthony DENNY

Sir Henry GUILDFORD

Sir Thomas CROMWELL

Sir Nicholas VAUX

CARDINAL WOLSEY

CARDINAL CAMPEIUS

Thomas CRANMER, later Archbishop of Canterbury

Stephen GARDINER, the King's new secretary, later Bishop of Winchester

Gardiner's PAGE

Bishop of LINCOLN (John Longland)

GRIFFITH, Queen Katherine's gentleman usher

PATIENCE, her waiting woman

An OLD LADY

Dr BUTTS, the King's Physician

BRANDON

BUCKINGHAM'S SURVEYOR

Three GENTLEMEN

GARTER King-of-Arms

Two SECRETARIES

SERJEANT-at-arms

Two SCRIBES

A CRIER

Lord Chamberlain's SERVANT

MESSENGER

A DOORKEEPER

A PORTER

His MAN

Lord Mayor of London

Six personages in Katherine's Vision

Others appearing at the Legatine Court:
Archbishop of Canterbury (William Warham), Bishop of Ely, Bishop of
Rochester, Bishop of Saint Asaph, two noblemen, two priests, two
vergers

Others appearing at the Coronation:
Countesses and ladies, Marquis Dorset, four Barons of the Cinque Ports,
Bishop of London (John Stokesley), two judges, choristers, trumpeters

Others appearing at the Christening:
The infant Princess Elizabeth, Marchioness Dorset, six noblemen, two
aldermen

Musicians, ladies, gentlemen, halberdiers, tipstaves, pages, pursuivants,
footboys, grooms, servants, guards, attendants, common people

King Henry VIII, or All is True

Prologue *Enter Prologue*

PROLOGUE

I come no more to make you laugh. Things now
That bear a weighty and a serious brow,
Sad, high, and working, full of state and woe—
Such noble scenes as draw the eye to flow
We now present. Those that can pity here   5
May, if they think it well, let fall a tear;
The subject will deserve it. Such as give
Their money out of hope they may believe,
May here find truth, too. Those that come to see
Only a show or two, and so agree   10
The play may pass—if they be still, and willing,
I'll undertake may see away their shilling
Richly in two short hours. Only they
That come to hear a merry, bawdy play,
A noise of targets, or to see a fellow   15
In a long motley coat guarded with yellow,
Will be deceived. For, gentle hearers, know—
To rank our chosen truth with such a show

Title *King . . . VIII*] The Famous History of the Life of King HENRY the Eight. F; *All is True* OXFORD

Prologue 0.1 *Enter Prologue* | PROLOGUE] OXFORD; *THE PROLOGVE*. F

Pro.1 **I . . . laugh** An allusion to an un-
identified comedy, which evidently
also began with a prologue used to intro-
duce the action. Here, the prologue
prepares the audience's attitude (4–7,
13–17).

3 **Sad, high, and working** solemn, important, and emotionally charged
state dignity, stateliness

9 **truth** Alludes to the original title, 'All is
True', re-emphasized at 18 and 20–1.

10 **show** spectacle

11 **pass** surpass
still, and willing attentive and inclined

12 **see away** spend in seeing
shilling (cost of an expensive seat in

the galleries)

13 **two short hours** A general or conventional reference to the length of a play, as
in *Romeo* Pro.12.

14–17 **a merry . . . deceived** May allude to
Rowley's play (see Introduction, p. 15),
which had low comic dialogue, battle
scenes, and Will Somers (Henry VIII's
fool).

15 **noise of targets** battle sounds. Targets are
shields.

16 **long . . . yellow** (clown's customary garb)
motley variegated, many-coloured
guarded trimmed

17 **deceived** disappointed

18 **rank** couple

As fool and fight is, beside forfeiting
Our own brains, and the opinion that we bring   20
To make that only true we now intend,
Will leave us never an understanding friend.
Therefore, for goodness' sake, and as you are known
The first and happiest hearers of the town,
Be sad as we would make ye. Think ye see   25
The very persons of our noble story
As they were living; think you see them great
And followed with the general throng and sweat
Of thousand friends; then, in a moment, see
How soon this mightiness meets misery.   30
And if you can be merry then, I'll say
A man may weep upon his wedding day.   *Exit*

I.I   *A cloth of state throughout the play. Enter the Duke of*
        Norfolk at one door; at the other door enter the Duke
        of Buckingham and the Lord Abergavenny

BUCKINGHAM (*to Norfolk*)

        Good morrow, and well met. How have ye done
        Since last we saw in France?

32 *Exit*] OXFORD; *not in* F
    I.I] *Actus Primus. Scoena Prima.* F   0.1 *A cloth . . . play*] OXFORD; *not in* F   0.2 *door enter*]
OXFORD; *not in* F

19–21 **beside . . . intend** i.e. apart from sur-
    rendering our own intelligence and the
    conviction that we carry to present only
    what is true
22 **understanding** A quibble on groundlings
    who stood around the stage in the yard.
    Cf. Jonson, *Bartholomew Fair* Ind.49
    (Foakes).
24 **first . . . hearers** 'the leading and
    best qualified audience' (Humphreys).
    The King's Men were the premier
    acting company in London and attracted
    a more distinguished audience than
    others.
25 **sad** serious
    Think ye see Cf. *Henry V* Pro.17–31, esp.
    26: 'Think, when we talk of horses, that
    you see them'. Comparing the two Pro-
    logues, S. C. Sen Gupta says that in
    Henry V Shakespeare was anxious
    whether his stage could contain 'the

vastness of his martial theme', whereas
in *Henry VIII* 'not the vastness of his
subject but its truth . . . engage[s] the
poet's attention' (*Shakespeare's Historical
Plays* (Oxford, 1964), 152).
27–8 **great . . . sweat** Pronounced similarly
(Kökeritz, 201; Cercignani, 78).
30 **How soon . . . misery** The fall from high to
low estate was a medieval conception of
tragedy, as exemplified in Chaucer's
'Monk's Tale' (see Introduction, p. 25).
The concept was still current in the early
seventeenth century.
I.I.0.I *cloth of state* F stage directions take
for granted the presence on stage of a seat
or state for the King (*TC*).
0.2 *one door . . . other door* Two stage
doors, one on either side, were usual in
London theatres until the end of the
eighteenth century.
2 **saw** i.e. saw each other

NORFOLK   I thank your grace,
Healthful, and ever since a fresh admirer
Of what I saw there.
BUCKINGHAM   An untimely ague
Stayed me a prisoner in my chamber when   5
Those suns of glory, those two lights of men,
Met in the vale of Ardres.
NORFOLK   'Twixt Guisnes and Ardres.
I was then present, saw them salute on horseback,
Beheld them when they lighted, how they clung
In their embracement as they grew together,   10
Which had they, what four throned ones could have
        weighed
Such a compounded one?
BUCKINGHAM   All the whole time
I was my chamber's prisoner.
NORFOLK   Then you lost
The view of earthly glory. Men might say
Till this time pomp was single, but now married   15
To one above itself. Each following day
Became the next day's master, till the last
Made former wonders its. Today the French,
All clinquant, all in gold, like heathen gods

6 suns] F1; Sons F3   7 Ardres] ROWE; Andren F   Guisnes] F (Guynes)   Ardres.] ROWE;
Arde, F   11 Which . . . weighed] ROWE; *as two lines divided* they,/ F   17 next . . . last] F; last .
. . next CAPELL

3 **fresh** untired; 'an admirer still feeling the
   impression as if it were hourly renewed'
   (Johnson)
4 **untimely ague** Buckingham was in fact
   present at the Field of the Cloth of Gold,
   but the dramatist invents his illness so
   that Norfolk (who was not present) may
   describe the event and Buckingham may
   register his reaction.
6–7 **Those suns . . . Ardres** Henry VIII and
   Francis I met from 7 to 24 June 1520. For
   the splendour of the meetings and
   Wolsey's part in them, see Holinshed,
   858–60, and Hall, 605–20.
6 **suns** As the sun was the primate of the
   heavens, so kings were primates on
   earth. (Cf. 33 below.) The F3 and Capell
   reading 'sons' suggests an intentional
   pun (Foakes).

7 **Guisnes and Ardres** Guisnes was English, Ardres French, with the valley between them in Picardy, where the kings
   met.
8 **salute** greet
9 **lighted** alighted
10 **as** as if
   grew together Cf. *Dream*, 3.2.209–10:
   'So we grew together, | Like to a double
   cherry'.
11–12 **Which . . . one** which, if they had
   grown into one, what four kings could
   have counted as much as that compounded one
16–18 **Each . . . its** each succeeding day instructed the next until the last one com-
   bined all the wonders into itself
19 **clinquant** glittering
   heathen gods Psalm 115: 4: 'Their idols

75

Shone down the English; and tomorrow they   20
Made Britain India. Every man that stood
Showed like a mine. Their dwarfish pages were
As cherubins all gilt; the madams, too,
Not used to toil, did almost sweat to bear
The pride upon them, that their very labour   25
Was to them as a painting. Now this masque
Was cried incomparable, and th'ensuing night
Made it a fool and beggar. The two kings
Equal in lustre, were now best, now worst,
As presence did present them. Him in eye   30
Still him in praise, and being present both,
'Twas said they saw but one, and no discerner
Durst wag his tongue in censure. When these suns—
For so they phrase 'em—by their heralds challenged
The noble spirits to arms, they did perform   35
Beyond thought's compass, that former fabulous story
Being now seen possible enough, got credit
That *Bevis* was believed.

BUCKINGHAM   O, you go far!

NORFOLK

As I belong to worship and affect

---

23 cherubins] F; cherubim OXFORD   madams] F (Madams); mesdames OXFORD   33 censure.
When] ROWE; ~, when F

---

are of silver and gold, even the work of
men's hands' (Foakes).

20 **Shone down** outshone
21–2 **Made Britain . . . mine** The wealth the
British displayed made them look like the
fabled mines of the East. Cf. *1 Henry IV*
3.1.164–5: 'as bountiful | As mines of
India'.
23 **madams** ladies of rank
25 **pride** splendid adornments
that i.e. so that; also at 36
25–6 **their . . . painting** Their exertions, like
cosmetics, coloured their cheeks.
26–8 **Now . . . beggar** Holinshed, Hall, and
other chroniclers comment on the extravagant masques used as entertainment. An allusion also perhaps to the
entertainments during the wedding festivities of Princess Elizabeth in 1613
(Foakes).
29–30 **now best . . . them** i.e. appeared best

or worst accordingly as one or the other
appeared on view
30–1 **Him . . . praise** 'the one seen was ever
the one praised' (Humphreys)
31–2 **being . . . but one** i.e. when both kings
appeared, they were each so splendid as
to be indistinguishable
32 **discerner** observer
33 **censure** judgement; i.e. could not distinguish which was superior.
36 **beyond thought's compass** unimagin-
ably
38 *Bevis* Early English romance, *Bevis of
Hampton*. The hero's chivalric feats were
now rendered credible by the performance of the knights at the Field of the
Cloth of Gold (i.e. in jousts and tourna-
ments). Drayton's *Poly-Olbion* (1613) celebrates his 'achievement great' (Pooler).
39–40 **As I . . . honesty** as I hold high
rank and love truthfulness in matters of
honour

In honour honesty, the tract of ev'rything   40
Would by a good discourser lose some life
Which action's self was tongue to. All was royal.
To the disposing of it naught rebelled.
Order gave each thing view. The office did
Distinctly his full function.

BUCKINGHAM   Who did guide—   45
I mean, who set the body and the limbs
Of this great sport together, as you guess?

NORFOLK

One, certes, that promises no element
In such a business.

BUCKINGHAM   I pray you who, my lord?

NORFOLK

All this was ordered by the good discretion   50
Of the right reverend Cardinal of York.

BUCKINGHAM

The devil speed him! No man's pie is freed
From his ambitious finger. What had he
To do in these fierce vanities? I wonder
That such a keech can, with his very bulk,   55
Take up the rays o'th' beneficial sun,
And keep it from the earth.

NORFOLK   Surely, sir,

42–5 All . . . function] THEOBALD; *assigned to Buckingham* F   47 together, as you guess?] F4
(*subs.*); ~? | *Nor.* As you guesse: F

40–2 **the tract . . . tongue to** the description
of everything even by a good narrator
would lose in the telling what the action
itself conveyed

40 **tract** description (Riverside)

41 **discourser** narrator

42–5 **All . . . function** Theobald rightly as-
signs these lines, which F impossibly
gives to Buckingham, who twice says he
was not present (4–6, 12–13).

44 **Order . . . view** Because everything was
well arranged, everything was visible.

44–5 **The office . . . function** The officials
properly carried out their assignments;
'office' = people holding official position
(Onions).

47 **as you guess?** NCS rejects the F4 emendation, arguing that Norfolk assumes

Buckingham can easily guess the truth.

48 **certes** (one syllable) certainly
element part, role. Schmidt paraphrases:
'of whom it would not be expected, that
he should find his proper sphere in such a
business'.

50 **ordered** arranged

52 **speed** prosper, meaning 'dispatch' (*OED*
v. 9c)

54 **fierce** wild, extravagant (Onions)

55 **keech** the fat of a slaughtered animal
rolled up into a lump (*OED*), with a
glance at Wolsey as a butcher's son. Perhaps Shakespeare thought of Wolsey as a
fat man (Foakes).

56 **Take . . . sun** Figuratively, absorb all the
attention of the monarch; 'take up' =
occupy entirely (Onions).

There's in him stuff that puts him to these ends.
For being not propped by ancestry, whose grace
Chalks successors their way, nor called upon   60
For high feats done to th' crown, neither allied
To eminent assistants, but spider-like,
Out of his self-drawing web, a gives us note
The force of his own merit makes his way—
A gift that heaven gives for him, which buys   65
A place next to the King.

ABERGAVENNY   I cannot tell
What heaven hath given him: let some graver eye
Pierce into that; but I can see his pride
Peep through each part of him. Whence has he that?
If not from hell, the devil is a niggard   70
Or has given all before, and he begins
A new hell in himself.

BUCKINGHAM   Why the devil,
Upon this French going out, took he upon him—
Without the privity o'th' King—t'appoint
Who should attend on him? He makes up the file   75
Of all the gentry, for the most part such
To whom as great a charge as little honour
He meant to lay upon; and his own letter,

63 web, a]; CAMBRIDGE 1892 (*conj.* Capell); Web. O F; ~, he CAPELL; ~, O, FOAKES
69–70 that? . . . hell,] THEOBALD (*subs.*); ~, . . . Hell? F

59–62 **For being . . . assistants** Norfolk comments on Wolsey's lack of noble descent, services, and connections.
59 **grace** beneficent virtue
60 **Chalks** marks
63 **self-drawing web** web spun from his own resources (Humphreys). Spiders were considered venomous.
  a he. *TC* gives good reason to accept Capell's conjecture, even though 'a' = he appears nowhere else in the play (a scribe might have changed others to 'he' and, in general, F modernizes). The *a/o* misreading is easy.
  gives us note informs us
70–2 **If not . . . himself** If Wolsey's pride derives not from hell, then the devil is stingy or has already given all the pride away, so that Wolsey must contrive a new hell

in himself. Abergavenny can see nothing of heaven's gifts in him, only sinful pride.
73 **going out** expedition
74 **privity** private knowledge
75 **file** list
77–8 **To whom . . . upon** on whom he meant to impose expenses as great as the honour intended to them is little (Humphreys). The first 'To' is redundant.
78–80 **his own letter . . . papers** Malone cites Holinshed: 'The peers of the realm (receiving letters to prepare themselves to attend the King in this journey . . .) seemed to grudge that such a costly journey should be taken in hand, to their importunate charges and expenses, without consent of the whole board of the Council' (855). Buckingham was especially angry at Wolsey's presumption.

The honourable board of council out,
Must fetch him in, he papers.
ABERGAVENNY   I do know   80
Kinsmen of mine—three at the least—that have
By this so sickened their estates that never
They shall abound as formerly.
BUCKINGHAM   O, many
Have broke their backs with laying manors on 'em
For this great journey. What did this vanity   85
But minister communication of
A most poor issue?
NORFOLK   Grievingly, I think
The peace between the French and us not values
The cost that did conclude it.
BUCKINGHAM   Every man,
After the hideous storm that followed, was   90
A thing inspired, and, not consulting, broke
Into a general prophecy—that this tempest,
Dashing the garment of this peace, aboded
The sudden breach on't.
NORFOLK   Which is budded out;
For France hath flawed the league and hath attached 95
Our merchants' goods at Bordeaux.

---

79 council out,] POPE (*subs.*); ~, ~, F   80 him in, he] F; in him he POPE

79 **out** not sitting (Johnson) or not mentioned (Steevens)
80 **papers** sets down on paper, writes in a list (Onions)
82 **sickened** weakened, i.e. impoverished
83 **abound** be wealthy, abundant
84 **broke . . . on 'em** A common expression (Tilley L452, W62), as in *K. John* 2.1.69–71. The nobility raised funds by selling or mortgaging houses and land.
85 **vanity** extravagant display; cf. today's 'conspicuous consumption'
86–7 **minister . . . issue** Perhaps, convey the idea of impoverishing heirs. Cf. Holinshed, 855: 'he knew not for what cause so much money should be spent about the sight of a vain talk to be had, and communication to be ministered of things of no importance.' Foakes sees a possible double pun on 'communication' =

sexual intercourse and hence the begetting of bastard children.
87 **Grievingly, I think** I grieve to think
88 **not values** is not worth
90–4 **hideous storm . . . breach on't** Cf. Holinshed, 860: 'On Monday the eighteenth of June was such an hideous storm of wind and weather that many conjectured it did prognosticate trouble and hatred shortly to follow between princes.' In fact, the peace did not last long (94–6).
91–2 **not consulting . . . prophecy** independently, each one prophesied the same thing
93 **Dashing** destroying
aboded foretold, with a possible pun on 'budded' (94).
95 **flawed** broken
attached seized by legal process

ABERGAVENNY   Is it therefore
Th'ambassador is silenced?
NORFOLK   Marry is't.
ABERGAVENNY

A proper title of a peace and purchased
At a superfluous rate.
BUCKINGHAM   Why, all this business
Our reverend Cardinal carried.
NORFOLK   Like it your grace,   100
The state takes notice of the private difference
Betwixt you and the Cardinal. I advise you—
And take it from a heart that wishes towards you
Honour and plenteous safety—that you read
The Cardinal's malice and his potency   105
Together; to consider further that
What his high hatred would effect wants not
A minister in his power. You know his nature,
That he's revengeful; and I know his sword
Hath a sharp edge—it's long, and't may be said   110
It reaches far; and where 'twill not extend,
Thither he darts it. Bosom up my counsel,
You'll find it wholesome. Lo, where comes that rock
That I advise your shunning.

> *Enter Cardinal Wolsey, the purse containing the*
> *Great Seal borne before him. With him certain of the*
> *guard, and two secretaries with papers. The Cardinal*
> *in his passage fixeth his eye on Buckingham and*
> *Buckingham on him, both full of disdain*

114.1–2 *containing . . . Seal*] OXFORD; *not in* F   114.2 *With him*] OXFORD; *not in* F

97 **silenced** Wolsey retaliated by putting the French ambassador under what amounted to house arrest and ordering the Mayor of London to attach all Frenchmen, 'body and goods and them to keep in prison' (Hall, 634).
98 **proper title** (used ironically)
99 **superfluous rate** excessive cost
100 **Like . . . grace** may it please your grace
105 **potency** power
107–8 **wants . . . power** i.e. does not lack an agent in his service

111 **It reaches far** Tilley K87: 'Kings have long arms'.
112 **Bosom up** hold close, keep secret
113 **that rock** (a nautical metaphor)
114.1–5 *Enter . . . disdain* Usually staged so that Wolsey and his entourage are distant from the others; their conversation is not overheard, while Wolsey and Buckingham glare at each other.
114.1 *purse* Bag in which the Great Seal is kept, an emblem of the Chancellor's office.

CARDINAL WOLSEY (*to a Secretary*)

  The Duke of Buckingham's surveyor? Ha?   115
  Where's his examination?

SECRETARY   Here, so please you.

CARDINAL WOLSEY

  Is he in person ready?

SECRETARY   Ay, please your grace.

CARDINAL WOLSEY

  Well, we shall then know more, and Buckingham
  Shall lessen this big look.   *Exeunt Wolsey and his train*

BUCKINGHAM

  This butcher's cur is venom-mouthed, and I   120
  Have not the power to muzzle him; therefore best
  Not wake him in his slumber. A beggar's book
  Outworths a noble's blood.

NORFOLK   What, are you chafed?

  Ask God for temp'rance; that's th'appliance only
  Which your disease requires.

BUCKINGHAM   I read in's looks   125

  Matter against me, and his eye reviled
  Me as his abject object. At this instant
  He bores me with some trick. He's gone to th' King;
  I'll follow and outstare him.

NORFOLK   Stay, my lord,

  And let your reason with your choler question   130
  What 'tis you go about. To climb steep hills
  Requires slow pace at first. Anger is like
  A full hot horse who, being allowed his way,

---

120 venom-mouthed] POPE (*after* Rowe); venom'd-mouth'd F   123 chafed] F (chaff'd)

115 **surveyor** Overseer of Buckingham's estates, his cousin Charles Knyvet (Knevet).

116 **examination** deposition, testimony

119 **big look** haughty stare

120 **butcher's cur** Wolsey's father was supposed to have been a butcher. Cf. Tilley B764: 'as surly as a butcher's dog' and B764.1 (Dent).

122 **Not wake him** 'Let sleeping dogs lie' (Tilley W7).

122–3 **A beggar's . . . blood** As a poor boy, Wolsey was an excellent scholar. His learning ('book'), Buckingham says, is valued more than a nobleman's lineage. Foakes suggests a pun, 'book'/'bulk' (mass or body) in opposition to 'blood' (cf. 55 above).

123 **chafed** angry, vexed

124 **temp'rance** self-restraint, one of the four cardinal virtues (*OED*). Tilley P107: 'Patience is a plaster for all sores' (Dent).
   appliance remedy, treatment

127 **abject object** rejected or cast-off thing; hence, object of contempt

128 **bores** cheats (*OED*), wounds (Johnson)

131–2 **To climb . . . first** Tilley C413: 'Hasty climbers have sudden falls' (Dent).

133–4 **A full . . . him** Tilley H642: 'A free horse will soon tire'.

Self-mettle tires him. Not a man in England
Can advise me like you. Be to yourself   135
As you would to your friend.

BUCKINGHAM   I'll to the King,
And from a mouth of honour quite cry down
This Ipswich fellow's insolence, or proclaim
There's difference in no persons.

NORFOLK   Be advised.
Heat not a furnace for your foe so hot   140
That it do singe yourself. We may outrun
By violent swiftness that which we run at,
And lose by over-running. Know you not
The fire that mounts the liquor till't run o'er
In seeming to augment it wastes it? Be advised.   145
I say again there is no English soul
More stronger to direct you than yourself,
If with the sap of reason you would quench
Or but allay the fire of passion.

BUCKINGHAM   Sir,
I am thankful to you, and I'll go along   150
By your prescription; but this top-proud fellow—
Whom from the flow of gall I name not, but
From sincere motions—by intelligence
And proofs as clear as founts in July when
We see each grain of gravel, I do know   155
To be corrupt and treasonous.

NORFOLK   Say not 'treasonous'.

134 **Self-mettle** his own vigour
135–6 **Be . . . friend** Tilley C688: 'He can give others good counsel but will take none himself' (Dent).
137 **from . . . honour** speaking as a nobleman
139 **difference** distinction of rank or quality, as at *Lear* 1.4.89 (Foakes).
   Be advised be careful
140–1 **Heat . . . yourself** Alludes to Daniel 3: 19, 22, the fiery furnace for Shadrach, Mishach, and Abednego, which in fact burned their would-be executioners (Shaheen).
141–3 **We may . . . over-running** i.e. we may run past our goal by going too fast. Tilley H192: 'Make haste slowly', and H98 'The more haste the less speed' (Dent). Norfolk's speeches are sententious.

144 **mounts the liquor** makes liquid rise
147 **More stronger** Double comparatives are common in Shakespeare (Abbott §11).
148–9 **sap of reason . . . passion** Norfolk offers conventional wisdom: reason should rule emotion, not vice versa.
149 **allay** moderate
151 **top-proud** excessively proud; cf. 'top-gallant'.
152–3 **Whom . . . motions** 'Whom I speak of not from personal rancour but from honest motives' (Humphreys). In medieval theory, choler, or anger, derived from gall, or bile.
153 **motions** motives (as at *Coriolanus* 2.1.50)
   intelligence secret information
154 **founts** springs

BUCKINGHAM

To th' King I'll say't and make my vouch as strong

As shore of rock. Attend: this holy fox,

Or wolf, or both—for he is equal rav'nous

As he is subtle, and as prone to mischief   160

As able to perform't, his mind and place

Infecting one another, yea, reciprocally—

Only to show his pomp as well in France

As here at home, suggests the King our master

To this last costly treaty, th'interview   165

That swallowed so much treasure and, like a glass,

Did break i'th' rinsing.

NORFOLK   Faith, and so it did.

BUCKINGHAM

Pray give me favour, sir. This cunning Cardinal,

The articles o'th' combination drew

As himself pleased, and they were ratified   170

As he cried 'Thus let be', to as much end

As give a crutch to th' dead. But our Count-Cardinal

Has done this, and 'tis well for worthy Wolsey,

Who cannot err, he did it. Now this follows—

Which, as I take it, is a kind of puppy   175

To th' old dam, treason—Charles the Emperor,

159–62 —for . . . perform't, . . . reciprocally—] CAPELL (*subs.*); (~ . . . ~) . . . ~, F   167 rinsing] F (wrenching)   172 Count-Cardinal] F; Court-Cardinal POPE   173 well, for] OXFORD; ~:~F; ~ — ~ ROWE

157 **vouch** assertion, allegation
158–60 **holy fox . . . subtle** Tilley F629: 'as wily as a fox' and W601 'as hungry as a wolf'. NCS suggests an echo of Matthew 7: 15: 'Beware of false prophets, which come to you in sheep's clothing, but inwardly they are ravening wolves'.
159 **equal** equally (Abbott §1)
160 **subtle** sly, cunning
161 **place** i.e. position of power (as Lord Chancellor)
164 **suggests** prompts, incites
165 **th'interview** the formal meeting (of the kings)
167 **rinsing** F 'wrenching' is a dialectal form of 'rinsing', usually emended, as here, following Pope (cf. *Kinsmen* 1.1.155). Some editions, e.g. Riverside, NCS, prefer the dialectal form as stronger and as suggesting 'distortion of meaning' (*OED v.* 7) (Foakes). Drinking glasses

were an expensive luxury.
169 **combination** treaty. Cf. Holinshed, 858: Henry gave Wolsey 'full authority, power, and liberty, to affirm and confirm, bind and unbind, whatsoever should be in question between him and the French king.' Francis I empowered him as well.
172 **Count-Cardinal** Foakes defends Pope's emendation, 'Court-Cardinal', arguing that the chronicles do not support Capell's 'ingenious solution', i.e. that Wolsey was 'Count-Palatine' by virtue of holding the bishopric of Durham *in commendam*. But cf. 'King-Cardinal' (2.2.19). Buckingham here mocks Wolsey's pretensions to aristocracy, not his service at court.
176 **dam** bitch
176–83 **Charles . . . menaced him** (See Introduction, pp. 13–14, for the international politics at this time.)

Under pretence to see the Queen his aunt—
For 'twas indeed his colour, but he came
To whisper Wolsey—here makes visitation.
His fears were that the interview betwixt   180
England and France might through their amity
Breed him some prejudice, for from this league
Peeped harms that menaced him; privily
Deals with our Cardinal and, as I trow—
Which I do well, for I am sure the Emperor   185
Paid ere he promised, whereby his suit was granted
Ere it was asked—but when the way was made,
And paved with gold, the Emperor thus desired
That he would please to alter the King's course
And break the foresaid peace. Let the King know,   190
As soon he shall by me, that thus the Cardinal
Does buy and sell his honour as he pleases,
And for his own advantage.

NORFOLK   I am sorry
To hear this of him and could wish ye were
Something mistaken in't.

BUCKINGHAM   No, not a syllable.   195
I do pronounce him in that very shape
He shall appear in proof.

      Enter Brandon, a serjeant-at-arms before him, and
      two or three of the guard

BRANDON

Your office, serjeant, execute it.

SERJEANT   Sir.
(*To Buckingham*) My lord the Duke of Buckingham
    and Earl

---

183 privily] F; He ~ F2; ~ he OXFORD   194 ye] This edition (*conj*. Oxford); he F1; you F4

178 **colour** pretext
181 **England and France** i.e. their kings
183 **privily** secretly, privately. The line is a
    syllable short, prompting some editors to
    follow F2 and emend; but the next lines
    also show metrical irregularity.
184 **trow** believe
189 **he** i.e. Wolsey
192 **buy and sell** traffic in (Pooler), as at
    Richard III 5.6.35.
195 **Something** somewhat

197 **in proof** in testing, experience
197.1 **Brandon** Although Holinshed, 863,
    identifies 'Sir Henry Marney, Captain of
    the Guard', Shakespeare here names the
    arresting officer Brandon. This may be
    Charles Brandon, Duke of Suffolk, who
    appears later in 2.2 but is there referred to
    as 'Suffolk'; inconsistency in such mat-
    ters is common in Shakespeare. Bucking-
    ham refers to 'lords' at 227 as he departs
    with Abergavenny under guard (Foakes).

Of Hereford, Stafford, and Northampton, I   200
Arrest thee of high treason in the name
Of our most sovereign King.
BUCKINGHAM (*to Norfolk*)   Lo you, my lord,
The net has fall'n upon me. I shall perish
Under device and practice.
BRANDON   I am sorry
To see you ta'en from liberty to look on   205
The business present. 'Tis his highness' pleasure
You shall to th' Tower.
BUCKINGHAM   It will help me nothing
To plead mine innocence, for that dye is on me
Which makes my whit'st part black. The will of heav'n
Be done in this and all things. I obey.   210
O, my lord Abergavenny, fare you well.
BRANDON
Nay, he must bear you company.
(*To Abergavenny*)   The King
Is pleased you shall to th' Tower till you know
How he determines further.
ABERGAVENNY   As the Duke said,
The will of heaven be done and the King's pleasure   215
By me obeyed.
BRANDON   Here is a warrant from
The King t'attach Lord Montague and the bodies
Of the Duke's confessor, John de la Car,
One Gilbert Perke, his chancellor—

---

200 Hereford] CAPELL; *Hertford* F   211 Abergavenny] F (*Aburgany; also at* 1.2.138)
217 Montague] ROWE, OXFORD; *Mountacute* F   219 Perke] Perk FOAKES; *Pecke* F (*also at* 2.1.21)
chancellor—] *after* POPE 1728 (*conj*. Theobald); Councellour. F

200 **Hereford** Disyllabic. Capell's correction
of F 'Hertford' (probably a compositor's
misreading) derives from Holinshed.
202 **Lo you** look you
203 **net . . . me** Alludes to catching birds
with nets; cf. *Macbeth* 4.2.34 (Foakes).
204 **device and practice** trickery and intrigue
205 **to look on** and to witness
207 **Tower** i.e. the Tower of London, where
prisoners accused of treason were held
209–10 **The will . . . things** Echoes the
Lord's Prayer, Matthew 6: 10: 'Thy will
be done even in earth as it is in heaven'
(Shaheen); also at 215.

211 **Abergavenny** Pronounced, as F spelling
indicates, 'Aburgany'.
217 **t'attach** to arrest
    Lord Montague According to Holinshed,
    863, Abergavenny and Montague were
    arrested later on charges of 'conceal-
    ment', i.e. suppression of truth (Hosley).
    Montague, or Montacute, was Henry
    Pole, Abergavenny's son-in-law, par-
    doned on this occasion but executed for
    treason in 1539 (Humphreys).
219 **Gilbert . . . chancellor** Theobald's and
    Foakes's emendations derive from Holin-
    shed although, as Humphreys notes,

BUCKINGHAM   So, so;

    These are the limbs o'th' plot. No more, I hope.   220

BRANDON

    A monk o'th' Chartreux.

BUCKINGHAM   O, Nicholas Hopkins?

BRANDON He.

BUCKINGHAM

    My surveyor is false. The o'er-great Cardinal

    Hath showed him gold. My life is spanned already.

    I am the shadow of poor Buckingham,   225

    Whose figure even this instant cloud puts on

    By dark'ning my clear sun. My lords, farewell.

                Exeunt Norfolk at one door, Buckingham and

                Abergavenny under guard at another

1.2   *Cornetts. Enter King Henry leaning on Cardinal*
       Wolsey's shoulder. With them Wolsey's two
       secretaries, the nobles, and Sir Thomas Lovell. The
       King ascends to his seat under the cloth of state;
       Wolsey places himself under the King's feet on his
       right side

KING HENRY (*to Wolsey*)

    My life itself and the best heart of it

    Thanks you for this great care. I stood i'th' level

221 Nicholas] POPE 1728 (*conj.* Theobald); *Michaell* F   227 lords] F; Lord ROWE
   1.2] *Scena Secunda.* F   0.2–3 *With . . . secretaries*] OXFORD; *not in* F   0.3–4 *The King . . .
state*] OXFORD; *not in* F

'Perke' is probably Holinshed's mistake
for 'clerk': contemporary records refer to
'Robert Gilbert, clerk' as Buckingham's
chancellor.

221 **Chartreux** Carthusian Order
   Nicholas Hopkins F's Compositor B probably mistook 'Nic.' or 'Nich.' for 'Mic.'
   or 'Mich.'
224–5 **My life . . . shadow** Cf. Psalm 39: 6–7
   (Prayer Book version): 'Behold, thou
   hast made my days as it were a span
   long. . . . For man walketh in a vain
   shadow' (Humphreys).
224 **spanned** (a) seized; (b) measured out,
   completed (Johnson)
225–7 **I am . . . sun** A difficult construction.
   'Shadow' = resemblance, reflection; 'figure' = form, shape; 'instant' may be a

noun or, more likely, an adjective =
now present (Onions); 'cloud' = trouble,
affliction; 'sun' = Buckingham or Henry.
Hence, Buckingham says either: (a) I am
the shadow of my former self, thanks to
the cloud that now darkens my erstwhile
blameless life; or (b) I am the shadow of
unfortunate Buckingham, whose form is
now shrouded by the trouble I have
caused my king.
1.2.0.1–2 **Enter . . . shoulder** Henry's
   stance suggests his dependency upon
   Wolsey. Stuart M. Kurland, '*Henry VIII
   and James I*', *SSt* 19 (1987), 205, compares James I's habit of leaning upon his
   courtiers' shoulders.
0.5 *Wolsey . . . feet* i.e. below the king
  1 **best heart** most precious part (Pooler)
  2 **level** direct aim

Of a full-charged confederacy and give thanks
To you that choked it. Let be called before us
That gentleman of Buckingham's; in person   5
I'll hear him his confessions justify,
And point by point the treasons of his master
He shall again relate.

⌈CRIER⌉ (*within*)

Room for the Queen, ushered by the Duke of Norfolk.

> *Enter Queen Katherine, the Duke of Norfolk, and the*
> *Duke of Suffolk. She kneels. King Henry riseth from*
> *his state, takes her up, and kisses her*

QUEEN KATHERINE

Nay, we must longer kneel. I am a suitor.   10

KING HENRY

Arise, and take place by us.

> *He placeth her by him*

                              Half your suit
Never name to us: you have half our power,
The other moiety ere you ask is given.
Repeat your will and take it.

QUEEN KATHERINE   Thank your majesty.

That you would love yourself, and in that love   15
Not unconsidered leave your honour nor
The dignity of your office, is the point
Of my petition.

KING HENRY   Lady mine, proceed.

QUEEN KATHERINE

I am solicited—not by a few,

5 Buckingham's; in person‿] JOHNSON; ~, ~ ~, F   9 ⌈CRIER⌉ (*within*)] OXFORD; *A noyse within crying* F   Room . . . Norfolk] OXFORD; *as part of stage direction* F   11 *He . . . him*] OXFORD; *at end of preceding stage direction* F

3 **full-charged** fully loaded
   confederacy conspiracy
4 **choked** i.e. suppressed
6 **justify** confirm, prove
9 CRIER . . . **Norfolk** Oxford's emendation
   regularizes F's stage direction (which anticipates Katherine's entry).
9.3 *state* chair of state, throne
10 **we** royal plural
11 **take place** take your seat
13 **moiety** half
14 **Repeat . . . it** state your desire and consider it granted

Thank (I) thank
15–18 **That you . . . petition** Katherine asks Henry to take regard for himself and in so doing surrender neither his honour nor the dignity of his position.
19–30 **I am . . . rebellion** Katherine's appeal on behalf of the commons is unhistorical and seems invented by Shakespeare to arouse sympathy at once for the Queen. The 'commissions', however, were both historical and notorious, though they came later, in 1525. Wolsey was universally blamed; Holinshed, 891, refers

And those of true condition—that your subjects   20
Are in great grievance. There have been commissions
Sent down among 'em which hath flawed the heart
Of all their loyalties; wherein, although,
My good lord Cardinal, they vent reproaches
Most bitterly on you, as putter-on   25
Of these exactions, yet the King our master—
Whose honour heaven shield from soil—even he
    escapes not
Language unmannerly; yea, such which breaks
The sides of loyalty and almost appears
In loud rebellion.
NORFOLK   Not 'almost appears'—   30
It doth appear; for upon these taxations
The clothiers all, not able to maintain
The many to them 'longing, have put off
The spinsters, carders, fullers, weavers, who,
Unfit for other life, compelled by hunger   35
And lack of other means, in desperate manner
Daring th' event to th' teeth, are all in uproar,
And danger serves among them.
KING HENRY   Taxation?
Wherein? And what taxation? My lord Cardinal,

---

to the 'strange commissions' Wolsey devised to pay for Henry's war in France (cf. Hall, 694–7).

20 **true condition** loyal nature or disposition

21 **grievance** distress
commissions writs of authority (to collect taxes)

22 **flawed** damaged, cracked

25 **putter-on** instigator

27 **soil** stain, moral blemish

28–9 **breaks . . . loyalty** i.e. bursts the bounds; a common metaphor in Shakespeare for the effect of strong passion (Maxwell), as at *Antony* 1.3.16–17.

31–8 **It doth . . . among them** For dramatic purposes Shakespeare transforms the rebellion in Suffolk that Holinshed records (891–2) into a general upheaval (Foakes).

33 **put off** dismissed from service (Onions). Cf. Holinshed, 891: 'the rich clothiers . . . went about to discharge and put from

them their spinners, carders, fullers, weavers, and other artificers'.

34 **spinsters** spinners, usually but not exclusively female
carders those who card, or comb, the wool
fullers men who beat cloth to clean and thicken it

35 **life** way of life, trade

37 **Daring . . . teeth** boldly facing the result of their rising (Pooler), as at *Hamlet* 3.3.63: 'Even to the teeth and forehead of our faults'.

38 **danger . . . them** Defiantly challenging the outcome. Danger is personified, just as Poverty and Necessity are in Holinshed's account ('Poverty was their captain, which with his cousin Necessity, had brought them to that doing').

38–9 **Taxation? . . . taxation?** Henry's protest of ignorance was genuine; Wolsey, not uncommonly, had kept him in the dark.

You that are blamed for it alike with us,   40
Know you of this taxation?
CARDINAL WOLSEY   Please you, sir,
I know but of a single part in aught
Pertains to th' state and front but in that file
Where others tell steps with me.
QUEEN KATHERINE   No, my lord?
You know no more than others? But you frame   45
Things that are known alike, which are not wholesome
To those which would not know them and yet must
Perforce be their acquaintance. These exactions,
Whereof my sovereign would have note, they are
Most pestilent to th' hearing, and to bear 'em   50
The back is sacrifice to th' load. They say
They are devised by you, or else you suffer
Too hard an exclamation.
KING HENRY   Still exaction!
The nature of it? In what kind, let's know,
Is this exaction?
QUEEN KATHERINE I am much too venturous   55
In tempting of your patience, but am boldened
Under your promised pardon. The subjects' grief
Comes through commissions which compels from each
The sixth part of his substance to be levied
Without delay, and the pretence for this   60
Is named your wars in France. This makes bold
          mouths.
Tongues spit their duties out, and cold hearts freeze
Allegiance in them. Their curses now
Live where their prayers did, and it's come to pass

44–5 lord? . . . others?] F; ~, . . . ~; F4, FOAKES

42 **a single part** one person's share
43–4 **front . . . me** i.e. am only more con-
    spicuous among those who are involved
    with me
44 **tell steps** march along (continuing the
    martial metaphor)
45–8 **you frame . . . acquaintance** i.e. you
    originate things that everyone (in Coun-
    cil) knows are not beneficial to those that
    would reject them but must accept them
49 **would** would like to, should (*OED*,

will, *v*. 40)
49 **note** knowledge
50–1 **to bear . . . load** carrying them is to
    sacrifice the bearer to the burden
53 **exclamation** reproach
54 **In what kind** what is the nature of
57 **grief** grievance
58 **commissions** See 19–30 n.
    compels For third person plurals ending
    in -*s*, see Abbott §333.
59 **substance** wealth

This tractable obedience is a slave   65
To each incensèd will. I would your highness
Would give it quick consideration, for
There is no primer business.
KING HENRY   By my life,
This is against our pleasure.
CARDINAL WOLSEY   And for me,
I have no further gone in this than by   70
A single voice, and that not passed me but
By learned approbation of the judges. If I am
Traduced by ignorant tongues—which neither know
My faculties nor person, yet will be
The chronicles of my doing—let me say   75
'Tis but the fate of place and the rough brake
That virtue must go through. We must not stint
Our necessary actions in the fear
To cope malicious censurers, which ever
As rav'nous fishes do a vessel follow   80
That is new trimmed, but benefit no further
Than vainly longing. What we oft do best,
By sick interpreters—once weak ones—is
Not ours or not allowed; what worst, as oft

68 business] HANMER (*conj.* Warburton); basenesse F   71 passed] F (past)   83 once] F; or
POPE

65–6 **This . . . will** i.e. wrath dominates
people's formerly compliant obedience
68 **primer** more important
business As Sisson says (98), emendation
is not obligatory and may seem to weaken
the sense; Foakes along with some other
editors concurs. But, as Sisson also says,
the emendation 'business' for 'baseness'
is more consonant with Katherine's request for 'quick consideration' and with
the adjective, *primer*. A misreading *a/u*,
moreover, is plausible.
69 **This** i.e. the taxation through commissions
71 **single voice** unanimous vote. Although
the *OED* does not record 'single' in this
sense, Foakes cites *Macbeth* 1.3.139
('single state of man') and Holinshed's
reference to the consent of the whole
Council in this action (891–2). Alterna-
tively, Wolsey may be saying that he ex-
ercised only one vote, as one among
many (Riverside).

72 **approbation of the judges** According to
Holinshed, the judges sitting in Council
had approved the legality of the commissions.
74 **faculties** personal qualities, disposition
(Onions)
person bearing, physical appearance
76 **place** rank, office
brake lit., thicket
77 **stint** withhold, curtail
79 **cope** encounter
censurers critics
81 **new trimmed** newly fitted out for sea duty
81–2 **benefit . . . longing** gain nothing beyond their futile hopes (because the new
ship is tightly fitted and secure)
82–4 **What . . . allowed** i.e. often what we
do well, unsound ('sick') interpreters—
in a word, unqualified ones—give us
no credit for or attribute it to others.
For 'weak' = feeble-minded, see *Errors*
3.2.35, *Twelfth Night* 1.5.111, etc.
(Schmidt).

Hitting a grosser quality, is cried up   85
For our best act. If we shall stand still
In fear our motion will be mocked or carped at,
We should take root here where we sit
Or sit state-statues only.
KING HENRY   Things done well
And with a care exempt themselves from fear;   90
Things done without example, in their issue
Are to be feared. Have you a precedent
Of this commission? I believe not any.
We must not rend our subjects from our laws
And stick them in our will. Sixth part of each?   95
A trembling contribution! Why, we take
From every tree lop, bark, and part o'th' timber;
And though we leave it with a root, thus hacked
The air will drink the sap. To every county
Where this is questioned send our letters with   100
Free pardon to each man that has denied
The force of this commission. Pray look to't;
I put it to your care.
CARDINAL WOLSEY (*to a secretary*) A word with you.
Let there be letters writ to every shire
Of the King's grace and pardon.
(*Aside to the secretary*)   The grievèd commons   105
Hardly conceive of me. Let it be noised
That through our intercession this revokement

92 precedent] F (President)   98 root,] THEOBALD (*conj.* Warburton); $\sim_\wedge$ F

85 **Hitting . . . quality** appealing to cruder
minds (Humphreys). But Foakes and NCS
regard the line as ambiguous, referring to
either the action or the reaction; hence, it
may signify achieving an inferior level of
attainment.
cried up praised
87 **motion** (a) proposal; (b) action
89 **state-statues** effigies of statesmen
(Humphreys)
91 **example** precedent
issue outcome
94–5 **We . . . will** i.e. we must not violate
our subjects' rights under the law to satisfy our desires. 'The figure is that of
plucking up a flower from the soil in

which it thrives and sticking it in one's
dress for mere personal gratification'
(Deighton; cited by Maxwell, who regards the interpretation as perhaps too
specific, noting that the whole passage
suggests branches rather than flowers;
see 96–9).
96 **trembling** fearful
97 **lop** 'the smaller branches and twigs of
trees' (*OED sb.* 1)
99–108 **To every . . . comes** As reported by
Holinshed, 891.
102 **force** validity
105 **grace** mercy
106 **Hardly conceive of** think ill of
noised bruited about

And pardon comes. I shall anon advise you
Further in the proceeding.   *Exit secretary*
   Enter Buckingham's Surveyor
QUEEN KATHERINE (*to the King*)
I am sorry that the Duke of Buckingham   110
Is run in your displeasure.
KING HENRY   It grieves many.
The gentleman is learned and a most rare speaker,
To nature none more bound; his training such
That he may furnish and instruct great teachers
And never seek for aid out of himself. Yet see,   115
When these so noble benefits shall prove
Not well disposed, the mind growing once corrupt,
They turn to vicious forms ten times more ugly
Than ever they were fair. This man so complete,
Who was enrolled 'mongst wonders—and when we   120
Almost with ravished list'ning could not find
His hour of speech a minute—he, my lady,
Hath into monstrous habits put the graces
That once were his, and is become as black
As if besmeared in hell. Sit by us. You shall hear—   125
This was his gentleman in trust—of him
Things to strike honour sad.
(*To Wolsey*)   Bid him recount

126 trust—of him] F (*subs.*); ~ ‿ ~ ~—— OXFORD

111 **Is run in** has incurred
111–27 **It grieves . . . sad** Although the examination of Buckingham's surveyor appears
in Holinshed, Wolsey not Henry questions
him. Henry's eulogy is not included.
Humphreys maintains that Shakespeare
probably wanted to strengthen Henry's
role at this point, as he does increasingly
later on, until Act 5 when, protecting
Cranmer, he shows himself 'unquestioned
and unrivalled ruler'.
112 **rare** excellent
113 **bound** indebted, i.e. for natural qualities (Foakes)
115 **out of himself** beyond his own ability
116–19 **When . . . fair** i.e. when the noble
attributes are ill directed, the mind grows
corrupted, and those very attributes become more vicious than they ever were

virtuous. *Sonnet* 94.10–14 makes a
similar comment; see also Tilley N317.
116 **benefits** natural gift or advantage
(Onions)
117 **disposed** directed
118 **They** i.e. the 'benefits' (116)
119 **complete** Accented on first syllable, as
often in Shakespeare when used attribu-
tively.
121 **ravished** enthralled
121–2 **could not . . . minute** i.e. an hour of
his speaking seemed like a minute
123 **habits** lit., clothes, dress; or, habits of
mind
124–5 **become as black . . . hell** Cf. *Othello*
3.3.391–3: 'My name, that was as fresh
| As Dian's visage, is now begrimed and
black | As mine own face' (Steevens).
126 **gentleman in trust** trusted servant

The fore-recited practices whereof
We cannot feel too little, hear too much.

CARDINAL WOLSEY (*to the Surveyor*)

Stand forth, and with bold spirit relate what you   130
Most like a careful subject have collected
Out of the Duke of Buckingham.

KING HENRY   Speak freely.

BUCKINGHAM'S SURVEYOR

First, it was usual with him, every day
It would infect his speech, that if the King
Should without issue die, he'll carry it so   135
To make the sceptre his. These very words
I've heard him utter to his son-in-law,
Lord Abergavenny, to whom by oath he menaced
Revenge upon the Cardinal.

CARDINAL WOLSEY   Please your highness note
His dangerous conception in this point,   140
Not friended by his wish to your high person.
His will is most malignant, and it stretches
Beyond you to your friends.

QUEEN KATHERINE   My learned Lord Cardinal,
Deliver all with charity.

KING HENRY (*to the Surveyor*) Speak on.
How grounded he his title to the crown   145
Upon our fail? To this point hast thou heard him
At any time speak aught?

BUCKINGHAM'S SURVEYOR   He was brought to this
By a vain prophecy of Nicholas Hopkins.

KING HENRY

What was that Hopkins?

BUCKINGHAM'S SURVEYOR   Sir, a Chartreux friar,

140 His] POPE; This F   140–1 point, . . . person.] F (*subs.*); ~: . . . ~, POPE   148, 149 Hop-
kins] POPE 1728 (*conj.* Theobald); *Henton* F

128 **practices** intrigues, plots
131 **careful** caring, full of care
131–2 **collected | Out of** gathered from (as
   evidence)
135 **carry it** manage it
140 **His** Pope's emendation may stand: 'the
   insistence in Wolsey's speech, as in the
   Surveyor's preceding speech, is throughout on *him*, *he*, *his*; and *this* weakens the
   line. It was probably attracted from *his* by

the second *this* in the line' (Sisson, 99).
141 **Not friended . . . person** not gratified in
   his wish regarding the King (i.e. that he
   should die childless)
142 **will** desire, wish
145 **grounded** based
146 **fail** failure to have children, implying
   also the King's death
149 **Hopkins** Theobald's emendation is necessary for internal consistency (*TC*). But

His confessor, who fed him every minute   150
With words of sovereignty.
KING HENRY   How know'st thou this?
BUCKINGHAM'S SURVEYOR
Not long before your highness sped to France,
The Duke, being at the Rose within the parish
Saint Lawrence Poultney, did of me demand
What was the speech among the Londoners   155
Concerning the French journey. I replied,
Men feared the French would prove perfidious,
To the King's danger; presently the Duke
Said 'twas the fear indeed, and that he doubted
'Twould prove the verity of certain words   160
Spoke by a holy monk that oft, says he,
'Hath sent to me, wishing me to permit
John de la Car, my chaplain, a choice hour
To hear from him a matter of some moment;
Whom after under the confession's seal   165
He solemnly had sworn that what he spoke
My chaplain to no creature living but
To me should utter, with demure confidence
This pausingly ensued: "neither the King nor's heirs",
Tell you the Duke, "shall prosper. Bid him strive   170

---

157 feared] POPE; feare F   165 confession's] THEOBALD; Commissions F

as Sisson notes (99), Buckingham made
the earlier reference (1.1.221), and the
monk was also known as 'Nicholas
Henton', Henton being the name of his
convent. He believes that Shakespeare's
inconsistency was deliberate, although
Maxwell argues it derives from a careless
reading of Holinshed: 'Nicholas Hopkins,
a monk of an house of the Chartreux
order, beside Bristow, called Henton'
(863). The surveyor's testimony (152 ff.)
closely follows Holinshed (864).

151 **words of sovereignty** i.e. talk of his succession to the throne
153 **the Rose** A manor once owned by Buckingham, converted in 1561 into the Merchant Taylors' School (Humphreys).
154 **Saint Lawrence Poultney** (a London
church)
157 **feared** F 'feare' probably derives from an

easy *d/e* misreading.
158 **presently** immediately
159 **doubted** suspected
163 **choice** chosen, appointed (Schmidt)
165 **confession's** Theobald emended according to Holinshed: 'The Duke in talk told
the Monk, that he had done very well to
bind his chaplain, John de la Court
[Car], under the seal of confession, to
keep secret such matter' (863). 'The Folio
reading could not be a mere misreading of
the copy, but may well have been an editorial change. The "seal of the confession" was by now less familiar than "a
commission under seal". It was hardly
likely to be a censorial change' (Sisson,
99–100).
168 **demure** grave, sober (Onions)
confidence assurance, certitude (*OED* 2),
as in *Winter's Tale* 1.2.414: 'He thinks,
nay, with all confidence he swears'.

To win the love o'th' commonalty. The Duke
Shall govern England."'

QUEEN KATHERINE   If I know you well,
You were the Duke's surveyor and lost your office
On the complaint o'th' tenants. Take good heed
You charge not in your spleen a noble person   175
And spoil your nobler soul. I say, take heed;
Yes, heartily beseech you.

KING HENRY   Let him on.
(*To the Surveyor*) Go forward.

BUCKINGHAM'S SURVEYOR   On my soul I'll speak but truth.
I told my lord the Duke, by th' devil's illusions
The monk might be deceived, and that 'twas dangerous   180
To ruminate on this so far until
It forged him some design which, being believed,
It was much like to do. He answered, 'Tush,
It can do me no damage', adding further
That had the King in his last sickness failed,   185
The Cardinal's and Sir Thomas Lovell's heads
Should have gone off.

KING HENRY   Ha? What, so rank? Ah, ha!
There's mischief in this man. Canst thou say further?

BUCKINGHAM'S SURVEYOR
I can, my liege.

KING HENRY   Proceed.

BUCKINGHAM'S SURVEYOR   Being at Greenwich,

---

171 win] SISSON (*conj.* White); *not in* F1; gain F4   176 nobler] F; Noble F2   177–8 Let . . . for-
ward] POPE; *as one line* F   181 To ruminate] MAXWELL (*anon. conj. in* Cambridge); For this ~ ~
F; For Him ~ ~ ROWE

171 **win** F omits the word, probably inadvertently. Both sense and metre require it
or 'gain' (F4).
173–4 **lost . . . tenants** Buckingham dismissed Knevet on complaint of his tenants
'for such bribing as he had used there
[in Kent] against them' (Holinshed, 856).
175 **spleen** malice. In early physiological
psychology, the spleen was the seat of
passions such as hate and anger.
175–6 **noble . . . nobler** As the soul is more
important than rank, Katherine's wordplay places them in opposition.
176 **spoil** ruin, destroy. Cf. *Othello* 5.1.55:
'O, I am spoiled, undone by villains'

(Foakes).
179 **illusions** deceptions, tricks
181 **To ruminate** 'For this to' (F) looks like a
false start (Maxwell), either undeleted
(*TC*) or too lightly marked.
182 **forged him** framed, fashioned for him
182–3 **which . . . to do** once the plan was
found feasible, it would lead him to act
184 **It** i.e. the prophecy
185 **failed** died; cf. 146, above.
187 **Ha?** Henry's characteristic exclamation, especially when angry or disturbed, as used often in Rowley's *When
You See Me, You Know Me*.
rank corrupt

After your highness had reproved the Duke   190
About Sir William Bulmer—

KING HENRY   I remember

Of such a time, being my sworn servant,

The Duke retained him his. But on—what hence?

BUCKINGHAM'S SURVEYOR

'If', quoth he, 'I for this had been committed'—

As to the Tower, I thought—'I would have played   195

The part my father meant to act upon

Th'usurper Richard who, being at Salisbury,

Made suit to come in's presence; which, if granted,

As he made semblance of his duty, would

Have put his knife into him.'

KING HENRY   A giant traitor!   200

CARDINAL WOLSEY (*to the Queen*)

Now, madam, may his highness live in freedom,

And this man out of prison?

QUEEN KATHERINE   God mend all.

KING HENRY (*to the Surveyor*)

There's something more would out of thee—what sayst?

BUCKINGHAM'S SURVEYOR

After 'the Duke his father', with 'the knife',

He stretched him, and with one hand on his dagger,   205

Another spread on's breast, mounting his eyes,

He did discharge a horrible oath, whose tenor

191 Bulmer] WRIGHT; *Blumer* F   191–2 I remember | Of such . . . servant] POPE; *as one line* F;
~ ~ | Such . . . ~ OXFORD

190–3 **reproved . . . his** Cf. Hall, 599: 'and especially the king rebuked Sir William Bulmer, Knight, because he being the king's servant sworn, refused the king's service, and became servant to the Duke of Buckingham'. Bulmer along with others was arraigned in 1519 for 'diverse riots, misdemeanours, and offences' but won the King's pardon.

192 **Of** Oxford drops the preposition, arguing that the line is unmetrical and the construction nowhere else appears in Shakespeare (*TC*). While the latter is true, the line with 'Of' contains a full ten syllables, as divided by Pope.

194–200 **'If' . . . him'** According to Holinshed, 864, after the Bulmer incident, Buckingham told Knevet that if he were

imprisoned, he would do what his father intended to do with Richard III at Salisbury, i.e. stick a knife into him as he pretended to show his loyalty.

199 **made . . . duty** i.e. knelt to the King, pretending obeisance

200 **giant** 'As often, with a glance at the rebellion of the giants against the gods'; cf. *Hamlet* 4.5.119–20: 'What is the cause, Laertes, | That thy rebellion looks so giant-like?' (Maxwell).

201 **may** can

205 **stretched him** i.e. rose to his full height; 'him' = himself (Abbott §223)

206 **mounting** raising

207 **a horrible oath** Holinshed, 864, records the oath: 'by the blood of our Lord'.

Was, were he evil used, he would outgo
His father by as much as a performance
Does an irresolute purpose.

KING HENRY   There's his period—   210

To sheathe his knife in us. He is attached.
Call him to present trial. If he may
Find mercy in the law, 'tis his; if none,
Let him not seek't of us. By day and night,
He's traitor to th' height.   *Flourish. Exeunt*   215

1.3   *Enter the Lord Chamberlain and Lord Sands*

LORD CHAMBERLAIN

Is't possible the spells of France should juggle
Men into such strange mysteries?

SANDS   New customs,

Though they be never so ridiculous—
Nay, let 'em be unmanly—yet are followed.

LORD CHAMBERLAIN

As far as I see, all the good our English   5
Have got by the late voyage is but merely
A fit or two o'th' face. But they are shrewd ones;
For when they hold 'em, you would swear directly

---

215 *Flourish*] OXFORD; *not in* F
  1.3] *Scena Tertia.* F   O.1 *Sands*] F (*Sandys*)

208 **evil used** treated severely
    outgo surpass, exceed
210 **irresolute** wavering, not firm
    period goal, also suggesting his end,
    finish
211 **attached** arrested
215 **to th' height** in the highest degree
1.3.0.1 *Enter . . . Sands* Historical events
    in this scene are compressed. Bucking-
    ham's trial (2.1) occurred in 1521.
    William Sands did not become Lord Sands
    until 1523. Holinshed (850) records the
    behaviour of the English deplored here in
    1520, before the Field of the Cloth of Gold,
    but the criticism of English affecting
    French manners is topical, 'reflecting a
    common complaint in James's reign, and
    one especially prevalent in and around
    1613' (Foakes). The Lord Chamberlain is
    never named in this play; in 1521 he was
    Charles Somerset, Earl of Worcester; in

1527 (the actual date of the episode in
    1.4) he was Lord Sands (Maxwell), al-
    though in 1.4 both Sands and the Lord
    Chamberlain appear (Saccio, 216).
1 **spells** enchantments
    juggle deceive, beguile
2 **mysteries** i.e. the fantastic court fashions
    (Warburton)
4 **unmanly** effeminate
6 **late voyage** The dramatic context sug-
    gests the expedition to France referred to
    in 1.1, but it probably derives historically
    to the events of 1520 recorded in Holin-
    shed (850) when Englishmen returned
    home after the handing over of Tournai
    'all French in eating, drinking, and ap-
    parel, and in French vices and brags'.
7 **fit . . . face** grimace or two; 'fit' literally =
    paroxysm
    shrewd cunning, clever
8 **hold 'em** i.e. the grimaces

Their very noses had been counsellors
To Pépin or Clotharius, they keep state so.   10

SANDS

They have all new legs, and lame ones; one would take it,
That never see 'em pace before, the spavin
Or spring-halt reigned among 'em.

LORD CHAMBERLAIN   Death, my lord,
Their clothes are after such a pagan cut to't
That sure they've worn out Christendom.

    Enter Sir Thomas Lovell

                     How now—   15

What news, Sir Thomas Lovell?

LOVELL   Faith, my lord,
I hear of none but the new proclamation
That's clapped upon the court gate.

LORD CHAMBERLAIN   What is't for?

LOVELL

The reformation of our travelled gallants
That fill the court with quarrels, talk, and tailors.   20

LORD CHAMBERLAIN

I'm glad 'tis there. Now I would pray our '*messieurs*'
To think an English courtier may be wise
And never see the Louvre.

11 They . . . it] POPE; *as two lines divided* legs,/ F   They have] F; They've POPE   13 Or] DYCE
(*conj.* Collier); A F; And POPE   15 *Enter . . . Lovell*] CAPELL (*after* 'how now?'); *after l.* 16,
'*Louell*?' F   21 I'm . . . '*messieurs*'] POPE; *as two lines divided* there;/ F   '*messieurs*'] OXFORD;
ₐMonsieursₐ F

9–10 **noses . . . so** Pépin and Clotharius were
early Frankish kings; the implication is of
French affectations, but grotesque and
barbarous ones (Humphreys).

11 **They . . . take it** An hexameter line, unless 'They have' and 'take it' are elided
(see collation).
    legs A quibble on 'leg' = bow, obeisance
and 'leg' = way of walking.

11–13 **lame . . . 'em** On affected gaits, Foakes
quotes Daniel Price, *Lamentations for the
death . . . of Prince Henry* (1613): 'The
quaint *Crane-paced* Courtiers of this time'.

12 **see** An old past tense form; hence,
emendation is unnecessary.
    spavin A disease causing swollen joints,
generally of horses.

13 **spring-halt** Stringhalt, a disease of a
horse's hind legs that causes muscles to

contract spasmodically (Onions).

13 **Death** An abbreviated oath, 'by God's
death'.

14–15 **Their clothes . . . Christendom** 'i.e.
they have tried out all the fashions of
Christendom and have now gone on to
pagan fashions' (NCS).

14 **to't** in addition to it; see Abbott §185, who
cites *K. John* 1.1.144 and *Macbeth* 3.1.53.

17–20 **new . . . tailors** Holinshed (852) records
that young courtiers who affected French
manners were banished from court, but
the reference to quarrels, i.e. duels, is more
likely a contemporary allusion (as Foakes
notes) to James's *Edict . . . against Private
Combats* (April 1613), which forbade private challenges and fights.

23 **Louvre** A royal palace in Paris, now an
art museum.

LOVELL   They must either—
    For so run the conditions—leave those remnants
    Of fool and feather that they got in France,   25
    With all their honourable points of ignorance
    Pertaining thereunto—as fights and fireworks,
    Abusing better men than they can be
    Out of a foreign wisdom, renouncing clean
    The faith they have in tennis and tall stockings,   30
    Short blistered breeches, and those types of travel—
    And understand again like honest men,
    Or pack to their old playfellows. There, I take it,
    They may, *cum privilegio*, 'oui' away
    The lag end of their lewdness and be laughed at.   35
SANDS
    'Tis time to give 'em physic, their diseases
    Are grown so catching.
LORD CHAMBERLAIN   What a loss our ladies
    Will have of these trim vanities!
LOVELL   Ay, marry,
    There will be woe indeed, lords. The sly whoresons

34 '*oui*'] COLLIER; wee F1; weare F2

25 **fool and feather** i.e. foolishness and osten-
    tatious display. Feathers worn in hats
    copied French fashions. 'A fool and his
    feather' became proverbial (Dent F451.1).
26 **honourable . . . ignorance** 'i.e. in all their
    ignorance they think that all these fash-
    ionable attributes are signs of honour.
    "Points" may also suggest laces' (NCS).
27 **fights and fireworks** duelling and whor-
    ing, with a possible allusion as well to the
    mock battles and pyrotechnical displays
    staged on the Thames as part of the
    wedding celebration of Princess Elizabeth
    (Foakes). Fireworks were associated with
    prostitutes, who transmitted venereal
    diseases; hence, in Marlowe's *Dr Faustus*
    'a hot whore' (B 539) is explained by the
    stage direction in A 595–6 as 'a devil
    dressed like a woman, with fireworks'
    (Maxwell, citing Greg's edn., 1950).
28–9 **Abusing . . . wisdom** 'Mocking better
    men than themselves, through the
    "wisdom" they have gained abroad'
    (Humphreys).
29 **renouncing** The parallelism with 'Abus-

ing' (28) is misleading; the phrase here
refers back to line 24, i.e. what the
courtiers must now do (Maxwell).
29 **clean** completely, without exception
30 **tennis** A fashionable sport during James's
    reign as in Henry's.
30–1 **tall . . . breeches** French fashions
    favoured short, puffed ('blistered')
    breeches, requiring long hose.
31 **types** distinguishing marks, signs
32 **understand** Playing on the sense 'stand
    under', referring to those standing in the
    yard around the stage.
33 **pack** pack up and go
34 *cum privilegio* with immunity. The
    phrase appeared on licences of monopoly
    granted to print some books, e.g. the
    Bible (Foakes).
    '*oui*' French for 'yes'; F 'wee' is a phon-
    etic spelling.
35 **lag end** latter part, remainder
    lewdness wickedness
36 **physic** medicine, especially a cathartic or
    purge (*OED* 4b)
38 **trim** fine, pretty (used ironically)

99

Have got a speeding trick to lay down ladies.   40
A French song and a fiddle has no fellow.

SANDS

The devil fiddle 'em! I am glad they are going,
For sure there's no converting of 'em. Now
An honest country lord, as I am, beaten
A long time out of play, may bring his plainsong   45
And have an hour of hearing and, by'r Lady,
Held current music, too.

LORD CHAMBERLAIN   Well said, Lord Sands.
Your colt's tooth is not cast yet?

SANDS   No, my lord,
Nor shall not while I have a stump.

LORD CHAMBERLAIN   Sir Thomas,
Whither were you a-going?

LOVELL   To the Cardinal's.   50
Your lordship is a guest too.

LORD CHAMBERLAIN   O, 'tis true.
This night he makes a supper, and a great one,
To many lords and ladies. There will be
The beauty of this kingdom, I'll assure you.

LOVELL

That churchman bears a bounteous mind indeed,   55
A hand as fruitful as the land that feeds us.
His dews fall everywhere.

---

42 The . . . going] POPE; *as two lines divided* 'em,/ F   I am] F; I'm POPE   55 That . . . indeed]
POPE; *as two lines divided* Churchman/ F

40 **speeding trick** successful device (Pooler), with a quibble on 'speedy'.
41 **A . . . fellow** An adaptation of a proverbial expression (Dent F181.1), with 'fiddle' quibbling obscenely with 'lay down ladies' (40) and the next line. Humphreys cites Fletcher's *The Honest Man's Fortune* 5.1.37–9, for another use of the sexual meaning of 'fiddle'.
has no fellow i.e. there is nothing to compare with it
43 **converting** i.e. to decent behaviour
45 **play** amorous dalliance (*OED* 6c), as at *Winter's Tale* 1.2.188–9.
plainsong simple melody without ornament, contrasting with French song, l. 41 above.
47 **current** accepted, good. Sands through-

out this passage contrasts plain English wooing with affected French style. Cf. Henry's wooing of the French princess in *Henry V*, esp. 5.2.123–32.
48 **colt's tooth** Proverbial for wanton inclinations and impulses (Tilley C525).
49 **Nor . . . not** For use of double negative see Abbott §406.
stump Sands continues the bawdy interchange.
52 **makes** i.e. holds, gives
56 **fruitful** bountiful
57 **His . . . everywhere** A common image, but its origin is probably biblical (Shaheen, 198, who compares Psalm 133: 3 and 'God's dew' at 2.4.78). Foakes suggests a pun on 'dues' = charges or impositions.

LORD CHAMBERLAIN   No doubt he's noble.
  He had a black mouth that said other of him.
SANDS
  He may, my lord; h'as wherewithal; in him
  Sparing would show a worse sin than ill doctrine.   60
  Men of his way should be most liberal;
  They are set here for examples.
LORD CHAMBERLAIN   True, they are so,
  But few now give so great ones. My barge stays.
  Your lordship shall along. Come, good Sir Thomas,
  We shall be late else, which I would not be,   65
  For I was spoke to, with Sir Henry Guildford,
  This night to be comptrollers.
SANDS   I am your lordship's.

Exeunt

I.4   *Hautboys. Enter servants with a small table for Cardinal*
     Wolsey which they place under the cloth of state, and
     a longer table for the guests. Then enter at one door
     Anne Boleyn and divers other ladies and gentlemen as
     guests, and at another door enter Sir Henry Guildford

GUILDFORD
  Ladies, a general welcome from his grace

59 He . . . him] ROWE 1714; *as two lines divided* Lord,/ F   H'as] F (ha's); 'has DYCE; he's OXFORD wherewithal; in him‸] THEOBALD (*conj.* Thirlby); ~‸ ~ ~; F   63 But . . . stays] ROWE 1714; *as two lines divided* ones:/ F

1.4] *Scena Quarta.* F   0.1 *Enter servants with*] OXFORD; *not in* F   0.1–2 *for Cardinal . . . state, and*] OXFORD; *vnder a State for the Cardinall* F   0.3 *at one door*] OXFORD; *after* 'Guests' F
0.4 *Boleyn*] F (*Bullen*), *throughout play*   0.5 *and*] OXFORD; *not in* F   1 Ladies . . . grace] POPE; *as two lines divided* Ladyes,/ F

58 **black mouth** wicked tongue; cf. *Macbeth* 1.4.51: 'my black and deep desires' and 2.1.86 below.
  other otherwise
59 **He may** The antecedent is Wolsey, not 'He' in l. 58.
  h'as he has. See *TC* for discussion of F 'ha's' and its implications for scribal copy.
61 **way** i.e. way of life; cf. Timothy 3: 2 and Titus 1: 8 (Shaheen), where Paul instructs bishops to be hospitable.
63 **stays** is waiting
64 **along** i.e. come along
67 **comptrollers** stewards, or masters of ceremonies (Pooler)

1.4.0.1 **Hautboys** An early form of oboes, often used with recorders and other instruments on festive occasions (NCS). The scene ultimately derives from Cavendish (29–8), who was present on the occasion, and is dated 1527 (see Introduction). Holinshed defers his description until after Wolsey's death and the summary of his achievements (921–2). Although historically Anne was not present at the feast, Cavendish speaks of Henry's infatuation with her in the pages immediately following (29–32), perhaps prompting her appearance here.
0.5 *Sir Henry Guildford* Henry VIII's

Salutes ye all. This night he dedicates
To fair content and you. None here, he hopes,
In all this noble bevy has brought with her
One care abroad. He would have all as merry   5
As feast, good company, good wine, good welcome
Can make good people.
          Enter the Lord Chamberlain, Lord Sands, and
          Sir Thomas Lovell
(*To the Lord Chamberlain*) O, my lord, you're tardy.
The very thought of this fair company
Clapped wings to me.
LORD CHAMBERLAIN   You are young, Sir Harry Guildford.
SANDS

Sir Thomas Lovell, had the Cardinal   10
But half my lay thoughts in him, some of these
Should find a running banquet, ere they rested,
I think would better please 'em. By my life,
They are a sweet society of fair ones.
LOVELL

O, that your lordship were but now confessor   15
To one or two of these.
SANDS   I would I were.
They should find easy penance.
LOVELL   Faith, how easy?
SANDS

As easy as a down bed would afford it.
LORD CHAMBERLAIN

Sweet ladies, will it please you sit?
(*To Guildford*)   Sir Harry,
Place you that side, I'll take the charge of this.   20
          They sit about the longer table. A noise within
His grace is ent'ring. Nay, you must not freeze—

---

6 feast] STAUNTON; first F   20.1 *They . . . within*] OXFORD; *not in* F

comptroller, apparently borrowed here
for the occasion along with Lord Sands
(1.3.66–7).

4 **bevy** company
6 **feast** Most editions retain F 'first', with
  'then' (which Hanmer inserted after
  'company') understood. But 'feast' is

consistent with the series and completes
it; a misreading *ir/ea* is possible.
11 **lay** i.e. layman's, perhaps punning on
  'lay down' (Foakes)
12 **running banquet** hasty refreshment,
  with a bawdy implication
14 **society** assemblage
20 **Place** i.e. arrange the seating

Two women placed together makes cold weather.
My lord Sands, you are one will keep 'em waking.
Pray sit between these ladies.

SANDS   By my faith,
And thank your lordship. By your leave, sweet ladies.   25
    He sits between Anne and another
If I chance to talk a little wild, forgive me.
I had it from my father.

ANNE   Was he mad, sir?

SANDS

O, very mad—exceeding mad—in love, too;
But he would bite none. Just as I do now,
He would kiss you twenty with a breath.
    He kisses her

LORD CHAMBERLAIN   Well said, my lord.   30
So now you're fairly seated. Gentlemen,
The penance lies on you if these fair ladies
Pass away frowning.

SANDS For my little cure,
Let me alone.   35

    Hautboys. Enter Cardinal Wolsey who takes his seat
    at the small table under the state

CARDINAL WOLSEY

You're welcome, my fair guests. That noble lady
Or gentleman that is not freely merry
Is not my friend. This, to confirm my welcome,
And to you all, good health!
    He drinks

SANDS   Your grace is noble.

---

25 ladies.] POPE; ~, F   25.1 *He sits . . . another*] CAPELL (*subs.*); *not in* F   30 *He kisses her*]
JOHNSON; *not in* F   35.1–2 *who . . . state*] OXFORD; *and takes his State.* F   39 *He drinks*]
THEOBALD; *not in* F

22 **Two . . . weather** Possibly proverbial; cf.
    Tilley W221 (Dent).
23 **waking** lively, excited
25 **And thank** I thank
28 **mad . . . in love** Cf. 'love is a madness'
    (Dent L505.2).
29 **bite** Madmen were thought liable to bite;
    cf. *Antony* 2.5.80: 'Though I am mad, I
    will not bite him' (Foakes).
30 **kiss you twenty** kiss twenty (i.e. many)

ladies; the 'you' is the ethical dative, as
often in Shakespeare (Humphreys).
with a breath without taking a second
breath
Well said well done
34 **cure** oversight of parishioners (*OED* 4a).
    Sands plays on the ecclesiastical
    metaphor in 32.
35 **Let me alone** leave it to me (Maxwell)
35.2 *state* chair of state

Let me have such a bowl may hold my thanks,   40
And save me so much talking.
CARDINAL WOLSEY   My lord Sands,
I am beholden to you. Cheer your neighbours.
Ladies, you are not merry! Gentlemen,
Whose fault is this?
SANDS   The red wine first must rise
In their fair cheeks, my lord, then we shall have 'em   45
Talk us to silence.
ANNE   You are a merry gamester,
My lord Sands.
SANDS   Yes, if I make my play.
Here's to your ladyship; and pledge it, madam,
For 'tis to such a thing—
ANNE   You cannot show me.
SANDS (*to Wolsey*)
I told your grace they would talk anon.
            Drum and trumpet. Chambers discharged
CARDINAL WOLSEY   What's that?   50
LORD CHAMBERLAIN (*to the servants*)
Look out there, some of ye.   *Exit a servant*
CARDINAL WOLSEY   What warlike voice,
And to what end is this? Nay, ladies, fear not.
By all the laws of war you're privileged.
            Enter the servant
LORD CHAMBERLAIN
How now, what is't?
SERVANT   A noble troop of strangers,
For so they seem. They've left their barge and landed,   55

42 beholden] F (beholding)   49 thing—] ROWE; ~. F   50 *Drum . . . discharged*] F (*after l.* 49)
51 *Exit a servant*] CAPELL (*subs.*);   *not in* F

42 **Cheer** entertain, make cheerful
44–5 **red wine . . . cheeks** Foakes cites contemporary references to the effect that red wine makes red blood and purifies it; e.g. Marlowe, 2 *Tamburlaine* 3.2.107–8: 'aery wine that being concocted, turns to crimson blood'. Wine, of course, can cause people's cheeks to become flushed; it also makes some garrulous.
46 **gamester** (a) frolicsome person (Onions); (b) sportsman; (c) lewd person. Sands plays on the second and third senses.

47 **make my play** win my hand (at cards, or in love). Foakes suggests a pun on 'plea', pronounced similarly.
49 **thing** Anne plays on the bawdy sense, 'sexual organ'.
50 *Chambers* small cannon used for salutes. It may have been here that the thatch caught fire and burned the Globe down in 1613 (see Introduction, p. 17).
51 **voice** i.e. noise of the cannon
54 **strangers** foreigners
55 **left their barge** Situated on the Thames,

And hither make as great ambassadors
From foreign princes.

CARDINAL WOLSEY   Good Lord Chamberlain,
Go give 'em welcome: you can speak the French tongue.
And pray receive 'em nobly and conduct 'em
Into our presence, where this heaven of beauty   60
Shall shine at full upon them. Some attend him.

>   *Exit Chamberlain, attended*
>   *All rise, and some servants remove the tables*

You have now a broken banquet, but we'll mend it.
A good digestion to you all, and once more
I shower a welcome on ye: welcome all.

>   *Hautboys. Enter, ushered by the Lord Chamberlain,*
>   *King Henry and others as masquers habited like*
>   *shepherds. They pass directly before Cardinal Wolsey*
>   *and gracefully salute him*

A noble company. What are their pleasures?   65

LORD CHAMBERLAIN
Because they speak no English, thus they prayed
To tell your grace that, having heard by fame
Of this so noble and so fair assembly
This night to meet here, they could do no less
Out of the great respect they bear to beauty   70
But leave their flocks and, under your fair conduct,
Crave leave to view these ladies and entreat
An hour of revels with 'em.

CARDINAL WOLSEY   Say, Lord Chamberlain,
They have done my poor house grace, for which I pay 'em
A thousand thanks, and pray 'em take their pleasures.   75

61.1 *Exit . . . attended*] CAPELL; *not in* F   61.2 *some . . . tables*] OXFORD; *Tables remov'd* F   64.1
ushered . . . Chamberlain] *after 'Shepheards'* F   74–5 They . . . pleasures] POPE; *as three lines di-*
vided . . . grace:/ . . . thankes,/ F

York House was accessible by water. For
a sketch of the palace showing the waterside entrance, see Halliwell, 100.

56 **make** are coming

58 **French tongue** (the language of diplo-
macy)

62 **broken banquet** (a) interrupted feast;
(b) remains of a feast; cf. 'eater of broken

meats', *Lear* 2.2.13 (Foakes).

64.2 *masquers* The masque was an elaborate, masked entertainment, involving
an intricate dance, often allegorical, performed by noble men and women and
even royalty, as here. It became especially popular at the court of James I.

67 **fame** rumour, report

71 **conduct** guidance, escort

The masquers choose ladies. The King chooses Anne
Boleyn

KING HENRY (*to Anne*)

The fairest hand I ever touched. O beauty,

Till now I never knew thee.

Music. They dance

CARDINAL WOLSEY (*to the Lord Chamberlain*) My lord.

LORD CHAMBERLAIN   Your grace.

CARDINAL WOLSEY   Pray tell 'em thus much from me: 80

There should be one amongst 'em by his person

More worthy this place than myself, to whom—

If I but knew him—with my love and duty

I would surrender it.

LORD CHAMBERLAIN   I will, my lord.

He whispers with the masquers

CARDINAL WOLSEY

What say they?

LORD CHAMBERLAIN   Such a one they all confess   85

There is indeed, which they would have your grace

Find out, and he will take it.

CARDINAL WOLSEY (*standing*)   Let me see then.

By all your good leaves, gentlemen; here I'll make

My royal choice.

He bows before the King

KING HENRY (*unmasking*) Ye have found him, Cardinal.

You hold a fair assembly. You do well, lord: 90

You are a churchman, or I'll tell you, Cardinal,

I should judge now unhappily.

CARDINAL WOLSEY   I am glad

Your grace is grown so pleasant.

KING HENRY   My Lord Chamberlain,

Prithee come hither.

(*Gesturing towards Anne*) What fair lady's that?

75.1–2 *The masquers . . . Boleyn*] OXFORD; *Choose Ladies, King and An Bullen.* F; *Musick. Dance form'd: King chooses* Anne Bullen. CAPELL   84.1 *He . . . masquers*] OXFORD; *Whisper.* F (*after surrender it*)   87 *standing*] OXFORD; *comes from his State* CAPELL; *not in* F   89 *He . . . King*] OXFORD; *not in* F   *unmasking*] CAPELL; *not in* F   94 *Gesturing towards Anne*] OXFORD; *not in* F

75.1–2 *King . . . Boleyn* Unhistorical. See
    I.4.0.1 n.
76 **beauty** i.e. personified in Anne
82 **this place** i.e. the chair of state. Wolsey
    senses the King is present in disguise. In

Cavendish's account and Holinshed's,
he picks Sir Edward Neville at 88.1.
87 **take it** i.e. the chair of state
92 **unhappily** unfavourably
93 **pleasant** humorous

LORD CHAMBERLAIN

An't please your grace, Sir Thomas Boleyn's daughter—   95
The Viscount Rochford—one of her highness' women.

KING HENRY

By heaven, she is a dainty one. (*To Anne*) Sweetheart,
I were unmannerly to take you out
And not to kiss you (*kisses her*). A health, gentlemen;
          He drinks
Let it go round.   100

CARDINAL WOLSEY

Sir Thomas Lovell, is the banquet ready
I'th' privy chamber?

LOVELL   Yes, my lord.

CARDINAL WOLSEY (*to the King*)   Your grace
I fear with dancing is a little heated.

KING HENRY   I fear too much.

CARDINAL WOLSEY   There's fresher air, my lord,   105
In the next chamber.

KING HENRY

Lead in your ladies, every one.—Sweet partner,
I must not yet forsake you.—Let's be merry,
Good my lord Cardinal. I have half a dozen healths
To drink to these fair ladies and a measure   110
To lead 'em once again, and then let's dream
Who's best in favour. Let the music knock it.

                    Exeunt with trumpets

2.1   *Enter two Gentlemen, at several doors*

FIRST GENTLEMAN

Whither away so fast?

95–6 An't . . . women] POPE; *as three lines divided . . . Grace,/ . . . Rochford,/* F   99 *kisses her*]
OXFORD; *not in* F   99.1 *He drinks*] OXFORD; *not in* F   108–9 merry, . . . Cardinal.] F (*subs.*);
~: . . . ~, WARBURTON
    2.1] *Actus Secundus. Scena Prima.* F

96 **Viscount   Rochford**   According   to
Cavendish (29), Henry made Sir Thomas
Boleyn a viscount after falling in love
with Anne. He later made him Earl of
Wiltshire and Lord Privy Seal.
    one . . . women a lady-in-waiting to the
Queen
98 **take you out** i.e. to dance
99 **kiss you** It was customary for men to kiss
their partner after dancing.

101 **banquet** dessert
110 **measure** stately dance
111 **dream** think, imagine
112 **best in favour** handsomest, best looking
    knock it strike up
2.1.0.1 *Enter two Gentlemen* Buckingham's trial (1521) is not dramatized, so
as not to detract from Katherine's trial,
the climax of this act.
    several different

SECOND GENTLEMAN   O, God save ye.
   Ev'n to the hall to hear what shall become
   Of the great Duke of Buckingham.
FIRST GENTLEMAN   I'll save you
   That labour, sir. All's now done but the ceremony
   Of bringing back the prisoner.
SECOND GENTLEMAN   Were you there?   5
FIRST GENTLEMAN
   Yes, indeed was I.
SECOND GENTLEMAN   Pray speak what has happened.
FIRST GENTLEMAN
   You may guess quickly what.
SECOND GENTLEMAN   Is he found guilty?
FIRST GENTLEMAN
   Yes, truly is he, and condemned upon't.
SECOND GENTLEMAN I am sorry for't.
FIRST GENTLEMAN So are a number more.   10
SECOND GENTLEMAN But pray, how passed it?
FIRST GENTLEMAN
   I'll tell you in a little. The great Duke
   Came to the bar, where to his accusations
   He pleaded still not guilty and alleged
   Many sharp reasons to defeat the law.   15
   The King's attorney, on the contrary,
   Urged on the examinations, proofs, confessions
   Of divers witnesses, which the Duke desired
   To him brought viva voce to his face;
   At which appeared against him his surveyor,   20
   Sir Gilbert Perke his chancellor, and John Car,

---

8 Yes . . . upon't] POPE; *as two lines divided* he, / F   19 him] F1; have F4

2 **hall** i.e. Westminster Hall
10 **So . . . more** According to Holinshed (864), Buckingham was well loved by the general public.
11 **passed it** did the trial proceed
12 **in a little** briefly
14 **alleged** put forward, advanced
15 **sharp reasons** acute arguments **defeat** refute
17 **proofs** written statements
18–19 **desired . . . brought** 'The construc-

tion is "desired brought to him *viva voce*, to his face", with "to his face" amplifying "to him". Modern English cannot say "desired brought", but it can say "wanted (or wished) brought"' (Maxwell). Emendation is therefore unnecessary.
21–3 **Sir Gilbert . . . Hopkins** See 1.1.219–21 n. and 1.2.165 n. 'Sir' was a courtesy title for a priest; cf. 'Sir Topas', *Twelfth Night* 4.2.22 (Foakes).

Confessor to him, with that devil-monk,
Hopkins, that made this mischief.
SECOND GENTLEMAN   That was he
That fed him with his prophecies.
FIRST GENTLEMAN   The same.
All these accused him strongly, which he fain   25
Would have flung from him, but indeed he could not.
And so his peers upon this evidence
Have found him guilty of high treason. Much
He spoke, and learnedly, for life; but all
Was either pitied in him or forgotten.   30
SECOND GENTLEMAN
After all this, how did he bear himself?
FIRST GENTLEMAN
When he was brought again to th' bar to hear
His knell rung out, his judgement, he was stirred
With such an agony he sweat extremely
And something spoke in choler, ill and hasty;   35
But he fell to himself again and sweetly
In all the rest showed a most noble patience.
SECOND GENTLEMAN
I do not think he fears death.
FIRST GENTLEMAN   Sure he does not.
He never was so womanish. The cause
He may a little grieve at.
SECOND GENTLEMAN   Certainly   40
The Cardinal is the end of this.
FIRST GENTLEMAN   'Tis likely
By all conjectures: first, Kildare's attainder,
Then deputy of Ireland, who, removed,

---

42 attainder] F (attendure)

---

30 **Was . . . forgotten** 'Either produced no effect, or produced only ineffectual pity'
(Malone).
33 **judgement** sentence
34 **sweat** sweated
35 **choler** anger
36 **fell to himself** regained his composure
38 **Sure** surely
41 **the end of** i.e. at the bottom of
42 **Kildare's attainder** To succeed in his action

against Buckingham, Wolsey felt the need
to get the Duke's closest allies, friends, and
kinsmen out of the way. He therefore had
the Earl of Kildare, then Lord Deputy of Ireland, accused of malfeasance in office and
imprisoned; whereupon he arranged that
the Earl of Surrey, Buckingham's son-in-
law, should take his place—in effect, sent
into exile. (See Holinshed, 855.)
43 **deputy** viceroy, governor

Earl Surrey was sent thither—and in haste, too,
Lest he should help his father.

SECOND GENTLEMAN   That trick of state   45
Was a deep envious one.

FIRST GENTLEMAN   At his return
No doubt he will requite it. This is noted,
And generally: whoever the King favours,
The Card'nal instantly will find employment—
And far enough from court, too.

SECOND GENTLEMAN   All the commons   50
Hate him perniciously and, o' my conscience,
Wish him ten fathom deep. This Duke as much
They love and dote on, call him 'bounteous
          Buckingham,
The mirror of all courtesy'—

> *Enter the Duke of Buckingham from his arraignment,*
> *tipstaves before him, the axe with the edge towards*
> *him, halberdiers on each side, accompanied with*
> *Sir Thomas Lovell, Sir Nicholas Vaux, Sir William*
> *Sands, and common people*

FIRST GENTLEMAN   Stay there, sir,
And see the noble ruined man you speak of.   55

SECOND GENTLEMAN
Let's stand close and behold him.

> *They stand apart*

BUCKINGHAM (*to the common people*)   All good people,
You that thus far have come to pity me,

---

54 courtesy'—] ~;— STEEVENS; ~. F   54.3 *halberdiers*] OXFORD; *Halberds* F   54.4 *William*]
THEOBALD (*after* Holinshed); *Walter* F   54.5 *people*] OXFORD; ~, *&c.* F   56.1 *They stand apart*]
OXFORD; *not in* F

45 **father** i.e. father-in-law
   trick of state political manoeuvre
46 **envious** malicious
   his return i.e. Surrey's
51 **perniciously** maliciously, so as to desire
   his death or ruin
54 **mirror** model, paragon, as at *Henry V*
   2.0.6. The Gentlemen talk over the stage
   action.
54.2 **tipstaves** Officials carrying staves
   tipped with metal, appointed to take custody of committed persons (Onions).
54.2–3 **axe . . . him** (signalling a condemned
   prisoner)
54.3 **halberdiers** (F Halberds) Guards carry-

ing weapons consisting of a long shaft
with a spearpoint and battleaxe mounted
at the top end.
54.4–5 **Sir William Sands** Theobald's
emendation follows Holinshed. The error
probably results from faulty expansion
of the authorial abbreviation 'W.' by
scribe or compositor (*TC*). Although referred to as 'Lord Sands' in 1.4, at the
time of Buckingham's trial and execution, Sands was a knight not yet elevated
to the peerage. Compression and reorder-
ing of events for dramatic purposes
probably led to this confusion (Foakes).
56 **close** silently out of sight

Hear what I say, and then go home and lose me.
I have this day received a traitor's judgement,
And by that name must die. Yet, heaven bear witness,　60
And if I have a conscience let it sink me,
Even as the axe falls, if I be not faithful.
The law I bear no malice for my death.
'T has done, upon the premises, but justice.
But those that sought it I could wish more Christians.　65
Be what they will, I heartily forgive 'em.
Yet let 'em look they glory not in mischief,
Nor build their evils on the graves of great men,
For then my guiltless blood must cry against 'em.
For further life in this world I ne'er hope,　70
Nor will I sue, although the King have mercies
More than I dare make faults. You few that loved me
And dare be bold to weep for Buckingham,
His noble friends and fellows, whom to leave
Is only bitter to him, only dying:　75
Go with me like good angels to my end
And, as the long divorce of steel falls on me,
Make of your prayers one sweet sacrifice
And lift my soul to heaven. (*To the guard*) Lead on, a
　　God's name.

LOVELL

I do beseech your grace, for charity,　80
If ever any malice in your heart
Were hid against me, now to forgive me frankly.

72 More . . . me] ROWE 1714; *as two lines divided* faults. / F　79 And . . . name] POPE; *as two lines divided* Heauen. / F　a] F; O' THEOBALD

58 **lose** forget (Onions). See Holinshed (865) for Buckingham's reaction to his sentence, here elaborated.
59 **judgement** sentence
61 **sink** ruin eternally (a Fletcherism)
64 **premises** evidence (Foakes); previous circumstances (*OED* 6, first citation)
65–6 **But . . . forgive 'em** Alludes to the Christian principle of loving one's enemies and freely forgiving those who hurt us; cf. Matthew 5: 44 and Colossians 3: 13 (Shaheen).
67 **look** watch out
68 **evils** Probably quibbling on the usual sense and an extended sense, 'brothels'

or 'privies' (*OED*, *evil*, *sb*.²); cf. *Measure* 2.2.177, where it appears in a similar construction. (Only recorded uses.)
69 **my . . . against 'em** Shaheen compares Genesis 4: 10: 'the voice of thy brother's blood crieth unto me from the earth'.
72 **make faults** commit offences
75 **only** alone (both uses); i.e. to leave his friends is the real bitterness and death to him
77 **long divorce of steel** i.e. the axe that will sever his soul and body
78 **sacrifice** offering; cf. Psalm 141: 2: 'let the lifting up of my hands be an evening sacrifice' (Shaheen)
79 **a** in

BUCKINGHAM

　　Sir Thomas Lovell, I as free forgive you
　　As I would be forgiven. I forgive all.
　　There cannot be those numberless offences   85
　　'Gainst me that I cannot take peace with. No black envy
　　Shall mark my grave. Commend me to his grace;
　　And if he speak of Buckingham, pray tell him
　　You met him half in heaven. My vows and prayers
　　Yet are the King's and, till my soul forsake,   90
　　Shall cry for blessings on him. May he live
　　Longer than I have time to tell his years;
　　Ever beloved and loving may his rule be;
　　And, when old Time shall lead him to his end,
　　Goodness and he fill up one monument.   95

LOVELL

　　To th' waterside I must conduct your grace,
　　Then give my charge up to Sir Nicholas Vaux,
　　Who undertakes you to your end.

VAUX (*to an attendant*)   Prepare there—
　　The Duke is coming. See the barge be ready,
　　And fit it with such furniture as suits   100
　　The greatness of his person.

BUCKINGHAM   Nay, Sir Nicholas,
　　Let it alone; my state now will but mock me.
　　When I came hither I was Lord High Constable
　　And Duke of Buckingham—now, poor Edward Bohun.
　　Yet I am richer than my base accusers,   105

86–7 'Gainst . . . grace] POPE; *as three lines divided . . . with:/ . . . Graue./* F   87 mark]
HANMER (*conj.* Warburton); make F   98 *to an attendant*] OXFORD; *not in* F

83–4 **I as free . . . all** Cf. Matthew 6: 14–15:
'For if ye forgive men their trespasses,
your heavenly father will also forgive
you' (Shaheen).
86 **take** make
90 **forsake** i.e. leave my body
92 **tell** count
94 **old Time** Time as an old man is a common
personification.
95 **fill up** i.e. (may they) occupy
monument tomb
98 **undertakes** takes charge of
100 **furniture** equipment, provision
104 **Bohun** Pronounced 'Boon'. The family

name was actually Stafford, but he was
descended from the Bohuns, Earls of
Hereford, and held the position of Lord
High Constable by heredity in that family
(Steevens, citing Tollet). Among the nobles opposed to the upstart Wolsey, only
Buckingham could claim a long aristo-
cratic lineage, going back to Edward III's
youngest son, Thomas of Woodstock,
who had married Eleanor Bohun. Buckingham was beheaded because, as his
Plantagenet lineage suggests, he represented a dynastic threat to the Tudors as
much as (perhaps more than) a threat to

That never knew what truth meant. I now seal it,
And with that blood will make 'em one day groan for't.
My noble father, Henry of Buckingham,
Who first raised head against usurping Richard,
Flying for succour to his servant Banister,   110
Being distressed, was by that wretch betrayed,
And without trial fell. God's peace be with him.
Henry the Seventh succeeding, truly pitying
My father's loss, like a most royal prince
Restored me to my honours and out of ruins   115
Made my name once more noble. Now his son,
Henry the Eighth, life, honour, name, and all
That made me happy, at one stroke has taken
For ever from the world. I had my trial,
And must needs say a noble one; which makes me   120
A little happier than my wretched father.
Yet thus far we are one in fortunes: both
Fell by our servants, by those men we loved most—
A most unnatural and faithless service.
Heaven has an end in all. Yet, you that hear me,   125
This from a dying man receive as certain:
Where you are liberal of your loves and counsels,
Be sure you be not loose; for those you make friends
And give your hearts to, when they once perceive
The least rub in your fortunes, fall away   130
Like water from ye, never found again
But where they mean to sink ye. All good people
Pray for me. I must now forsake ye. The last hour

Wolsey, especially since Henry so far had
no living, legitimate son (Saccio, 216–17).

106 **truth** loyalty
   seal attest to, ratify (as if a legal document)
108–16 **My noble . . . noble** (as recorded in
   Holinshed, 869–70)
109 **raised head** gathered an army, rebelled
   usurping Richard Richard III
112 **without trial** Buckingham's father was
   beheaded 'without arraignment or trial'
   (Holinshed).
118 **one stroke** Possibly a punning allusion
   to his execution (Foakes).

125 **end** purpose, goal
126 **This . . . certain** Persons on the point of
   death were believed bound to speak truly;
   cf. *Cymbeline* 5.6.41 (Foakes). Maxwell
   suggests a hint of the different notion that
   dying men are inspired (Tilley M514).
   Cf. *Richard II* 2.1.5–6.
128 **loose** lax, wanting restraint
130 **rub** check, impediment. The metaphor
   is from the game of bowls, which Shakespeare uses elsewhere, as at *Henry V*
   5.2.33 and *Hamlet* 3.1.67.
130–1 **fall . . . ye** Shaheen compares Psalm
   58: 7: 'Let them melt like the waters, let
   them pass away'.

Of my long weary life is come upon me.
Farewell, and when you would say something that is sad,   135
Speak how I fell. I have done, and God forgive me.

> *Exeunt Buckingham and train*
> *The two Gentlemen come forward*

FIRST GENTLEMAN
  O, this is full of pity, sir; it calls,
  I fear, too many curses on their heads
  That were the authors.
SECOND GENTLEMAN   If the Duke be guiltless,
  'Tis full of woe. Yet I can give you inkling   140
  Of an ensuing evil, if it fall,
  Greater than this.
FIRST GENTLEMAN   Good angels keep it from us.
  What may it be? You do not doubt my faith, sir?
SECOND GENTLEMAN
  This secret is so weighty, 'twill require
  A strong faith to conceal it.
FIRST GENTLEMAN   Let me have it;   145
  I do not talk much.
SECOND GENTLEMAN   I am confident;
  You shall, sir. Did you not of late days hear
  A buzzing of a separation
  Between the King and Katherine?
FIRST GENTLEMAN   Yes, but it held not.
  For when the King once heard it, out of anger   150
  He sent command to the Lord Mayor straight
  To stop the rumour and allay those tongues
  That durst disperse it.
SECOND GENTLEMAN   But that slander, sir,

---

135 Farewell] F; *as separate line* CAPELL, FOAKES, MAXWELL   136 Speak . . . me] POPE; *as two
lines divided* fell./ F   I have] F; I've POPE   136.2 *The two . . . forward*] OXFORD; *not in* F

---

134 **long weary life** Buckingham was 43
  years old when he died in 1521.
140 **inkling** hint
143 **faith** trustworthiness
146 **I am confident** i.e. of your discretion
  and trustworthiness
147 **shall** i.e. have it (the 'inkling')
148 **buzzing** whispering, rumour. The
  Gentlemen thus provide a link between
  Buckingham's fall and Katherine's

(NCS). Although in fact the events were
  separated by several years, they are
  dramatically juxtaposed here.
149 **held not** ceased (Pooler)
150–3 **For when . . . disperse it** As recorded
  by Holinshed, 897.
151 **straight** straightaway
152 **allay** restrain
153–4 **slander . . . truth** Cf. Tilley S520: 'It
  may be a slander but it is no lie' (Dent).

Is found a truth now, for it grows again
Fresher than e'er it was and held for certain   155
The King will venture at it. Either the Cardinal
Or some about him near have, out of malice
To the good Queen, possessed him with a scruple
That will undo her. To confirm this, too,
Cardinal Campeius is arrived, and lately,   160
As all think, for this business.
FIRST GENTLEMAN   'Tis the Cardinal;
And merely to revenge him on the Emperor
For not bestowing on him at his asking
The Archbishopric of Toledo this is purposed.
SECOND GENTLEMAN
I think you have hit the mark. But is't not cruel   165
That she should feel the smart of this? The Cardinal
Will have his will, and she must fall.
FIRST GENTLEMAN   'Tis woeful.
We are too open here to argue this.
Let's think in private more.   *Exeunt*

2.2   *Enter the Lord Chamberlain, with a letter*
LORD CHAMBERLAIN (*reads*) 'My lord, the horses your lordship sent for, with all the care I had, I saw well chosen,
ridden, and furnished. They were young and handsome,
and of the best breed in the north. When they were ready
to set out for London, a man of my lord Cardinal's, by   5
commission and main power, took 'em from me with

165 I . . . cruel] POPE; *as two lines divided* thinke/ F
  2.2] *Scena Secunda.* F   0.1] *with a letter*] OXFORD; *reading this Letter* F   1 reads] OXFORD; *not in* F

155 **held** maintained
156 **venture at** hazard, risk
157 **some . . . near** his intimates
158 **possessed** imbued (perhaps hinting at di-
    abolical possession)
    scruple doubt, suspicion, i.e. that the
    marriage was invalid (see Introduction,
    p. 4 n. 3)
160 **Cardinal Campeius** He arrived in 1528
    as the Pope's legate to hear the case with
    Wolsey; see Introduction, p. 7.
162 **the Emperor** Charles V, Holy Roman
    Emperor and King of Spain, Katherine's
    nephew.
165 **have . . . mark** are right. The metaphor,

now dead, is from archery.
168 **open** exposed, out in the open
2.2.1–8 **My . . . sir** The letter, like most of
    the scene, is original. Holinshed suggests
    a few hints, but D. Nichol Smith (cited by
    Maxwell) says the germ of the letter may
    be in Rowley's *When You See Me, You
    Know Me*, 1268–9, where a citizen com-
    plains that Wolsey's emissary has 'taken
    up | Commodities valued at a thousand
    pound' for the Cardinal's advantage.
3 **ridden** broken in
    furnished equipped
6 **commission . . . power** warrant and sheer
    force

this reason: his master would be served before a subject,
if not before the King; which stopped our mouths, sir.'
I fear he will indeed. Well, let him have them.
He will have all, I think.   10

    Enter to the Lord Chamberlain the Dukes of Norfolk
    and Suffolk

NORFOLK Well met, my lord Chamberlain.

LORD CHAMBERLAIN Good day to both your graces.

SUFFOLK

How is the King employed?

LORD CHAMBERLAIN   I left him private,
Full of sad thoughts and troubles.

NORFOLK   What's the cause?

LORD CHAMBERLAIN

It seems the marriage with his brother's wife   15
Has crept too near his conscience.

SUFFOLK   No, his conscience
Has crept too near another lady.

NORFOLK   'Tis so.
This is the Cardinal's doing. The King-Cardinal,
That blind priest, like the eldest son of fortune
Turns what he list. The King will know him one day.   20

SUFFOLK

Pray God he do. He'll never know himself else.

NORFOLK

How holily he works in all his business,
And with what zeal! For now he has cracked the league
Between us and the Emperor, the Queen's great-nephew,

9–10 I fear . . . think] THEOBALD; *as prose* F   21 Pray . . . else] POPE; *as two lines divided*
doe,/ F

---

14 **sad** serious

15–16 **marriage . . . conscience** See Introduction for the causes of Henry's concern over his marriage to his brother's
wife.

16–17 **No . . . lady** Many editors mark an
aside here, perhaps rightly, since Norfolk's reply is to the Lord Chamberlain,
not Suffolk.

18 **This . . . doing** Although Wolsey helped
Henry to seek the divorce, he did not suggest it. (See Introduction, p. 3, n. 2.)

19–20 **That . . . list** Norfolk compares

Wolsey to the senior offspring of Fortune, inheriting her blindness and careless controlling of the destinies of
others. Cf. *Henry V* 3.6.28–36, where
Fluellen describes Fortune's characteris-
tics (Foakes).

19 **blind** (a) (like Fortune); (b) regardless of
others (Maxwell)

21 **know himself** Cf. 'Know thyself', Tilley,
K175 (Dent).

23 **cracked the league** See Introduction for
Wolsey's role in international politics
and 1.1.176–90, 2.1.161–4, above.

He dives into the King's soul and there scatters   25
Dangers, doubts, wringing of the conscience,
Fears, and despairs—and all these for his marriage.
And out of all these, to restore the King,
He counsels a divorce—a loss of her
That like a jewel has hung twenty years   30
About his neck, yet never lost her lustre;
Of her that loves him with that excellence
That angels love good men with; even of her
That, when the greatest stroke of fortune falls,
Will bless the King. And is not this course pious?   35

LORD CHAMBERLAIN
Heaven keep me from such counsel! 'Tis most true—
These news are everywhere, every tongue speaks 'em,
And every true heart weeps for't. All that dare
Look into these affairs see this main end:
The French King's sister. Heaven will one day open   40
The King's eyes that so long have slept upon
This bold bad man.

SUFFOLK   And free us from his slavery.

NORFOLK   We had need pray,
And heartily, for our deliverance,   45
Or this imperious man will work us all
From princes into pages. All men's honours
Lie like one lump before him to be fashioned
Into what pitch he please.

SUFFOLK   For me, my lords,
I love him not, nor fear him—there's my creed.   50
As I am made without him, so I'll stand,
If the King please. His curses and his blessings

44–5 We . . . deliverance] F; ~ . . . deliv'rance POPE

30–1 **jewel . . . neck** Gentlemen wore costly ornaments on gold chains around their necks.
34–5 **when . . . King** Cf. 4.2.164–5, below.
34 **stroke** Perhaps a punning allusion to execution, as at 2.1.118 (Foakes).
37 **These news** (commonly plural at this time)
39 **main end** chief object (Pooler)
40 **French King's sister** Duchess of Alençon, Wolsey's candidate for Henry's second marriage (see Introduction).

41 **slept upon** i.e. been closed to
43 **his slavery** Cf. 1.1.72–9.
47–9 **All . . . please** Foakes and Shaheen cite Romans 9: 21: 'Hath not the potter the power of the clay to make of the same lump one vessel to honour, and another to dishonour?' Cf. also Wisdom of Solomon 15: 7 (Shaheen).
48 **lump** i.e. of clay
49 **pitch** level, stature (Foakes); lit., height
51 **made** i.e. a nobleman

Touch me alike; they're breath I not believe in.
I knew him, and I know him; so I leave him
To him that made him proud—the Pope.

NORFOLK   Let's in,   55
And with some other business put the King
From these sad thoughts that work too much upon him.
My lord, you'll bear us company?

LORD CHAMBERLAIN   Excuse me,
The King has sent me otherwhere. Besides,
You'll find a most unfit time to disturb him.   60
Health to your lordships.

NORFOLK   Thanks, my good lord Chamberlain.
                              Exit the Lord Chamberlain
            King Henry draws the curtain, and sits reading
            pensively

SUFFOLK
How sad he looks! Sure he is much afflicted.

KING HENRY
Who's there? Ha?

NORFOLK   Pray God he be not angry.

KING HENRY
Who's there, I say? How dare you thrust yourselves
Into my private meditations!   65
Who am I? Ha?

NORFOLK
A gracious king that pardons all offences
Malice ne'er meant. Our breach of duty this way
Is business of estate, in which we come
To know your royal pleasure.

KING HENRY   Ye are too bold.   70
Go to, I'll make ye know your times of business.
Is this an hour for temporal affairs? Ha?
            Enter Cardinal Wolsey and Cardinal Campeius, the
            latter with a commission

72.1–2 *the latter*] OXFORD; *not in* F

53 **breath** airy words
55 **him . . . Pope** This is somewhat misleading, revealing the anti-papal attitude of
Protestants; it was Henry who empowered Wolsey and won the cardinal's hat
for him from the Pope.
61.2 *draws the curtain* i.e. the curtain

separating the inner stage, or discovery
space, from the rest of the stage
68 **this way** in this respect
69 **business of estate** state affairs
72 **temporal** secular (implying that he has
been reading a religious book)
72.2 *a commission* i.e. from the Pope, em-

Who's there? My good lord Cardinal? O, my Wolsey,
The quiet of my wounded conscience,
Thou art a cure fit for a king. (*To Campeius*) You're
    welcome,   75
Most learned reverend sir, into our kingdom.
Use us, and it. (*To Wolsey*) My good lord, have great
    care
I be not found a talker.
CARDINAL WOLSEY   Sir, you cannot.
I would your grace would give us but an hour
Of private conference.
KING HENRY (*to Norfolk and Suffolk*) We are busy; go.   80
    Norfolk and Suffolk speak privately to one another as
    they depart

NORFOLK
This priest has no pride in him!
SUFFOLK   Not to speak of.
I would not be so sick, though, for his place.
But this cannot continue.
NORFOLK   If it do
I'll venture one have-at-him.
SUFFOLK   I another.
                  Exeunt Norfolk and Suffolk

CARDINAL WOLSEY
Your grace has given a precedent of wisdom   85
Above all princes in committing freely
Your scruple to the voice of Christendom.
Who can be angry now? What envy reach you?

---

80. 1–2 *Norfolk . . . depart*] OXFORD (*after* Capell); *not in* F   83–4 If . . . him] POPE; *as one line* F
84 one$_\wedge$] MALONE; ~; F

powering both cardinals to hear the case
regarding Henry's marriage to Katherine
(see Holinshed, 906)

74 **quiet** quieter; hence, balm
75 **cure** (implying spiritual care as well;
cf. 1.4.34)
78 **a talker** i.e. a mere flatterer, boaster.
Cf. Tilley, W64: 'The greatest talkers are
the least doers', and W820: 'Not words
but deeds' (Dent).
81 **This . . . of** Spoken ironically and con-
temptuously; cf. 49–55, above.

82 **sick** envious (Onions)
84 **one have-at-him** a stroke, attack
(Onions). Malone's emendation of F's
punctuation (dropping the comma but
not adding hyphens) makes 'have-
at-you' a noun, supported by Suffolk's
response (Maxwell).
87 **voice of Christendom** Henry requested
England's and Europe's most learned ec-
clesiastics to send him their views
concerning his marriage (see Holinshed,
906, and Introduction, p. 4).
88 **envy** malice, ill-will

The Spaniard, tied by blood and favour to her,
Must now confess, if they have any goodness,   90
The trial just and noble. All the clerks—
I mean the learnèd ones in Christian kingdoms—
Have their free voices. Rome, the nurse of judgement,
Invited by your noble self, hath sent
One general tongue unto us: this good man,   95
This just and learnèd priest, Card'nal Campeius,
Whom once more I present unto your highness.
KING HENRY (*embracing Campeius*)
And once more in mine arms I bid him welcome,
And thank the holy conclave for their loves.
They have sent me such a man I would have wished for.   100
CARDINAL CAMPEIUS
Your grace must needs deserve all strangers' loves,
You are so noble. To your highness' hand
I tender my commission, by whose virtue—
The Court of Rome commanding—you, my lord
Cardinal of York, are joined with me their servant   105
In the unpartial judging of this business.
KING HENRY
Two equal men. The Queen shall be acquainted
Forthwith for what you come. Where's Gardiner?
CARDINAL WOLSEY
I know your majesty has always loved her
So dear in heart not to deny her that   110
A woman of less place might ask by law—
Scholars allowed freely to argue for her.
KING HENRY
Ay, and the best she shall have, and my favour

---

98 *embracing Campeius*] OXFORD; *not in* F   104 commanding—you] F4 (~, ~); ~. You FI

91 **clerks** clerics, scholars
93 **Have . . . voices** may vote freely (Foakes)
    judgement faculty of discerning truth (Schmidt)
95 **One general tongue** one to speak for all
97 **once more** Campeius was the (absentee) Bishop of Salisbury and had worked with Wolsey in negotiating a peace treaty among the European powers in 1518
    (Elton, 70–1).
99 **holy conclave** i.e. of cardinals in Rome
100 **They . . . for** Another hexameter line, unless 'They have' and I would' are elided; cf. 1.3.11.
103 **virtue** power, authority
106 **unpartial** impartial
107 **equal** just, impartial
110 **that** that which
111 **less place** lower rank

To him that does best, God forbid else. Cardinal,
Prithee call Gardiner to me, my new secretary.   115
    Cardinal Wolsey goes to the door and summons
    Gardiner
I find him a fit fellow.
    Enter Gardiner
CARDINAL WOLSEY (*aside to Gardiner*)
  Give me your hand. Much joy and favour to you.
  You are the King's now.
GARDINER (*aside to Wolsey*) But to be commanded
  For ever by your grace, whose hand has raised me.
KING HENRY Come hither, Gardiner.   120
    The King walks with Gardiner and whispers with him
CARDINAL CAMPEIUS
  My lord of York, was not one Doctor Pace
  In this man's place before him?
CARDINAL WOLSEY   Yes, he was.
CARDINAL CAMPEIUS
  Was he not held a learnèd man?
CARDINAL WOLSEY   Yes, surely.
CARDINAL CAMPEIUS
  Believe me, there's an ill opinion spread then,
  Even of yourself, Lord Cardinal.
CARDINAL WOLSEY   How? Of me?   125
CARDINAL CAMPEIUS
  They will not stick to say you envied him,
  And fearing he would rise—he was so virtuous—
  Kept him a foreign man still; which so grieved him
  That he ran mad and died.

115.1–2 *Cardinal . . . Gardiner*] OXFORD (*subs.*); *not in* F   120.1 *The King . . . him*] OXFORD;
Walkes and whispers. F

---

115 **Gardiner** Historical time is again compressed, as Dr Stephen Gardiner was not
appointed Henry's secretary until 28 July
1529. He had been Wolsey's agent in
Rome and secured the papal commission
authorizing the Blackfriars trial (Saccio,
227). He became Bishop of Winchester in
1531.
116 **fit** suitable

121 **Doctor Pace** Gardiner replaced Pace,
who 'fell out of his right wits' by being
sent frequently abroad on assignments,
often unnecessarily, by Wolsey (Holinshed, 907). He died in 1536, six years
after Wolsey, not as indicated at l. 129.
126 **stick** hesitate
128 **a foreign man still** i.e. always travelling
abroad

CARDINAL WOLSEY   Heav'n's peace be with him:
That's Christian care enough. For living murmurers   130
There's places of rebuke. He was a fool,
For he would needs be virtuous.
(*Gesturing towards Gardiner*)   That good fellow,
If I command him, follows my appointment.
I will have none so near else. Learn this, brother:
We live not to be griped by meaner persons.   135
KING HENRY (*to Gardiner*)
Deliver this with modesty to th' Queen.   *Exit Gardiner*
The most convenient place that I can think of
For such receipt of learning is Blackfriars;
There ye shall meet about this weighty business.
My Wolsey, see it furnished. O, my lord,   140
Would it not grieve an able man to leave
So sweet a bedfellow? But conscience, conscience;
O, 'tis a tender place, and I must leave her.   *Exeunt*

2.3   *Enter Anne Boleyn and an Old Lady*
ANNE

Not for that neither. Here's the pang that pinches:
His highness having lived so long with her, and she
So good a lady that no tongue could ever
Pronounce dishonour of her—by my life,
She never knew harm-doing—O now, after   5

---

132 *Gesturing towards Gardiner*] OXFORD; *not in* F
2.3] *Scena Tertia*. F

131–2 **He . . . virtuous** Wolsey's machia-
vellian character is nowhere better expressed.
133 **appointment**   direction,   instruction
(Onions)
134 **near** i.e. close to the King
135 **griped** 'caught hold of disrespectfully,
with improper familiarity' (Maxwell)
136 **Deliver** make known
modesty due moderation, mildly
138 **receipt** reception
Blackfriars Then a Dominican mon-
astery; later used as a private theatre
by children's companies from 1600 and
by the King's Men from 1609 to 1642. If
the play was performed here in the seven-

teenth century, the scene would have
been staged in its original historical
setting.
141 **able** vigorous, lusty
142–3 **So sweet . . . her** Anderson (128–9)
explores the possible ambiguities in these
lines, e.g. those the association between
'sweet a bedfellow' and 'tender place'
suggests; 'her' presumably refers to
Katherine, but Henry's doubled use of
'conscience' may also point to Anne.
2.3 The scene is the dramatist's invention
and begins in the middle of a conversation.
1 **pinches** torments, hurts
4 **Pronounce** speak, utter

So many courses of the sun enthroned,
Still growing in a majesty and pomp the which
To leave a thousandfold more bitter than
'Tis sweet at first t'acquire—after this process,
To give her the avaunt, it is a pity   10
Would move a monster.

OLD LADY   Hearts of most hard temper
Melt and lament for her.

ANNE   O, God's will! Much better
She ne'er had known pomp; though't be temporal,
Yet if that quarrel, fortune, do divorce
It from the bearer, 'tis a sufferance panging   15
As soul and bodies severing.

OLD LADY   Alas, poor lady!
She's a stranger now again.

ANNE   So much the more
Must pity drop upon her. Verily,
I swear, 'tis better to be lowly born
And range with humble livers in content   20
Than to be perked up in a glist'ring grief
And wear a golden sorrow.

OLD LADY   Our content
Is our best having.

ANNE   By my troth and maidenhead,
I would not be a queen.

OLD LADY   Beshrew me, I would,
And venture maidenhead for't; and so would you,   25
For all this spice of your hypocrisy.
You, that have so fair parts of woman on you,

14 quarrel, fortune, do] F2; ~. Fortune, ~ F1; quarreler ~, ~, ~ HANMER (quarr'ler)

6 **courses of the sun** years
7–8 **the which . . . leave** i.e. which to surrender is. NCS notes the irony here, given Anne's own fate.
9 **process** course of events
10 **avaunt** the order to go, rejection
pity matter for compassion
11 **temper** disposition (lit. 'tempering', as of steel)
14 **quarrel** quarreller (Johnson)
15 **sufferance panging** injury as painful
16 **soul . . . severing** Cf. *Antony* 4.14.5–6: 'The soul and body rive not more in parting | Than greatness going off'

(Humphreys).
17 **stranger** alien
20 **range . . . livers** occupy a rank with humble folk
21 **perked up** trimmed out (Onions)
glist'ring glittering, sparkling
22–3 **Our . . . having** Cf. Tilley C624: 'Content is happiness' (Dent); 'having' = possession.
23 **troth** faith
24 **Beshrew me** A mild oath: the devil take me.
26 **spice** dash, touch
27 **fair parts** (a) beauty; (b) fine personal attributes

Have, too, a woman's heart, which ever yet
Affected eminence, wealth, sovereignty;
Which, to say sooth, are blessings; and which gifts,   30
Saving your mincing, the capacity
Of your soft cheveril conscience would receive,
If you might please to stretch it.

ANNE   Nay, good troth.

OLD LADY

Yes, troth and troth. You would not be a queen?

ANNE

No, not for all the riches under heaven.   35

OLD LADY

'Tis strange. A threepence bowed would hire me,
Old as I am, to queen it. But I pray you,
What think you of a duchess? Have you limbs
To bear that load of title?

ANNE   No, in truth.

OLD LADY

Then you are weakly made. Pluck off a little;   40
I would not be a young count in your way
For more than blushing comes to. If your back
Cannot vouchsafe this burden, 'tis too weak
Ever to get a boy.

ANNE   How you do talk!

---

29 **Affected** loved, desired
30 **sooth** truth
31 **mincing** affectation (Onions)
32 **cheveril** kid-leather, proverbial for softness and stretching qualities and often applied to conscience; cf. Tilley C608: 'He has a conscience like a cheveril's skin' (Dent). The image recalls Henry's tenderness of conscience (2.2.142–3) and summarizes the impression of conscience that dominates Acts 1 and 2; the question of conscience and of the truth to which it answers lies at the core of this play (Anderson, 129–30).
34 **troth and troth** faith, possibly punning on 'trot' = a contemptuous term for old lady (Foakes); cf. *Shrew* 1.2.78.
36 **threepence bowed** i.e. a bent and therefore worthless coin, with a possible pun on 'bawd'. Since no threepenny pieces were coined until after Henry's reign,

this is an anachronism (Pooler).
36 **hire** (disyllabic)
37 **queen** Punning on 'quean' = strumpet.
40 **Pluck off** lit., disrobe; hence, come down in rank (Onions)
41 **count** rank lower than a duke. For a pun on 'cunt', here used for 'countess', cf. Camden, *Machyn's Diary*, 1553: 'Phelyp and Marie . . . kyng and queen of England . . . prynsses of Spayne . . . archesduke of Austherege . . . Contes of Haspurge' (cited *OED* under *count, sb.*² 1).
in your way Quibbling on the senses path and condition, i.e. virgin (cf. 23, above).
42 **For . . . to** i.e. I would not remain a young countess and a virgin like you for more than a blush cost me. Cf. the similar dialogue between Emilia and Desdemona, *Othello* 4.3.60–84.
43 **vouchsafe** deign to accept
burden (refers to sexual intercourse)

I swear again, I would not be a queen   45
For all the world.
OLD LADY   In faith, for little England
You'd venture an emballing; I myself
Would for Caernarvonshire, although there 'longed
No more to th' crown but that. Lo, who comes here?
          Enter the Lord Chamberlain

LORD CHAMBERLAIN
Good morrow, ladies. What were't worth to know   50
The secret of your conference?
ANNE   My good lord,
Not your demand; it values not your asking.
Our mistress' sorrows we were pitying.

LORD CHAMBERLAIN
It was a gentle business, and becoming
The action of good women. There is hope   55
All will be well.
ANNE   Now I pray God, amen.

LORD CHAMBERLAIN
You bear a gentle mind, and heav'nly blessings
Follow such creatures. That you may, fair lady,
Perceive I speak sincerely, and high note's
Ta'en of your many virtues, the King's majesty   60
Commends his good opinion of you, and
Does purpose honour to you no less flowing
Than Marchioness of Pembroke; to which title

48 Caernarvonshire] F (*Carnaruanshire*)   59 note's] THEOBALD; notes F   61 of you, and]
CAPELL; ~ ~, to you; and F; to ~, ~ POPE

46 **little England** (a) England itself; (b) Pembrokeshire, often referred to by that name because people there generally spoke English (instead of Welsh, as in the rest of Wales; Steevens, citing John Taylor the Water Poet, *A Short Relation of a Long Journey*). The reference anticipates Anne's elevation as Marchioness of Pembroke at l. 63.

47 **emballing** (a) investiture with the ball or orb as the emblem of royalty (Johnson); (b) used in indelicate sense (Onions)

48 **Caernarvonshire** A poor county in western Wales. Foakes suggests a quibble, alluding to its shape, which is wedge-shaped, 'long and narrow towards the south' (Speed, *Theatre of the Empire*, 1611, Hh1).
'**longed** belonged

51 **conference** conversation
52 **Not your demand** (explained in the rest of the line)
   values not is not worth
59 **note's** note is
61 **Commends . . . you** i.e. presents his compliments (Pooler)
   of you Capell's emendation corrects F; Compositor I apparently caught 'to you' from the following line.
62 **flowing** brimming, abundant. Cf. *Troilus* 4.5.77–8: 'with gifts of nature flowing, | And swelling o'er with arts and exercise'.
63 **Marchioness of Pembroke** Anne was elevated to this rank on 1 September 1532 and given a thousand pounds annually (see Holinshed, 928). Again, time is

A thousand pound a year annual support
Out of his grace he adds.

ANNE   I do not know   65
What kind of my obedience I should tender.
More than my all is nothing; nor my prayers
Are not words duly hallowed, nor my wishes
More worth than empty vanities; yet prayers and wishes
Are all I can return. Beseech your lordship,   70
Vouchsafe to speak my thanks and my obedience
As from a blushing handmaid to his highness,
Whose health and royalty I pray for.

LORD CHAMBERLAIN   Lady,
I shall not fail t'approve the fair conceit
The King hath of you. (*Aside*) I have perused her well.   75
Beauty and honour in her are so mingled
That they have caught the King, and who knows yet
But from this lady may proceed a gem
To lighten all this isle.—I'll to the King
And say I spoke with you.   80

ANNE My honoured lord.   *Exit Lord Chamberlain*

OLD LADY Why, this it is: see, see!
I have been begging sixteen years in court,
Am yet a courtier beggarly, nor could
Come pat betwixt too early and too late   85
For any suit of pounds; and you—O, fate!—
A very fresh fish here—fie, fie upon

---

75 *Aside*] POPE; *not in* F   81 *Exit Lord Chamberlain*] F (*after l.* 80)   87 fie, fie] POPE; fye, fye, fye F

compressed for dramatic purposes, as
Henry begins his wooing of Anne. According to S. T. Bindoff, Anne was cre-
ated Marquess, not Marchioness; see
Tudor England (1950), 90 n.

67–9 **More . . . vanities** 'Could I do more
than my utmost it would still be as nothing, my prayers not holy enough, my
wishes no more than worthless, ineffectual words' (Humphreys). Anne appears
extremely modest or naive, or both.

67–8 **nor . . . not** The double negative is for
emphasis (Abbott §406).

74 **t'approve . . . conceit** confirm the good
opinion

75 **peruse** examine, inspect (as at *Romeo*

5.3.74)

78–9 **But . . . isle** Alludes to the birth of Elizabeth I and anticipates 5.4.16–47.

79 **lighten** shed light upon. In Renaissance
physics, precious stones gave off light. Cf.
Titus 2.3.227: 'A precious ring that
lightens all this hole' (Humphreys).

82 **this it is** i.e. thus it is, as at *Antony* 2.7.11
(Foakes)

85 **pat** quite to the purpose, fitly (Schmidt);
cf. *Lear* 1.2.131.

86 **suit of pounds** petition for money
(Onions). 'Pounds' also = ponds (*OED
sb.²* 4a) and may have suggested the
metaphor in the next line (Foakes).

87 **fie, fie** Pope's emendation of F's apparent
dittography corrects the metre.

This compelled fortune!—have your mouth filled up
Before you open it.

ANNE   This is strange to me.

OLD LADY

How tastes it? Is it bitter? Forty pence, no.   90
There was a lady once—'tis an old story—
That would not be a queen, that would she not,
For all the mud in Egypt. Have you heard it?

ANNE

Come, you are pleasant.

OLD LADY   With your theme I could
O'ermount the lark. The Marchioness of Pembroke?   95
A thousand pounds a year, for pure respect?
No other obligation? By my life,
That promises more thousands. Honour's train
Is longer than his foreskirt. By this time
I know your back will bear a duchess. Say,   100
Are you not stronger than you were?

ANNE   Good lady,
Make yourself mirth with your particular fancy,
And leave me out on't. Would I had no being,
If this salute my blood a jot. It faints me
To think what follows.   105
The Queen is comfortless, and we forgetful
In our long absence. Pray do not deliver
What here you've heard to her.

OLD LADY   What do you think me?

Exeut

98 more] F (mo)   108 me?] GLOBE; ~ — F

88 **compelled fortune** fortune thrust upon
one ('compelled' accented on first
syllable)
90 **Forty pence** Proverbial for a small sum
(Steevens; Tilley F618). Cf. *Richard II*
5.5.68: 'The cheapest of us is ten groats
too dear' (10 groats = 40 (old) pence).
93 **mud in Egypt** Source of Egypt's fertility
and therefore wealth. The Old Lady harks
back to their earlier conversation,
24–49.
94 **pleasant** merry
   With your theme 'if I had the subject
(your advancement) that you have'
(Deighton, cited by Maxwell)

95 **O'ermount** rise above
98 **more** i.e. in number
98–9 **Honour's . . . foreskirt** i.e. more rewards and honours will follow, like the
train of an elaborate dress becoming
longer with increasing rank, the foreskirt
remaining necessarily much shorter
(NCS)
100 **your . . . duchess** Cf. 38–44 above.
102 **particular** private, personal
103 **on't** of it
104 **salute** affect, act upon (Onions)
   blood passion, emotion
   faints me makes me faint
107 **deliver** make known, relate

2.4   *Trumpets: sennet. Then cornetts. Enter two vergers*
with short silver wands; next them two Scribes in the
habit of doctors; after them the Archbishop of
Canterbury alone; after him the Bishops of Lincoln,
Ely, Rochester, and Saint Asaph; next them, with   0.5
some small distance, follows a gentleman bearing both
the purse containing the great seal and a cardinal's
hat; then two priests bearing each a silver cross; then
a gentleman usher, bare-headed, accompanied with a
serjeant-at-arms bearing a silver mace; then two   0.10
gentlemen bearing two great silver pillars; after them,
side by side, the two cardinals, Wolsey and
Campeius; then two noblemen with the sword and
mace. The King ascends to his seat under the cloth of
state; the two cardinals sit under him as judges; the   0.15
Queen, attended by Griffith her gentleman usher,
takes place some distance from the King; the Bishops
place themselves on each side the court in the manner
of a consistory; below them, the Scribes. The lords sit
next the Bishops. The rest of the attendants stand in   0.20
convenient order about the stage

CARDINAL WOLSEY
Whilst our commission from Rome is read
Let silence be commanded.

2.4] *Scena Quarta.* F   0.1 *Trumpets: sennet. Then cornetts*] OXFORD; ~, ~, *and* ~ F
0.3 *Archbishop*] JOHNSON; *Bishop* F   0.6 *both*] OXFORD; *not in* F   0.7 *containing*] OXFORD;
with F   0.12–13 *Wolsey and Campeius; then*] OXFORD; *not in* F   0.14 *ascends to his seat*]
OXFORD; *takes place* F   0.16 *attended . . . usher*] OXFORD; *not in* F

2.4 The events in this scene occurred in June
1529 and closely follow Holinshed's account, 907–8. The number of supers for
the procession—at least sixteen—is unusually large.

0.1 **sennet** fanfare; notes played on a trumpet or cornet to signal approach or
departure of a ceremonial procession
vergers officials who carry a rod or similar symbol (here, silver wands) before the
dignitaries of a cathedral (*OED*)

0.3 **habit of doctors** i.e. the furred, black
gowns and flat hats of doctors of law; cf.
Lear 4.5.161: 'Robes and furred gowns
hide all'.

0.8 **two . . . cross** Wolsey had two large silver
crosses, one as an emblem of his archbishopric, the other of his position as papal

legate, carried before him always (Foakes,
citing Stow's *Annals* (1592), 838).

0.11 **pillars** Portable ensigns of office in the
form of an ornamented pillar or column
borne before Wolsey as a cardinal
(Onions). The mace (0.10) was also an
emblem of his office.

0.16 **attended . . . usher** Humphreys identi-
fies Griffith as the 'gentleman usher' at
0.9; Oxford places him later in the procession with Katherine as her gentleman
usher (see 4.2). F does not name him at
124, but both Humphreys and Oxford
follow Malone in that identification.

0.19 **consistory** College of cardinals presided
over by the Pope (Onions), or tribunal,
court of judgement (NCS).

1 **commission** See 2.2.103.

KING HENRY   What's the need?

It hath already publicly been read,

And on all sides th'authority allowed.

You may then spare that time.

CARDINAL WOLSEY   Be't so. Proceed.   5

SCRIBE (*to the Crier*)

Say, 'Henry, King of England, come into the court'.

CRIER

Henry, King of England, come into the court.

KING HENRY   Here.

SCRIBE (*to the Crier*)

Say, 'Katherine, Queen of England, come into the
        court'.

CRIER

Katherine, Queen of England, come into the court.   10

The Queen makes no answer, rises out of her chair,
goes about the court, comes to the King, and kneels
at his feet; then speaks

QUEEN KATHERINE

Sir, I desire you do me right and justice,

And to bestow your pity on me, for

I am a most poor woman, and a stranger,

Born out of your dominions, having here

No judge indifferent, nor no more assurance   15

Of equal friendship and proceeding. Alas, sir,

In what have I offended you? What cause

Hath my behaviour given to your displeasure

That thus you should proceed to put me off

And take your good grace from me? Heaven witness,   20

7, 10 come into the court] HUMPHREYS; &c. F   9 Say, Katherine . . . court] *as one verse line*
FOAKES; *as prose* CAPELL; *as two lines divided* England / F   11 QUEEN KATHERINE Sir] WARBUR-
TON; Sir F

---

3 **It . . . read** According to Hall (756–7),
the commission was read ('openly declared') at an earlier assembly on 28
May, the day after the feast of Corpus
Christi.

10.1–3 *The Queen . . . speaks* The direction
is borrowed from Holinshed (907), and its
dramatic effect is obvious. Katherine does
not respond to the Crier, but addresses

Henry directly.

11–55 **Sir . . . fulfilled** Essentially Holinshed
versified, with significant changes at
29–32 and 39–42 (Foakes).

15 **indifferent** impartial

16 **equal friendship** i.e. in the court as Henry
has; 'equal' = fair

19 **put me off** discard me

20 **good grace** person as well as favour

I have been to you a true and humble wife,
At all times to your will conformable,
Ever in fear to kindle your dislike,
Yea, subject to your countenance, glad or sorry
As I saw it inclined. When was the hour   25
I ever contradicted your desire?
Or made it not mine too? Or which of your friends
Have I not strove to love, although I knew
He were mine enemy? What friend of mine
That had to him derived your anger did I   30
Continue in my liking—nay, gave notice
He was from thence discharged? Sir, call to mind
That I have been your wife in this obedience
Upward of twenty years and have been blessed
With many children by you. If, in the course   35
And process of this time, you can report—
And prove it, too—against mine honour aught,
My bond to wedlock, or my love and duty
Against your sacred person, in God's name
Turn me away, and let the foul'st contempt   40
Shut door upon me, and so give me up
To the sharp'st kind of justice. Please you, sir,
The King your father was reputed for
A prince most prudent, of an excellent
And unmatched wit and judgement. Ferdinand   45
My father, King of Spain, was reckoned one
The wisest prince that there had reigned by many
A year before. It is not to be questioned
That they had gathered a wise council to them
Of every realm, that did debate this business,   50

---

22 **conformable** compliant, submissive (Onions)

24 **countenance** A richly ambiguous word that may mean disposition, bearing, favour, face, or any combination of these senses.

28 **strove** Old form of past participle, 'striven' (Abbott §343).

30 **derived** drawn

35 **many children** (all of whom, except Mary, died at birth or soon afterwards)

39 **Against** towards

39–42 **in . . . justice** As Foakes notes, Holinshed's expression is far more subdued. Cf. *All's Well* 2.1.170–4, where Helena invokes a similar harsh punishment if she is wrong.

40–1 **let . . . upon me** i.e. with utter contempt shut me out

45 **wit** intelligence, wisdom

46 **one** Used to emphasize superlatives (Abbott §18).

49–51 **they . . . lawful** Henry VII and Ferdinand had consulted widely about

Who deemed our marriage lawful. Wherefore I humbly
Beseech you, sir, to spare me till I may
Be by my friends in Spain advised, whose counsel
I will implore. If not, i'th' name of God,
Your pleasure be fulfilled.

CARDINAL WOLSEY   You have here, lady,   55
And of your choice, these reverend fathers, men
Of singular integrity and learning,
Yea, the elect o'th' land, who are assembled
To plead your cause. It shall be therefore bootless
That longer you desire the court, as well   60
For your own quiet, as to rectify
What is unsettled in the King.

CARDINAL CAMPEIUS   His grace
Hath spoken well and justly. Therefore, madam,
It's fit this royal session do proceed,
And that without delay their arguments   65
Be now produced and heard.

QUEEN KATHERINE (*to Wolsey*)   Lord Cardinal,
To you I speak.

CARDINAL WOLSEY   Your pleasure, madam.

QUEEN KATHERINE   Sir,
I am about to weep, but thinking that
We are a queen—or long have dreamed so, certain
The daughter of a king—my drops of tears   70
I'll turn to sparks of fire.

CARDINAL WOLSEY   Be patient yet.

QUEEN KATHERINE
I will when you are humble. Nay, before,

67 madam.] F; ~? THEOBALD   67–8 Sir . . . that] POPE; *as one line* F

the marriage and obtained a papal
dispensation.

56 **reverend fathers** i.e. the churchmen
Katherine had selected as her counsel:
the Archbishop of Canterbury, William
Warham, and the Bishops of Ely
(Nicholas West), Rochester (John Fisher),
and St Asaph (Henry Standish)
57 **singular** unmatched
59 **bootless** useless, unavailing

60 **longer . . . court** you entreat the court
any more (for a postponement of the trial)
61 **quiet** peace of mind
66 **produced** brought forward, exhibited
69 **certain** certainly
71 **Be patient** The usual advice in adversity,
with which for example Albany counsels
Lear (*Lear* 1.4.240); cf. 1.1.124 n.,
above, and 3.2.459, below.
72 **before** i.e. before you turn humble (for
you will never be) (Pooler)

Or God will punish me. I do believe,
Induced by potent circumstances, that
You are mine enemy, and make my challenge   75
You shall not be my judge. For it is you
Have blown this coal betwixt my lord and me,
Which God's dew quench. Therefore, I say again,
I utterly abhor, yea, from my soul,
Refuse you for my judge, whom yet once more   80
I hold my most malicious foe and think not
At all a friend to truth.
CARDINAL WOLSEY   I do profess
You speak not like yourself, who ever yet
Have stood to charity and displayed th'effects
Of disposition gentle and of wisdom   85
O'er-topping woman's power. Madam, you do me
          wrong.
I have no spleen against you, nor injustice
For you or any. How far I have proceeded,
Or how far further shall, is warranted
By a commission from the consistory,   90
Yea, the whole consistory of Rome. You charge me
That I 'have blown this coal'. I do deny it.
The King is present: if it be known to him
That I gainsay my deed, how may he wound,
And worthily, my falsehood—yea, as much   95
As you have done my truth. If he know
That I am free of your report, he knows
I am not of your wrong. Therefore in him
It lies to cure me, and the cure is to

74 **Induced** persuaded
75 **make my challenge** A legal term for raising an objection (Johnson).
77 **blown this coal** Proverbial for stirring up trouble (Tilley C465).
79 **abhor** protest against, reject (canon law term; Humphreys)
82 **profess** declare openly (Onions)
84 **stood to** upheld, stood up for
   charity Christian love
85–6 **wisdom . . . woman's power** That women had inferior intellectual abilities was a common Renaissance view, not one peculiar to Wolsey. Cf. 104–5, below.

87 **spleen** malice, antagonism. This speech may be indebted to Hall (755), where Wolsey defends himself against Katherine's claim that he is responsible for Henry's action in seeking the divorce (Foakes).
90 **consistory** college of cardinals
94 **gainsay my deed** deny what I have done
95 **worthily** rightly
96–8 **If . . . wrong** If he knows that I am innocent of your accusation, he also knows that I am not innocent of the wrong you have done me.
99 **cure** Cf. 2.2.75 and 'wound', 94.

Remove these thoughts from you. The which before   100
His highness shall speak in, I do beseech
You, gracious madam, to unthink your speaking,
And to say so no more.
QUEEN KATHERINE   My lord, my lord,
I am a simple woman, much too weak
T'oppose your cunning. You're meek and humble-
          mouthed;   105
You sign your place and calling, in full seeming,
With meekness and humility: but your heart
Is crammed with arrogancy, spleen, and pride.
You have by fortune and his highness' favours
Gone slightly o'er low steps and now are mounted   110
Where powers are your retainers, and your words—
Domestics to you—serve your will as't please
Yourself pronounce their office. I must tell you,
You tender more your person's honour than
Your high profession spiritual; that again   115
I do refuse you for my judge; and here,
Before you all, appeal unto the Pope
To bring my whole cause fore his holiness,
And to be judged by him.
          She curtsies to the King and offers to depart
CARDINAL CAMPEIUS   The Queen is obstinate,
Stubborn to justice, apt to accuse it, and   120
Disdainful to be tried by't. 'Tis not well.
She's going away.
KING HENRY (*to the Crier*) Call her again.
CRIER
Katherine, Queen of England, come into the court.
GRIFFITH Madam, you are called back.

124 GRIFFITH] MALONE; *Gent. Ush.* F

101 **in** in reference to
102 **unthink your speaking** i.e. annul what
   you have spoken, withdraw your accusations
105–7 **You're . . . humility** As Shaheen
   notes, these are the qualities that should
   be characteristic of Christians, especially
   churchmen.
106 **sign** mark
   in full seeming in all outward appearance
   (NCS)

110 **slightly** lightly, easily
111 **powers . . . retainers** the highest officers of
   state are subservient to your will (Steevens)
111–13 **your words . . . office** your words act
   like domestic servants and carry out your
   wishes as soon as you utter them
114 **tender** care for
118 **cause** case
120 **Stubborn** unyielding
124 GRIFFITH See 2.4.0.16n. and cf.
   Holinshed, 907: 'With that (quoth

QUEEN KATHERINE

What need you note it? Pray you keep your way.   125
When you are called, return. Now the Lord help.
They vex me past my patience. Pray you, pass on.
I will not tarry; no, nor ever more
Upon this business my appearance make
In any of their courts.

Exeunt Queen Katherine and her attendants

KING HENRY   Go thy ways, Kate.   130
That man i'th' world who shall report he has
A better wife, let him in naught be trusted
For speaking false in that. Thou art alone—
If thy rare qualities, sweet gentleness,
Thy meekness saint-like, wife-like government,   135
Obeying in commanding, and thy parts
Sovereign and pious else could speak thee out—
The queen of earthly queens. She's noble born,
And like her true nobility she has
Carried herself towards me.

CARDINAL WOLSEY   Most gracious sir,   140
In humblest manner I require your highness
That it shall please you to declare in hearing
Of all these ears—for where I am robbed and bound,
There must I be unloosed, although not there
At once and fully satisfied—whether ever I   145
Did broach this business to your highness, or
Laid any scruple in your way which might
Induce you to the question on't, or ever
Have to you, but with thanks to God for such
A royal lady, spake one the least word that might   150

130 *Exeunt*] ROWE; *Exit* F   143 robbed] F (rob'd)

Master Griffith), Madam, you be called
again'.

125 **keep your way** keep on going. Katherine
addresses all her attendants here as at
127, but the next line refers to Griffith
only.
134 **rare** excellent
135 **government** control (of self and others)
(Humphreys)
136 **Obeying in commanding** obeying the
dictates of self-restraint even when giving

commands (Maxwell, citing Deighton)
parts qualities, attributes
137 **Sovereign** (a) royal, princely; (b) excellent
speak thee out describe you fully
140 **Carried** behaved
141 **require** request
145 **satisfied** compensated, repaid. The King
may exonerate Wolsey here, but his
reputation will not be fully restored.
147 **scruple** doubt
150 **one** See l. 46 n. above.

Be to the prejudice of her present state,
Or touch of her good person?

KING HENRY   My lord Cardinal,
I do excuse you; yea, upon mine honour,
I free you from't. You are not to be taught
That you have many enemies that know not   155
Why they are so, but, like to village curs,
Bark when their fellows do. By some of these
The Queen is put in anger. You're excused.
But will you be more justified? You ever
Have wished the sleeping of this business, never desired   160
It to be stirred, but oft have hindered, oft,
The passages made toward it. On my honour
I speak my good lord Card'nal to this point,
And thus far clear him. Now, what moved me to't,
I will be bold with time and your attention.   165
Then mark th'inducement. Thus it came; give heed to't.
My conscience first received a tenderness,
Scruple, and prick, on certain speeches uttered
By th' Bishop of Bayonne, then French Ambassador,
Who had been hither sent on the debating   170
A marriage 'twixt the Duke of Orleans and
Our daughter Mary. I'th' progress of this business,
Ere a determinate resolution, he—
I mean the Bishop—did require a respite
Wherein he might the King his lord advertise   175
Whether our daughter were legitimate,
Respecting this our marriage with the dowager,
Sometimes our brother's wife. This respite shook
The bosom of my conscience, entered me,

---

164 And . . . to't] ROWE 1714; *as two lines divided* him. / F   171 A] ROWE 1714; And F

151 **prejudice** injury, impairment
152 **touch** taint, sullying (Onions)
156–7 **curs . . . do** Proverbial: cf. Tilley D539.
158 **excused** exonerated
162 **passages** proceedings
163 **speak** bear witness in favour of (Maxwell). Here, Henry addresses the whole court.
167 **tenderness** sensitivity. Cf. Tilley C598: 'The conscience and the eye are tender parts' (Dent).

169 **Bishop . . . Ambassador** On Henry's scruples, see Introduction and Holinshed, 907, closely followed here.
171 **Duke of Orleans** Second son of Francis I and later Henry II, King of France.
173 **determinate resolution** final decision
175 **advertise** take counsel with (accented on second syllable)
177 **dowager** i.e. Katherine as Arthur's widow
178 **Sometimes** formerly
179 **bosom** inmost recesses. Theobald's

Yea, with a spitting power, and made to tremble   180
The region of my breast, which forced such way
That many mazed considerings did throng
And pressed in with this caution. First, methought
I stood not in the smile of heaven, who had
Commanded nature that my lady's womb,   185
If it conceived a male child by me, should
Do no more offices of life to't than
The grave does to the dead. For her male issue
Or died where they were made, or shortly after
This world had aired them. Hence I took a thought   190
This was a judgement on me that my kingdom,
Well worthy the best heir o'th' world, should not
Be gladded in't by me. Then follows that
I weighed the danger which my realms stood in
By this my issue's fail, and that gave to me   195
Many a groaning throe. Thus hulling in
The wild sea of my conscience, I did steer
Toward this remedy, whereupon we are
Now present here together—that's to say
I meant to rectify my conscience, which   200
I then did feel full sick, and yet not well,

---

180 spitting] F1; splitting F2   188 does to the] ROWE 1714; does to th' F; ~ yield to th'
OXFORD   196 throe] POPE; throw F

emendation, 'bottom', is unnecessary,
as Foakes says, although Holinshed actually uses the phrase 'the secret bottom of
my conscience' in Henry's speech.

180 **spitting** transfixing (as on a spit)
(Onions). Again, emendation to 'splitting'
(F2) is unnecessary (Foakes, Sisson).
182 **mazed** confused, bewildered (as in a
maze) (Onions)
182–3 **throng . . . pressed in** i.e. like a crowd
of people; cf. *Lucrece* 1301–2: 'Much like
a press of people at a door | Throng her
inventions' (Maxwell).
184–8 **I stood . . . dead** Henry alludes to the
fact that Katherine and he have produced
no surviving male heir, as the following
lines make plain. Accordingly, he feels he
lacks heaven's favour ('the smile of
heaven').
187 **offices** (a) services; (b) rites due to the
dead (Foakes)

189 **Or** either
190 **aired** exposed to public view (Onions)
193 **gladded** made glad
196 **throe** extreme pain, pang (Schmidt)
196–7 **hulling . . . steer** For the wide use of
the metaphor of navigation in Shakespeare and his contemporaries, see Philip
Edwards, *Seamark: The Metaphor of Voy-
aging: Spenser to Milton* (Liverpool, 1997),
esp. 101–48 on Shakespeare.
196 **hulling** floating or drifting by the force of
the wind or current acting on the hull
alone, the sails being furled (Onions)
197 **steer** As Pooler notes, a hulling ship
cannot be steered. Humphreys suggests
that either Shakespeare is writing loosely
here, or his mind has passed to a later
state when the ship is under control and
moving towards safety.
200 **rectify** set right
201 **full** very, extremely
   yet even now, still

By all the reverend fathers of the land
And doctors learned. First I began in private
With you, my lord of Lincoln. You remember
How under my oppression I did reek   205
When I first moved you.

LINCOLN   Very well, my liege.

KING HENRY

I have spoke long. Be pleased yourself to say
How far you satisfied me.

LINCOLN   So please your highness,
The question did at first so stagger me,
Bearing a state of mighty moment in't   210
And consequence of dread, that I committed
The daring'st counsel which I had to doubt,
And did entreat your highness to this course,
Which you are running here.

KING HENRY   I then moved you,
My lord of Canterbury, and got your leave   215
To make this present summons. Unsolicited
I left no reverend person in this court,
But by particular consent proceeded
Under your hands and seals. Therefore, go on,
For no dislike i'th' world against the person   220
Of the good Queen, but the sharp thorny points
Of my allegèd reasons drives this forward.
Prove but our marriage lawful, by my life
And kingly dignity, we are contented
To wear our mortal state to come with her,   225

216 summons. Unsolicited͜] THEOBALD (*subs*.); ~͜ vnsolicited. F

203 **doctors learned** i.e. learned men
204 **lord of Lincoln** According to Holinshed, 906, John Longland, Bishop of Lincoln, was Henry's confessor.
205 **under . . . reek** i.e. my distress caused me to sweat; cf. *Lear* 2.2.206: 'came there a reeking post'
206 **moved** appealed to (Maxwell)
210–11 **Bearing . . . dread** concerning a state of things of great importance and fearful outcome (Foakes)
211–12 **I committed . . . doubt** I questioned the most extreme advice that I had to offer (i.e. to seek a divorce). Holinshed says (897) that Longland was popularly be-

lieved to be among the first to suggest to Henry that the marriage was not lawful (Maxwell).
218 **particular** individual
219 **Under . . . seals** A formal expression referring to written consent properly ratified.
222 **allegèd** proffered
drives The third person plural in *-s* is common in F (Abbott §333).
223–4 **my life . . . we are** Note the shift from first person singular to the royal plural, as at 5.1.98–108.
225 **mortal . . . come** the rest of my life on earth

137

Katherine, our queen, before the primest creature
That's paragoned o'th' world.
CARDINAL CAMPEIUS   So please your highness,
The Queen being absent, 'tis a needful fitness
That we adjourn this court till further day.
Meanwhile must be an earnest motion   230
Made to the Queen to call back her appeal
She intends unto his holiness.
KING HENRY (*aside*)   I may perceive
These cardinals trifle with me. I abhor
This dilatory sloth and tricks of Rome.
My learnèd and well-beloved servant, Cranmer,   235
Prithee return. With thy approach I know
My comfort comes along.—Break up the court.
I say, set on.   *Exeunt in manner as they entered*

3.1   *Enter Queen Katherine and her women, as at work*
QUEEN KATHERINE

Take thy lute, wench. My soul grows sad with troubles.
Sing, and disperse 'em if thou canst. Leave working.

---

232 *aside*] CAPELL (*subs.*); F *omits*   236 return. With thy approach‸] OXFORD (*after* F4); ~, ~
~ ~: F
   3.1] *Actus Tertius. Scena Prima.* F   1 Take . . . troubles] POPE; *as two lines divided* wench,/ F

---

226 **primest** most excellent
227 **paragoned** set forth as a paragon or per-
    fect model (Onions)
229 **further** a future
230 **motion** request, proposal
231–2 **her appeal . . . holiness** For Kather-
    ine's appeal to the Pope, see Introduc-
    tion.
232–4 **I may . . . Rome** Cf. Holinshed, 908:
    'The King would gladly have an end in
    the matter, but when the legates drove
    time and determined upon no certain
    point, he conceived a suspicion that this
    was done of purpose, that their doings
    might draw to none effect or conclusion'.
    See also Hall (758) and Introduction, pp.
    4, 8, for the political situation causing the
    delay.
235 **Cranmer** The apostrophe to Cranmer,
    who succeeded Warham as Archbishop
    of Canterbury in 1532, marks the King's
    transfer of trust away from Wolsey

(Humphreys). Hall (758) says Henry cast
Wolsey out of favour at this point, believ-
ing that he with Campeius unfaithfully
dissimulated with him to have the matter
heard in the court of Rome 'for the main-
tenance of their authority'.
236–7 **Prithee . . . along** Cranmer was trav-
    elling in Europe at this time, gathering
    opinions to support Henry's divorce.
238 **set on** advance
3.1 This scene expands and sharpens the
    version in Holinshed, 908, where Queen
    Katherine is described at work with her
    maids, a 'skein of white thread about her
    neck'. It is also thus described by
    Cavendish, 87–8, with whose account
    Holinshed's is almost identical.
  1 **lute** An Elizabethan not a Grecian instru-
    ment, played by a boy actor accompany-
    ing his singing as one of the Queen's
    women (Humphreys).
  2 **Leave** stop

GENTLEWOMAN (*sings*)

    Orpheus with his lute made trees

    And the mountain tops that freeze

      Bow themselves when he did sing.   5

    To his music plants and flowers

    Ever sprung, as sun and showers

      There had made a lasting spring.

    Everything that heard him play,

    Even the billows of the sea,   10

      Hung their heads and then lay by.

    In sweet music is such art,

    Killing care and grief of heart

      Fall asleep, or hearing, die.

    Enter ⌈Griffith,⌉ a gentleman

QUEEN KATHERINE How now?   15

⌈GRIFFITH⌉

  An't please your grace, the two great cardinals

  Wait in the presence.

QUEEN KATHERINE   Would they speak with me?

⌈GRIFFITH⌉

  They willed me say so, madam.

QUEEN KATHERINE   Pray their graces

  To come near.   ⌈*Exit Griffith*⌉

      What can be their business

  With me, a poor weak woman, fall'n from favour?   20

  I do not like their coming, now I think on't;

---

3 GENTLEWOMAN (*sings*)] HUMPHREYS; SONG F   14.1 *Griffith*] OXFORD; *not in* F   16, 18 GRIFFITH] OXFORD; *Gent.* F   16 An't] OXFORD; And't F   19 *Exit Griffith*] CAPELL (*subs.*); *not in* F
21 coming, . . . on't;] CAPELL (*subs.*); ~; . . . ~, F

3 **Orpheus** Orpheus and his lute had power to enchant even insentient things. For the story of his descent to the underworld to retrieve his wife, Eurydice, and his death at the hands of the Thracian women, see Ovid, *Metamorphoses*, Bks. X and XI. The substance of the song also appears in Beaumont and Fletcher, *The Captain* (1612) 3.1.31–8.

7 **as** as if

9–10 **play . . . sea** Kökeritz, 197–9, maintains that these words rhyme, like 'please'/'grace', 'peace'/'days', and

compares the puns 'raisins'–'reasons', 'stealer'–'staler', etc.; but Cercignani (10, 155) disagrees.

11 **lay by** came to a standstill (Onions), rested (Pooler)

13 **Killing** deadly

17 **presence** presence-chamber, reception room in which a sovereign receives guests (Onions)

21 **coming, . . . on't;** Capell is right in correcting F punctuation and thus clarifying Katherine's thought (cf. Sisson, 101).

They should be good men, their affairs as righteous—
But all hoods make not monks.

    Enter the two cardinals, Wolsey and Campeius,
    ⌈*ushered by Griffith*⌉

CARDINAL WOLSEY   Peace to your highness.

QUEEN KATHERINE

Your graces find me here part of a housewife—
I would be all—against the worst may happen.   25
What are your pleasures with me, reverend lords?

CARDINAL WOLSEY

May it please you, noble madam, to withdraw
Into your private chamber, we shall give you
The full cause of our coming.

QUEEN KATHERINE   Speak it here.

There's nothing I have done yet, o' my conscience,   30
Deserves a corner. Would all other women
Could speak this with as free a soul as I do.
My lords, I care not—so much I am happy
Above a number—if my actions
Were tried by ev'ry tongue, ev'ry eye saw 'em,   35
Envy and base opinion set against 'em,
I know my life so even. If your business
Seek me out and that way I am wife in,
Out with it boldly. Truth loves open dealing.

CARDINAL WOLSEY

Tanta est erga te mentis integritas, Regina serenissima—   40

23 *Campeius*] F4; *Campian* F1   *ushered by Griffith*] OXFORD; *not in* F   26 reverend] F2; reuerent F1   40, 49 CARDINAL WOLSEY] ROWE (*subs.*); *Card.* F

22 **their . . . righteous** and the business on which they come should be as good (Maxwell)
23 **hoods . . . monks** Proverbial (Tilley H586); Shakespeare uses the Latin form in *Measure* 5.1.260: '*Cucullus non facit monachum*'.
24 **part of** partly
25 **I . . . all** F's parentheses around this expression are usually dropped in modern editions, but the words are certainly parenthetical. Katherine says is she preparing for the worst, i.e. the divorce, which may mean earning her own living, 'a jesting exaggeration of the dangers before her' (Pooler).
31 **corner** i.e. to hide in (Riverside). Cf. Tilley T587: 'Truth seeks no corners'

(Dent), used again at 39.
32 **free** innocent, free from sin
34 **Above a number** more than many others
36 **Envy** malice
37 **even** pure, without a blemish (Schmidt). Cf. *Caesar* 2.1.132: 'The even virtue of our enterprise'.
38 **Seek . . . wife in** concerns me and my condition as a wife
39 **Truth . . . dealing** Cf. Tilley P383: 'Plain dealing is best' (Dent) and 31 n.
40 *Tanta . . . serenissima* So great is (my) integrity of mind towards you, most serene queen (Riverside); cf. 50, below. In neither Holinshed nor Cavendish are these words found; they simply say the cardinals began to speak in Latin.

QUEEN KATHERINE O, good my lord, no Latin.
 I am not such a truant since my coming
 As not to know the language I have lived in.
 A strange tongue makes my cause more strange,
   suspicious:
 Pray, speak in English. Here are some will thank you, 45
 If you speak truth, for their poor mistress' sake.
 Believe me, she has had much wrong. Lord Cardinal,
 The willing'st sin I ever yet committed
 May be absolved in English.
CARDINAL WOLSEY   Noble lady,
 I am sorry my integrity should breed—   50
 And service to his majesty and you—
 So deep suspicion where all faith was meant.
 We come not by the way of accusation
 To taint that honour every good tongue blesses,
 Nor to betray you any way to sorrow—   55
 You have too much, good lady—but to know
 How you stand minded in the weighty difference
 Between the King and you, and to deliver
 Like free and honest men our just opinions
 And comforts to your cause.
CARDINAL CAMPEIUS   Most honoured madam, 60
 My lord of York, out of his noble nature,
 Zeal, and obedience he still bore your grace,
 Forgetting, like a good man, your late censure
 Both of his truth and him—which was too far—
 Offers, as I do, in a sign of peace,   65
 His service and his counsel.
QUEEN KATHERINE (*aside*) To betray me.—
 My lords, I thank you both for your good wills.

---

60 your] F2; our F1 66 *aside*] CAPELL (*subs.*); *not in* F1

42 **truant** idle rogue or knave
 my coming i.e. to England
48 **willing'st** most wilful, deliberate
51 **And . . . you** These words should follow
 'integrity' in 50, but Foakes may be
 right: they sound like Wolsey's after-
 thought. Cyrus Hoy (*SB* 15 (1962), 82–3)
 shows that the construction is 'distinctly
 Fletcherian' (Foakes).

52 **all** nothing but
 faith loyalty
55 **any** in any
57 **stand minded in** i.e. what your view is
 concerning
59 **free** honourable, guiltless
62 **still** always
64 **too far** too extreme, taken too far
65 **in a sign** i.e. as a token (Onions)

Ye speak like honest men—pray God ye prove so.
But how to make ye suddenly an answer
In such a point of weight so near mine honour   70
(More near my life, I fear) with my weak wit—
And to such men of gravity and learning—
In truth I know not. I was set at work
Among my maids, full little—God knows—looking
Either for such men or such business.   75
For her sake that I have been—for I feel
The last fit of my greatness—good your graces,
Let me have time and counsel for my cause.
Alas, I am a woman friendless, hopeless.

CARDINAL WOLSEY
Madam, you wrong the King's love with these fears.   80
Your hopes and friends are infinite.

QUEEN KATHERINE   In England,
But little for my profit. Can you think, lords,
That any Englishman dare give me counsel,
Or be a known friend 'gainst his highness' pleasure—
Though he be grown so desperate to be honest—   85
And live a subject? Nay, forsooth, my friends,
They that must weigh out my afflictions,
They that my trust must grow to, live not here.
They are, as all my other comforts, far hence,
In mine own country, lords.

CARDINAL CAMPEIUS   I would your grace   90
Would leave your griefs and take my counsel.

QUEEN KATHERINE   How, sir?

CARDINAL CAMPEIUS
Put your main cause into the King's protection.

---

80 Madam . . . fears] POPE; *as two lines divided* Madam,/ F   82 profit. Can] F2 (*subs.*); ~‿ can F1

69 **suddenly** extempore (Onions)
71 **wit** mental capacity, faculty of reasoning
73 **set** seated (as at *Coriolanus* 4.5.197)
76 **For . . . been** Katherine speaks of herself
    in the third person as one who no
    longer exists, i.e. as Henry's wife and
    queen.
77 **fit** spell, e.g. of an illness
79 **friendless, hopeless** Here the account of
    the conversation ends in Cavendish and
    Holinshed.

82 **profit** benefit, advantage
85 **so . . . honest** A cynical or sardonic refer-
    ence to someone's becoming so reckless
    or crazy as to tell the truth.
87 **weigh out** assess at their full weight
    (Maxwell), counterbalance (Johnson),
    cause to rise in the scale, outweigh (*OED*
    20)
88 **grow to** become closely, vitally united to
    (Onions)
92 **main** principal, chief

He's loving and most gracious. 'Twill be much
Both for your honour better and your cause;
For if the trial of the law o'ertake ye,   95
You'll part away disgraced.

CARDINAL WOLSEY   He tells you rightly.

QUEEN KATHERINE

Ye tell me what ye wish for both—my ruin.
Is this your Christian counsel? Out upon ye!
Heaven is above all yet; there sits a judge
That no king can corrupt.

CARDINAL CAMPEIUS   Your rage mistakes us.   100

QUEEN KATHERINE

The more shame for ye! Holy men I thought ye;
Upon my soul, two reverend cardinal virtues:
But cardinal sins and hollow hearts I fear ye.
Mend 'em, for shame, my lords! Is this your comfort,
The cordial that ye bring a wretched lady?   105
A woman lost among ye, laughed at, scorned?
I will not wish ye half my miseries;
I have more charity. But say I warned ye.
Take heed, for heaven's sake take heed, lest at once
The burden of my sorrows fall upon ye.   110

CARDINAL WOLSEY

Madam, this is a mere distraction.
You turn the good we offer into envy.

QUEEN KATHERINE

Ye turn me into nothing. Woe upon ye,

111, 137, 141, 152 CARDINAL WOLSEY] ROWE (*subs.*); *Car.* F

94 **better** An inverted construction; syntactically follows 'much'.
96 **part away** depart, leave
97 **ye . . . both** Another inversion; 'both' follows 'ye'.
99 **Heaven . . . all** Proverbial: Tilley H348 (Dent).
100 **mistakes** i.e. makes you misjudge
101 **The . . . ye** 'If I mistake you, it is by your fault, not mine; for I thought you good' (Johnson).
102 **two . . . virtues** The cardinal virtues were justice, prudence, temperance, and fortitude, though obviously Katherine has justice uppermost in mind.
102–3 **cardinal . . . cardinal** The obvious

pun may be compounded by a pronunciation that elides medial -*d*-; thus, 'cardinal' = 'carnal' (Kökeritz, 63, 299). See *OED*, *carnal*, *sb.*[2] for three sixteenth-century instances of wordplay on carnal/cardinal.
103 **cardinal sins** An allusion to the seven deadly sins.
105 **cordial** lit., restorative medicine
106 **lost** Either (a) perplexed, bewildered, or (b) brought to ruin.
109 **at once** all at once. The line is irregular; Vaughan proposed omitting 'at' (Pooler), which would change the sense somewhat.
111 **mere distraction** sheer madness, frenzy
112 **envy** hatred

And all such false professors. Would you have me—
If you have any justice, any pity,   115
If ye be anything but churchmen's habits—
Put my sick cause into his hands that hates me?
Alas, he's banished me his bed already—
His love, too long ago. I am old, my lords,
And all the fellowship I hold now with him   120
Is only my obedience. What can happen
To me above this wretchedness? All your studies
Make me accursed like this.

CARDINAL CAMPEIUS   Your fears are worse.

QUEEN KATHERINE

Have I lived thus long—let me speak myself,
Since virtue finds no friends—a wife, a true one?   125
A woman—I dare say without vainglory—
Never yet branded with suspicion?
Have I with all my full affections
Still met the King, loved him next heav'n, obeyed him,
Been—out of fondness—superstitious to him,   130
Almost forgot my prayers to content him?
And am I thus rewarded? 'Tis not well, lords.
Bring me a constant woman to her husband,
One that ne'er dreamed a joy beyond his pleasure,

---

118 he's] F (ha's); 'has DYCE   119 love, too‿] F; ~‿ ~, ROWE   123 accursed] OXFORD (_conj._
Foakes); a Curse F

114 **professors** i.e. persons who profess Christianity, hypocrites
116 **habits** robes, the outward appearance of churchmen (cf. 23)
118 **he's . . . bed** Hall, 756: 'The King notwithstanding that his mind was unquiet, yet he kept a good countenance toward the Queen, with as much love, honour, and gentleness, as could be showed to such a princess, but he abstained from her bed, till the truth was tried, accordingly as his ghostly counsel had advised him'.
119 **old** Katherine was 43 years old.
120 **fellowship** familiar intercourse, communication (Schmidt)
122 **studies** diligence (possibly alluding to learned inquiries that were being solicited; see 2.4.236–7 n.)

123 **accursed** Foakes suggested but did not adopt the emendation; but a misreading _e/t_ would be easy, and the author might have written it as two words, i.e. 'a curst' (_TC_).
123 **worse** i.e. than your 'wretchedness' (122)
124 **speak** speak for
125 **virtue . . . friends** Cf. Tilley N117: 'He dwells far from neighbors (has ill neighbors) that is fain to praise himself' (Maxwell); also V81: 'Virtue is its own reward'.
128 **full affections** complete love
130 **fondness** (a) tenderness; (b) foolishness
superstitious extravagantly devoted (_OED_ 2b)
133 **constant** steady, faithful. A transposed adjective (Abbott §419a).

And to that woman when she has done most   135
Yet will I add an honour—a great patience.

CARDINAL WOLSEY

Madam, you wander from the good we aim at.

QUEEN KATHERINE

My lord, I dare not make myself so guilty
To give up willingly that noble title
Your master wed me to. Nothing but death   140
Shall e'er divorce my dignities.

CARDINAL WOLSEY   Pray, hear me.

QUEEN KATHERINE

Would I had never trod this English earth,
Or felt the flatteries that grow upon it.
Ye have angels' faces, but heaven knows your hearts.
What will become of me now, wretched lady?   145
I am the most unhappy woman living.
(*To her women*) Alas, poor wenches, where are now
        your fortunes?
Shipwrecked upon a kingdom where no pity,
No friends, no hope, no kindred weep for me?
Almost no grave allowed me? Like the lily,   150
That once was mistress of the field and flourished,
I'll hang my head and perish.

CARDINAL WOLSEY   If your grace
Could but be brought to know our ends are honest,
You'd feel more comfort. Why should we, good lady,
Upon what cause, wrong you? Alas, our places,   155

---

137 Madam . . . at] ROWE 1714; *as two lines divided* good / F   138 My . . . guilty] ROWE 1714; *as two lines divided* Lord, / F

135–6 **to . . . patience** compared to such a woman after she has done her utmost, I can add a further honourable attribute—great patience.

137 **the good . . . at** As Henry's emissaries, the cardinals hoped to gain Katherine's acquiescence in the divorce, in return for which she would be handsomely provided as Arthur's dowager queen and honoured accordingly, instead of the dishonour she risked by not complying.

144 **angels' faces . . . hearts** Cf. Tilley F3: 'Fair face, foul heart' and an allusion to the legend of St Gregory who saw some beautiful boys being sold as slaves in Rome. Informed they were 'Angli' (English), he said they had the faces of 'angeli' (angels) but was concerned 'that they which carry such grace in their countenances, should be void of grace in their hearts' (Foakes, citing Camden, *Remains*, 1605).

150–2 **Like . . . perish** Cf. Matthew 6: 28–9 on the lilies of the field and Psalm 103: 15–16 on the flowers of the field that soon perish (Shaheen); also Spenser, *Faerie Queene* 2.6.16: 'The lily, Ladie of the flowring field' (Foakes, citing Singer).

The way of our profession, is against it.
We are to cure such sorrows, not to sow 'em.
For goodness' sake, consider what you do,
How you may hurt yourself; ay, utterly
Grow from the King's acquaintance by this carriage.   160
The hearts of princes kiss obedience,
So much they love it, but to stubborn spirits
They swell and grow as terrible as storms.
I know you have a gentle, noble temper,
A soul as even as a calm. Pray, think us   165
Those we profess—peacemakers, friends, and servants.

CARDINAL CAMPEIUS
Madam, you'll find it so. You wrong your virtues
With these weak women's fears. A noble spirit,
As yours was put into you, ever casts
Such doubts as false coin from it. The King loves you.   170
Beware you lose it not. For us, if you please
To trust us in your business, we are ready
To use our utmost studies in your service.

QUEEN KATHERINE
Do what ye will, my lords, and pray forgive me;
If I have used myself unmannerly,   175
You know I am a woman, lacking wit
To make a seemly answer to such persons.
Pray do my service to his majesty.
He has my heart yet, and shall have my prayers
While I shall have my life. Come, reverend fathers,   180
Bestow your counsels on me. She now begs
That little thought, when she set footing here,
She should have bought her dignities so dear.

Exeunt

167 Madam . . . virtues] POPE; *as two lines divided* so:/ F   174 Do . . . me] ROWE 1714; *as two lines divided* Lords:/ F   174–5 me; . . . unmannerly,] F1; ~, . . . ~; F4

158 **For goodness' sake** out of your good nature (Humphreys)
159–60 **How . . . carriage** This in fact happened, as Katherine maintained her resistance: see Cavendish, 92, and Hall, 781–2.
160 **carriage** conduct, comportment
164 **temper** temperament
170 **The King loves you** See Hall (756, 780)
for the love Henry expressed during this difficult period.
173 **studies** endeavours
175 **used myself** behaved
178 **do my service** pay my respects
180–3 **Come . . . dear** A return to Cavendish and Holinshed; the conversation that ensued was not recorded.

3.2   *Enter the Duke of Norfolk, the Duke of Suffolk, the*
        Earl of Surrey, and the Lord Chamberlain

NORFOLK

If you will now unite in your complaints
And force them with a constancy, the Cardinal
Cannot stand under them. If you omit
The offer of this time, I cannot promise
But that you shall sustain more new disgraces   5
With these you bear already.

SURREY   I am joyful
To meet the least occasion that may give me
Remembrance of my father-in-law the Duke
To be revenged on him.

SUFFOLK   Which of the peers
Have uncontemned gone by him, or at least   10
Strangely neglected? When did he regard
The stamp of nobleness in any person
Out of himself?

LORD CHAMBERLAIN My lords, you speak your pleasures.
What he deserves of you and me I know;
What we can do to him—though now the time   15
Gives way to us—I much fear. If you cannot
Bar his access to th' King, never attempt
Anything on him, for he hath a witchcraft
Over the King in's tongue.

NORFOLK   O, fear him not.
His spell in that is out. The King hath found   20
Matter against him that for ever mars
The honey of his language. No, he's settled—
Not to come off—in his displeasure.

3.2] *Scena Secunda*. F   5, 55 more] F (moe)

3.2.0.2 *Earl of Surrey* Actually, Thomas
Howard, Earl of Surrey, had in 1524 succeeded his father as Duke of Norfolk
(Riverside).
2 **force . . . constancy** press them with per-
sistence
3 **omit** neglect
4 **offer of this time** present opportunity
8 **Duke** i.e. Buckingham
10 **uncontemned** not despised (*OED*, first

use cited)
11 **neglected** disregarded, snubbed
13 **Out of** except
16 **Gives way** favours
18 **on** against
19 **in's** in his
20 **out** finished, at an end. Cf. *Antony*
4.10.31–2: 'Our hour | Is fully out' (Onions).
23 **come off** escape (if Wolsey), desist (if
Henry) (Maxwell)

SURREY   Sir,
    I should be glad to hear such news as this
    Once every hour.
NORFOLK   Believe it, this is true.   25
    In the divorce his contrary proceedings
    Are all unfolded, wherein he appears
    As I would wish mine enemy.
SURREY   How came
    His practices to light?
SUFFOLK   Most strangely.
SURREY   O, how? how?
SUFFOLK
    The Cardinal's letters to the Pope miscarried,   30
    And came to th'eye o'th' King, wherein was read
    How that the Cardinal did entreat his holiness
    To stay the judgement o'th' divorce; for if
    It did take place, 'I do', quoth he, 'perceive
    My king is tangled in affection to   35
    A creature of the Queen's, Lady Anne Boleyn'.
SURREY
    Has the King this?
SUFFOLK   Believe it.
SURREY   Will this work?
LORD CHAMBERLAIN
    The King in this perceives him—how he coasts
    And hedges his own way. But in this point
    All his tricks founder, and he brings his physic   40
    After his patient's death. The King already
    Hath married the fair lady.
SURREY   Would he had.

---

26 **contrary proceedings** i.e. Wolsey's
    machinations opposed to Henry's; specif-
    ically, his letters to the Pope urging delay
    (30–3, below; Holinshed, 908)
27 **unfolded** disclosed, exposed
29 **practices** intrigues
30 **letters . . . miscarried** Cf. Cavendish, 94;
    Holinshed, 909; 'letters' = letter.
36 **creature** servant, dependant (Schmidt)
38 **coasts** travels circuitously (as if following
    a coastline) (Onions)
39 **hedges** dodges, shifts, as along hedge-

rows
40 **founder** miscarry
40–1 **he brings . . . death** Cf. Tilley D133:
    'After death the doctor' (Dent).
41–2 **The King . . . lady** i.e. in January 1533
    (14 November 1532 in Holinshed, 929;
    see Introduction, p. 5). The marriage
    was kept secret until Anne's pregnancy
    was unmistakable.
42 **Would he had** Surrey is sceptical but is
    immediately reassured that the marriage
    in fact has occurred.

SUFFOLK

   May you be happy in your wish, my lord,

   For I profess you have it.

SURREY   Now all my joy

   Trace the conjunction.

SUFFOLK   My amen to't.

NORFOLK   All men's.   45

SUFFOLK

   There's order given for her coronation.

   Marry, this is yet but young and may be left

   To some ears unrecounted. But, my lords,

   She is a gallant creature and complete

   In mind and feature. I persuade me, from her   50

   Will fall some blessing to this land, which shall

   In it be memorized.

SURREY   But will the King

   Digest this letter of the Cardinal's?

   The Lord forbid!

NORFOLK   Marry, amen.

SUFFOLK   No, no—

   There be more wasps that buzz about his nose   55

   Will make this sting the sooner. Cardinal Campeius

   Is stol'n away to Rome—hath ta'en no leave,

   Has left the cause o'th' King unhandled, and

   Is posted as the agent of our Cardinal

   To second all his plot. I do assure you   60

   The King cried 'Ha!' at this.

LORD CHAMBERLAIN   Now God incense him,

   And let him cry 'Ha!' louder.

58 Has] F (H'as)

45 **Trace the conjunction** follow the marriage
47 **Marry** A common exclamation, deriving from the Virgin Mary.
48 **unrecounted** The only use cited by *OED* (Foakes).
49 **gallant** splendid (used of both sexes)
    complete perfect, accomplished (Onions)
50-2 **I . . . memorized** Cf. 2.3.75-9.
50 **I persuade me** I am convinced
51 **fall** (a) befall, come to pass; (b) be born
52 **memorized** made memorable

53 **Digest** stomach, put up with
56-7 **Cardinal . . . leave** Holinshed and others report that Campeius in fact did take leave of the King; the dramatist resorted to Foxe instead, who says the cardinal 'craftily shifted himself out of the realm' (Humphreys).
58 **unhandled** unresolved, not dealt with (Onions)
59 **posted** dispatched
60 **his plot** See 26 n. above.
61 **Ha!** See 1.2.187 n.

NORFOLK   But, my lord,
　　When returns Cranmer?
SUFFOLK
　　He is returned in his opinions, which
　　Have satisfied the King for his divorce,   65
　　Together with all famous colleges,
　　Almost, in Christendom. Shortly, I believe,
　　His second marriage shall be published, and
　　Her coronation. Katherine no more
　　Shall be called 'Queen', but 'Princess Dowager'   70
　　And 'widow to Prince Arthur'.
NORFOLK   This same Cranmer's
　　A worthy fellow and hath ta'en much pain
　　In the King's business.
SUFFOLK   He has, and we shall see him
　　For it an archbishop.
NORFOLK   So I hear.
SUFFOLK   'Tis so.
　　　　Enter Cardinal Wolsey and Cromwell
　　The Cardinal.
NORFOLK   Observe, observe; he's moody.   75
　　　　They stand apart and observe Wolsey and Cromwell
CARDINAL WOLSEY
　　The packet, Cromwell—gave't you the King?
CROMWELL
　　To his own hand, in's bedchamber.
CARDINAL WOLSEY   Looked he
　　O'th' inside of the paper?

75.1 *They . . . Cromwell*] OXFORD; *not in* F   76–8 The packet . . . Presently] FOAKES; *as five lines divided* . . . Cromwell,/ . . . King?/ . . . Bed-chamber./ . . . Paper?/ F

64 **returned in his opinions** i.e. he has not arrived but has sent ahead his 'opinions' (Malone, citing Tyrwhitt). The views are those Cranmer obtained abroad (see 2.4.236–7 n.), or possibly the views he originally held and which remain unchanged (Steevens). Later in the scene (401) Cromwell says Cranmer has returned, but that may be another example of dramatic compression of events (cf. Humphreys and 73–4, below). Cranmer's journey may be indebted to Foxe (edn. 1563, 1471) (Foakes).

66–7 **Together . . . Christendom** See 2.2.87 n.

68 **published** publicly proclaimed

69–71 **Katherine . . . Arthur** As reported by Holinshed, 929; Henry had already secretly married Anne.

73–4 **we shall . . . archbishop** As Cromwell announces, 402 below. That he has not been so appointed further argues that he has not yet returned to England. In fact, Henry had already named him Archbishop of Canterbury but he was not consecrated until after his return in January 1533.

76 **packet** i.e. of letters, usually of official or state papers (*OED* 1)

78 **paper** wrapper

CROMWELL   Presently
He did unseal them, and the first he viewed.
He did it with a serious mind: a heed   80
Was in his countenance. You he bade
Attend him here this morning.
CARDINAL WOLSEY   Is he ready
To come abroad?
CROMWELL I think by this he is.
CARDINAL WOLSEY Leave me a while.   *Exit Cromwell*   85
(*Aside*) It shall be to the Duchess of Alençon,
The French King's sister; he shall marry her.
Anne Boleyn? No, I'll no Anne Boleyns for him.
There's more in't than fair visage. Boleyn?
No, we'll no Boleyns. Speedily I wish   90
To hear from Rome. The Marchioness of Pembroke?
         The nobles speak among themselves

NORFOLK
He's discontented.
SUFFOLK   Maybe he hears the King
Does whet his anger to him.
SURREY   Sharp enough,
Lord, for thy justice.
CARDINAL WOLSEY (*aside*)
The late Queen's gentlewoman? A knight's daughter   95
To be her mistress' mistress? The Queen's queen?
This candle burns not clear; 'tis I must snuff it,

82–3 Is . . . abroad?] HANMER; *as one line* F   91.1 *The nobles . . . themselves*] OXFORD; *not in* F
95 The . . . daughter] POPE; *as two lines divided* Gentlewoman?/ F

78 **Presently** at once
80 **heed** careful attention
83 **abroad** i.e. out of his bedchamber
86–7 **Duchess . . . her** See 2.2.40 n. Wolsey by now is totally out of the King's confidence, knowing nothing of Henry's secret marriage to Anne, which in fact took place after Wolsey's scheme. Again, as Humphreys notes, the dramatist telescopes history for dramatic effect.
88–90 **Anne . . . Boleyns** Wolsey was opposed to Anne Boleyn partly because of her Protestant proclivities (see 100–1 below) and partly because he wanted to use the marriage to the French princess

instead for political purposes (see Introduction).
91 **Marchioness of Pembroke** See 2.3.63 and n.
95 **late Queen's** Cf. 69–70 above.
knight's daughter Wolsey refers to Sir Thomas Boleyn's original status, before Henry elevated him. Cf. 1.4.96 n.
97–8 **This . . . goes** Tilley C49: 'To go out like a candle in a snuff' (Dent).
97 **snuff it** trim the wick. Wolsey believes he is expected to remove the snags to Henry's marriage with Anne, but he will stop it altogether, he says (Maxwell, Humphreys).

Then out it goes. What though I know her virtuous
And well deserving? Yet I know her for
A spleeny Lutheran and not wholesome to   100
Our cause, that she should lie i'th' bosom of
Our hard-ruled King. Again, there is sprung up
An heretic, an arch-one, Cranmer, one
Hath crawled into the favour of the King
And is his oracle.

NORFOLK   He is vexed at something.   105

Enter King Henry reading a schedule, and Lovell
with him

SURREY

I would 'twere something that would fret the string,
The master-cord on's heart!

SUFFOLK   The King, the King!

KING HENRY (*aside*)

What piles of wealth hath he accumulated
To his own portion? And what expense by th' hour
Seems to flow from him? How i'th' name of thrift   110
Does he rake this together?—Now, my lords,
Saw you the Cardinal?

105.1–2 *and . . . him*] THEOBALD (*subs.*); *not in* F   109 portion?] F; ~! ROWE   110 him?] F;
~! ROWE   111 together?] F; ~! ROWE

---

100 **spleeny Lutheran** passionate Protestant
('Lutheran' was a generic term for
Protestants). Cf. Foxe, 959: 'the cardinal
of York perceived the King to cast favour
to the Lady Anne, whom he knew to be a
Lutheran' (Foakes).
wholesome profitable, salutary (as at
Othello 1.1.147: 'wholesome to my
place')

101 **lie i'th' bosom** (a) marry; (b) share the
secrets (Foakes)

102 **hard-ruled** managed with difficulty

103 **heretic** Wolsey knew Cranmer's sympathies with Protestant reforms (see Introduction).
arch-one chief, with an unconscious play
on 'archbishop' (cf. 73–4 above)

105 **oracle** 'one who expounds or interprets
the will of God; a divine teacher' (*OED*
3c)

105.1 *schedule* a paper or scroll containing
writing (Onions). It is unclear whether
the schedule is the inventory he gives

Wolsey at 202 below (as Steevens believed), or the nobles' list of grievances
(see Holinshed, 909).

106–7 **fret . . . heart** The primary sense is
that of *fret*, *v.*¹, to gnaw, bite through the
strings which in early physiology supported the heart (cf. Q *Lear* 24.213–14:
'the strings of life | Began to crack'). The
reference is to Wolsey, who up to now
has been Henry's 'master-cord', i.e. his
main support. The secondary sense is
that of *fret*, *v.*⁵, to furnish (a guitar) with
frets, i.e. pieces of gut or wood used to
regulate the fingering of the instrument.
In this sense, the wish is that Wolsey
would come under control. Cf. *Hamlet*
3.2.359–60: 'though you can fret me,
you cannot play upon me'.

107 **on's** of his

109 **portion** share

109–10 **what . . . him** On Wolsey's lavish
manner of life, see Holinshed, 920–1,
and Cavendish, 17–25.

NORFOLK   My lord, we have
  Stood here observing him. Some strange commotion
  Is in his brain. He bites his lip, and starts,
  Stops on a sudden, looks upon the ground,   115
  Then lays his finger on his temple; straight
  Springs out into fast gait, then stops again,
  Strikes his breast hard, and anon he casts
  His eye against the moon. In most strange postures
  We have seen him set himself.
KING HENRY   It may well be   120
  There is a mutiny in's mind. This morning
  Papers of state he sent me to peruse
  As I required, and wot you what I found
  There—on my conscience—put unwittingly?
  Forsooth, an inventory thus importing   125
  The several parcels of his plate, his treasure,
  Rich stuffs, and ornaments of household, which
  I find at such proud rate that it outspeaks
  Possession of a subject.
NORFOLK   It's heaven's will.
  Some spirit put this paper in the packet   130
  To bless your eye withal.

124 There—on my conscience—put unwittingly?] This edition; ~, ~ ~ ~ ~ ~? POPE; ~ (~ ~
~ ̮ ~ ~ ̮) F

113 **commotion** agitation, perturbation; cf.
       121 below
114–20 **He . . . himself** As Foakes notes,
       these lines supply excellent stage direc-
       tions for the actor playing Wolsey, who is
       standing by out of earshot of this dialogue
       but visible to the audience. David
       Bevington (*Action Is Eloquence* (1984), 95)
       also cites this passage and says Wolsey is
       unaware that he is observed. True, but
       the cause of his agitation is not, as
       Bevington says, the horror that he has
       permitted a letter to the pope to be seen by
       Henry; it is the perturbation caused, as
       he himself says (95–105), by the
       marriage to Anne and the promotion of
       Cranmer.
116 **straight** straightaway
121 **mutiny in's mind** A common metaphor;
       cf. *Caesar* 2.1.63–9 (Pooler). Henry be-
       lieves that the 'mutiny' is *in* his mind, not
       on it, though he does not know the cause,

nor has he yet given him one. He does not
imagine that Wolsey is fomenting a plan
of rebellion; but cf. 95–105.
123 **wot** know
125 **an inventory** See 211–17 below. The
       dramatist has adapted an earlier incident
       involving the Bishop of Durham, Thomas
       Ruthall, which led to his downfall.
       See Holinshed (796) and Introduction,
       p. 16.
       importing signifying
126 **several parcels** various items
       plate utensils for table and domestic use;
       in a great house, usually of silver or gold
       (NCS)
127 **stuffs** fabrics
       ornaments of household furniture and
       the like
128 **proud rate** high value
128–9 **outspeaks . . . subject** proclaims more
       than a subject should possess
131 **withal** with this

KING HENRY   If we did think
His contemplation were above the earth
And fixed on spiritual object, he should still
Dwell in his musings. But I am afraid
His thinkings are below the moon, not worth   135
His serious considering.
          The King takes his seat and whispers with Lovell,
          who then goes to the Cardinal
CARDINAL WOLSEY   Heaven forgive me!—
Ever God bless your highness!
KING HENRY   Good my lord,
You are full of heavenly stuff and bear the inventory
Of your best graces in your mind, the which
You were now running o'er. You have scarce time   140
To steal from spiritual leisure a brief span
To keep your earthly audit. Sure, in that,
I deem you an ill husband and am glad
To have you therein my companion.
CARDINAL WOLSEY   Sir,
For holy offices I have a time; a time   145
To think upon the part of business which
I bear i'th' state; and nature does require
Her times of preservation which, perforce,
I, her frail son, amongst my brethren mortal,
Must give my tendance to.
KING HENRY   You have said well.   150

136 *and whispers with Lovell, who then*] OXFORD; *whispers Louell, who* F   143 glad] F2; gald F1

135 **below the moon** sublunary, worldly
136 **Heaven forgive me!** Wolsey is startled by the King's presence.
138 **stuff** matter (of thought) (Onions), but with 'inventory' ironically echoing 125 and 127, above.
139 **graces** virtues. In a theological sense, virtues are divine in origin (NCS).
141 **spiritual leisure** time devoted to religious duties and meditation (Onions), with perhaps a quibble implying that Wolsey treats as leisure the time he should devote to spiritual affairs (Foakes).
142 **earthly audit** i.e. as opposed to heavenly audit of Judgement Day
143 **ill husband** bad manager

143–4 **am glad . . . companion** Henry is not, as Foakes suggests, coupling himself with Wolsey as an 'ill husband' (he to Katherine, Wolsey to his earthly affairs); he is saying (with disguised irony) that he is glad to have so spiritual and unworldly a person as his fellow.
145 **a time; a time** Maxwell suggests an allusion to Ecclesiastes 3: 1–8 (not noted by Shaheen): 'To all things there is an appointed time, and a time to every purpose under the heaven. A time to be born, and a time to die', etc., and 'There is a time for all things' (Tilley T314).
148 **times of preservation** e.g. eating, sleeping
150 **tendance** attendance, care

CARDINAL WOLSEY

And ever may your highness yoke together,
As I will lend you cause, my doing well
With my well-saying.

KING HENRY   'Tis well said again,
And 'tis a kind of good deed to say well.
And yet words are no deeds. My father loved you.   155
He said he did, and with his deed did crown
His word upon you. Since I had my office,
I have kept you next my heart, have not alone
Employed you where high profits might come home,
But pared my present havings to bestow   160
My bounties upon you.

CARDINAL WOLSEY (*aside*)   What should this mean?

SURREY (*aside*)

The Lord increase this business!

KING HENRY   Have I not made you
The prime man of the state? I pray you tell me
If what I now pronounce you have found true,
And, if you may confess it, say withal   165
If you are bound to us or no. What say you?

CARDINAL WOLSEY

My sovereign, I confess your royal graces
Showered on me daily have been more than could
My studied purposes requite, which went
Beyond all man's endeavours. My endeavours   170
Have ever come too short of my desires,
Yet filled with my abilities. Mine own ends

172 filled] F (fill'd); filed HANMER

152–3 **doing well . . . well-saying** cf. Tilley
   S119: 'Saying and doing are two things'
   (Dent), and W802: 'From words to deeds
   is a great space' (Foakes). Henry picks up
   the proverb at 155.
155–7 **My . . . you** Wolsey's career began
   under Henry VII, who recognized his
   abilities and made him his chaplain,
   ambassador, almoner, and Dean of
   Lincoln Cathedral. (See Cavendish, 4–10.)
156 **crown** complete, perfect
158–61 **have not . . . you** I have not only
   used you where you might achieve great
   gains for yourself, but I have even re-

duced my own wealth to bestow some of
   it on you
160 **havings** possessions
163 **prime man of the state** As Lord Chancellor, Wolsey held the highest office under
   the king.
164 **pronounce** declare
165 **withal** in addition
169 **studied purposes** deliberate efforts
169–72 **which . . . abilities** which exceeded
   all human efforts, but which still came
   short of what I wished to do, even though
   I used my abilities to the utmost
172 **filled** Hanmer's emendation, 'fil'd', has

Have been mine so, that evermore they pointed
To th' good of your most sacred person and
The profit of the state. For your great graces   175
Heaped upon me, poor undeserver, I
Can nothing render but allegiant thanks,
My prayers to heaven for you, my loyalty,
Which ever has and ever shall be growing,
Till death, that winter, kill it.
KING HENRY   Fairly answered.   180
A loyal and obedient subject is
Therein illustrated. The honour of it
Does pay the act of it, as, i' th' contrary,
The foulness is the punishment. I presume
That as my hand has opened bounty to you,   185
My heart dropped love, my power rained honour more
On you than any; so your hand and heart,
Your brain, and every function of your power
Should, notwithstanding that your bond of duty,
As 'twere in love's particular, be more   190
To me, your friend, than any.
CARDINAL WOLSEY   I do profess
That for your highness' good I ever laboured
More than mine own; that am, have, and will be—
Though all the world should crack their duty to you
And throw it from their soul; though perils did   195
Abound as thick as thought could make 'em and
Appear in forms more horrid—yet, my duty,
As doth a rock against the chiding flood,

been widely accepted (e.g. NCS, Oxford),
but the F reading, as Sisson argues (101),
has 'clear and relevant sense'. He interprets: 'yet fulfilled to the best of my
abilities'.

173 **so** to this extent
177 **Can . . . thanks** can return only loyal
gratitude. *OED* cites 'allegiant' here as its
earliest use.
182–3 **The honour . . . act of it** 'Honour is
the reward of virtue' (Tilley H571).
184 **foulness** disgrace, as at *Lear* 1.1.227:
'no vicious, blot, murder, or foulness'.
185 **opened bounty** given bountifully
188 **function . . . power** activity of your fac-

ulties. Cf. *Hamlet* 3.2.165: 'My operant
powers their functions leave to do'.
189–90 **notwithstanding . . . particular** 'Besides the general bond of duty, by which
you are obliged to be a loyal and obedient
subject, you owe a particular devotion of
yourself to me, as your particular bene-
factor' (Johnson). As Maxwell argues, the
contrast is between 'duty' and 'love', not
(as Foakes suggests) between Wolsey's
obligations to church and pope as opposed to king and state.
190 **love's particular** for the special reason of
love (Humphreys)
193 **have** i.e. have been. Cf. 'has' 179,
above (NCS).

Should the approach of this wild river break,
And stand unshaken yours.
KING HENRY   'Tis nobly spoken.   200
Take notice, lords, he has a loyal breast,
For you have seen him open't. (*Giving Wolsey papers*)
        Read o'er this,
And after, this; and then to breakfast with
What appetite you have.

>   *Exit King Henry, frowning upon the Cardinal.*
>   *The nobles throng after the King, smiling and*
>   *whispering*

CARDINAL WOLSEY   What should this mean?
What sudden anger's this? How have I reaped it?   205
He parted frowning from me, as if ruin
Leaped from his eyes. So looks the chafèd lion
Upon the daring huntsman that has galled him,
Then makes him nothing. I must read this paper—
I fear, the story of his anger.

>   *He reads one of the papers*
                                'Tis so.   210
This paper has undone me. 'Tis th'account
Of all that world of wealth I have drawn together
For mine own ends—indeed, to gain the popedom,
And fee my friends in Rome. O negligence,
Fit for a fool to fall by! What cross devil   215
Made me put this main secret in the packet
I sent the King? Is there no way to cure this?
No new device to beat this from his brains?
I know 'twill stir him strongly; yet I know
A way, if it take right, in spite of fortune   220

---

202 *Giving . . . papers*] POPE (*subs.*); *not in* F   203 after, this;] THEOBALD; ~ ̭ ~, F   210 fear,]
ROWE; ~ ̭ F   *He . . . papers*] OXFORD (*conj.* Capell); *not in* F   211 account] ̭F (Accompt)

---

199 **this wild river** i.e. the 'perils' of 195–7
    taken figuratively
    break stem, as a breakwater (Foakes)
207 **chafèd** angry
208 **galled** wounded
209 **makes him nothing** annihilates him
211 **undone** ruined
    th'account Cf. 125 above.

212 **world** mass, huge quantity
213–14 **to gain . . . Rome** See Introduction,
    pp. 6–9.
215 **cross** perverse (Onions)
216 **main** highly important, momentous
    (Onions)
218 **device** contrivance, stratagem
220 **take right** succeeds

Will bring me off again. What's this?
   He reads another paper

                       'To th' Pope'?
The letter, as I live, with all the business
I writ to's holiness. Nay then, farewell.
I have touched the highest point of all my greatness,
And from that full meridian of my glory   225
I haste now to my setting. I shall fall
Like a bright exhalation in the evening,
And no man see me more.
   Enter to Cardinal Wolsey the Dukes of Norfolk and
   Suffolk, the Earl of Surrey, and the Lord Chamberlain

NORFOLK
Hear the King's pleasure, Cardinal, who commands
    you
To render up the Great Seal presently   230
Into our hands, and to confine yourself
To Asher House, my lord of Winchester's,
Till you hear further from his highness.

CARDINAL WOLSEY   Stay—
Where's your commission, lords? Words cannot carry
Authority so weighty.

SUFFOLK   Who dare cross 'em   235
Bearing the King's will from his mouth expressly?

CARDINAL WOLSEY
Till I find more than will or words to do it—

---

221 *He . . . paper*] OXFORD (*subs.*; *conj.* Capell); *not in* F   229 Hear . . . you] POPE; *as two lines divided* Cardinall,/ F   234 commission, lords?] ROWE; ~? ~, F

221 **bring me off** rescue, save me
222 **The letter** See Introduction, p. 8.
224–8 **I have . . . more** Cf. Speed's *History of Great Britain* (1611), 769: 'Cardinal Wolsey fell likewise in great displeasure of the King . . . but now his sun having passed the meridian of his greatness, began by degrees to decline, till lastly it set under the cloud of his fatal eclipse' (Foakes).
225 **meridian** highest point; lit., the point at which the sun reaches its highest altitude
227 **exhalation** meteor, falling star
228.1–2 *Enter . . . Chamberlain* Although Holinshed (909) mentions only Norfolk and Suffolk in this interview, the others are those who began the scene. Cf.

3.2.0.1–2. On Norfolk and Surrey, see 3.2.0.2 n.
232 **Asher House . . . Winchester's** Asher (an old form of Esher) House near Hampton Court belonged to the Bishop of Winchester, the benefice that Wolsey held at this time. Either Wolsey is being ordered to house arrest, or the dramatist has in mind Stephen Gardiner, who succeeded Wolsey as bishop and who appears as such in Act 5.
234 **commission** written warrant. On the controversy between Wolsey and the lords, cf. Holinshed, 909.
235 **cross** oppose
237 **to do it** i.e. render up the Great Seal

I mean your malice—know, officious lords,
I dare and must deny it. Now I feel
Of what coarse metal ye are moulded—envy.   240
How eagerly ye follow my disgraces
As if it fed ye, and how sleek and wanton
Ye appear in everything may bring my ruin!
Follow your envious courses, men of malice;
You have Christian warrant for 'em, and no doubt   245
In time will find their fit rewards. That seal
You ask with such a violence, the King—
Mine and your master—with his own hand gave me,
Bade me enjoy it with the place and honours
During my life, and to confirm his goodness   250
Tied it by letters patents. Now, who'll take it?

SURREY

The King that gave it.

CARDINAL WOLSEY   It must be himself then.

SURREY

Thou art a proud traitor, priest.

CARDINAL WOLSEY   Proud lord, thou liest.
Within these forty hours Surrey durst better
Have burnt that tongue than said so.

SURREY   Thy ambition,   255
Thou scarlet sin, robbed this bewailing land
Of noble Buckingham, my father-in-law.

---

240 moulded—envy.] ROWE (*subs*.); ~, Enuy, F

---

238 **officious** meddling, interfering
240 **coarse metal** (F 'Mettle') 'Metal' and
'mettle' were interchangeable spellings
of the same word, often resulting in ambiguities, or wordplay. Wolsey refers at one
and the same time to the lords' disposition or character and to the material
they are made from; hence 'moulded'.
242 **it** i.e. following his disgraces (Maxwell,
citing Vaughan). The imagery suggests
greyhounds pursuing a prey.
sleek and wanton unctuous and unprin-
cipled (Humphreys)
245 **Christian warrant** Wolsey is being bitterly ironical or satirical, for of course
Christians are bidden to be charitable to
their enemies. Foakes suggests an allusion to Tilley W947: 'Wrong has no war-

rant'. The 'rewards' (246) are the pun-
ishments they will receive for being
unchristian and following their 'envious
courses' (244).
249 **enjoy it** i.e. use it and have the benefits
of it
251 **Tied** ratified
letters patents open documents conferring a right or power (*OED, patent, adj*. 1)
254 **forty** Used indefinitely to convey a large
number (*OED* A. b), as at *Coriolanus*
3.1.242 (Onions).
256 **scarlet sin** A play on the colour of the
Cardinal's robes and Isaiah 1: 18:
'Though your sins were as crimson, they
shall be made white as snow: though
they were red like scarlet, they shall be as
wool' (Foakes).

The heads of all thy brother cardinals
With thee and all thy best parts bound together
Weighed not a hair of his. Plague of your policy,   260
You sent me deputy for Ireland,
Far from his succour, from the King, from all
That might have mercy on the fault thou gav'st him,
Whilst your great goodness, out of holy pity,
Absolved him with an axe.
CARDINAL WOLSEY   This, and all else   265
This talking lord can lay upon my credit,
I answer is most false. The Duke by law
Found his deserts. How innocent I was
From any private malice in his end,
His noble jury and foul cause can witness.   270
If I loved many words, lord, I should tell you
You have as little honesty as honour,
That in the way of loyalty and truth
Toward the King, my ever royal master,
Dare mate a sounder man than Surrey can be,   275
And all that love his follies.
SURREY   By my soul,
Your long coat, priest, protects you; thou shouldst feel
My sword i'th' life-blood of thee else. My lords,
Can ye endure to hear this arrogance?
And from this fellow? If we live thus tamely,   280
To be thus jaded by a piece of scarlet,

---

273 That in the] F; ~ I, i'th' THEOBALD   277 Your . . . feel] ROWE 1714; *as two lines divided you,/* F

259 **parts** qualities
260 **Weighed not** were not equal in weight to, i.e. were not worth. Cf. Tilley H19: 'Not worth a hair' (Dent).
   of on
261 **deputy for Ireland** See 2.1.42 n. 'Ireland' is trisyllabic.
263 **fault** offence
   gav'st attributed to, assigned (Onions)
264–5 **Whilst . . . axe** Surrey speaks with heavy sarcasm, using appropriate religious terms.
266 **credit** good name, reputation (*OED* 5b)
269 **From** i.e. of
270 **noble jury** i.e. jury comprised of nobility, with an obvious pun

273 **That** The construction is compressed; the relative pronoun is governed by 'I' (271): 'I . . . That . . . Dare' (Maxwell).
275 **mate** rival, vie with (Onions)
277 **long coat** An allusion to Wolsey's priestly garment, but perhaps also glancing at a fool's long coat (cf. Pro.16).
277–8 **protects . . . else** Surrey cannot challenge a priest to a duel.
280 **fellow** Here, a term of disrespect.
281 **jaded** made ridiculous (Onions), with wordplay on green (jade) and red (scarlet). But 'tamely' (280) suggests also 'jaded' = 'befooled', as in *Twelfth Night* 2.5.159, or possibly 'cowed' (Foakes).

Farewell nobility. Let his grace go forward
And dare us with his cap, like larks.

CARDINAL WOLSEY   All goodness

Is poison to thy stomach.

SURREY   Yes, that goodness

Of gleaning all the land's wealth into one,   285
Into your own hands, Card'nal, by extortion;
The goodness of your intercepted packets
You writ to th' Pope against the King; your goodness—
Since you provoke me—shall be most notorious.
My lord of Norfolk, as you are truly noble,   290
As you respect the common good, the state
Of our despised nobility, our issues—
Whom if he live will scarce be gentlemen—
Produce the grand sum of his sins, the articles
Collected from his life.—I'll startle you   295
Worse than the sacring bell when the brown wench
Lay kissing in your arms, Lord Cardinal.

CARDINAL WOLSEY (*aside*)

How much, methinks, I could despise this man,
But that I am bound in charity against it.

293 Whom] F1; Who F2   298 *aside*] OXFORD; *not in* F

283 **dare . . . larks** Surrey refers to the practice of dazzling or confusing larks with pieces of scarlet cloth, or small mirrors, or small hawks, which riveted their attention while nets were dropped over them. (See *OED*, *dare*, *v.*² 5 = to daze.) For a possible allusion to Wolsey's concubine, 'Mistress Lark', see 296–7 n.

288 **writ . . . King** Cf. 222, above; 'writ' is the usual past tense form in Shakespeare.

292 **issues** sons (Pooler)

293 **Whom** Often emended to 'Who' by editors, following F2. But *OED* notes confusion between the two forms in the seventeenth century (*TC*).

294 **articles** items (in an indictment). See Hall, 767–8, and Holinshed, 912, where the chief 'articles' are listed. In the dialogue that follows, only a few are mentioned.

296 **sacring bell** 'The little bell, which is rung to give notice of the Host approaching when it is carried in procession, as also in other offices of the Romish church, is called the *sacring*, or *consecration* bell' (Theobald); used here anachronistically in post-Reformation sense of a bell rung to summon parishioners to morning prayers (Foakes).

296–7 **brown wench . . . arms** Wolsey's lechery was notorious and was satirized by John Skelton in *Why come ye not to court?* (1522) and by others. He had a mistress, or concubine, called 'Mistress Lark', who bore him two children: a daughter, Dorothy, who was sent to Shaftesbury Abbey, and a son, Thomas Winter, whom Wolsey acknowledged as his 'nephew' (Peter Gwyn, *The King's Cardinal* (1990), p. xv, citing A. F. Pollard, *Wolsey* (1929)). Thomas Winter became Dean of Lincoln (Foakes).

NORFOLK

Those articles, my lord, are in the King's hand,   300
But thus much—they are foul ones.

CARDINAL WOLSEY   So much fairer
And spotless shall mine innocence arise
When the King knows my truth.

SURREY   This cannot save you.
I thank my memory I yet remember
Some of these articles, and out they shall.   305
Now, if you can blush and cry 'Guilty', Cardinal,
You'll show a little honesty.

CARDINAL WOLSEY   Speak on, sir,
I dare your worst objections. If I blush,
It is to see a nobleman want manners.

SURREY

I had rather want those than my head. Have at you!   310
First, that without the King's assent or knowledge
You wrought to be a legate, by which power
You maimed the jurisdiction of all bishops.

NORFOLK

Then, that in all you writ to Rome, or else
To foreign princes, '*Ego et Rex meus*'   315
Was still inscribed—in which you brought the King
To be your servant.

SUFFOLK   Then, that without the knowledge
Either of King or Council, when you went
Ambassador to the Emperor, you made bold
To carry into Flanders the Great Seal.   320

310 I . . . you] ROWE; *as two lines divided* head;/ F

300 **in . . . hand** Not in Henry's handwriting, but in his possession.
301 **But thus much** i.e. I can say this much
305 **out they shall** i.e. I shall mention them
306 **Now . . . Cardinal** Another hexameter, or an irregular line improved by eliding 'you can' and 'Cardinal' (as Card'nal).
308 **objections** accusations
309 **want** lack
310 **Have at you** A challenge for an attack. Cf. 2.2.84 n.
311–13 **First . . . bishops** On Wolsey's appointment as papal legate, which gave him power over even the Archbishop of Canterbury, see Introduction, p. 7.

312 **wrought** worked, contrived
315 '*Ego et Rex meus*' 'In Latin the pronoun of the first person is placed before other pronouns and before nouns. Wolsey's offence, if any, consisted in mentioning himself at all, not in putting him first' (Pooler). Norfolk's interpretation (316–17), following the wording in the chronicles, is that by putting himself first, Wolsey implies that the King is his servant, not the other way round. Wolsey should not have mentioned himself at all.
316 **still inscribed** always written conspicuously
319 **Ambassador to the Emperor** Wolsey

SURREY

Item, you sent a large commission
To Gregory de Cassado to conclude,
Without the King's will or the state's allowance,
A league between his highness and Ferrara.

SUFFOLK

That out of mere ambition you have caused   325
Your holy hat to be stamped on the King's coin.

SURREY

Then, that you have sent innumerable substance—
By what means got, I leave to your own conscience—
To furnish Rome, and to prepare the ways
You have for dignities to the mere undoing   330
Of all the kingdom. Many more there are,
Which since they are of you, and odious,
I will not taint my mouth with.

LORD CHAMBERLAIN   O, my lord,
Press not a falling man too far. 'Tis virtue.
His faults lie open to the laws; let them,   335
Not you, correct him. My heart weeps to see him
So little of his great self.

SURREY   I forgive him.

SUFFOLK

Lord Cardinal, the King's further pleasure is—

326 to] F; *not in* POPE

often served as Henry's ambassador (see,
e.g., 1.1.176–93); his offence was to
take the Great Seal out of the realm when
he travelled abroad to visit the Emperor,
Charles V. Cf. Hall, 624–7, although
nothing is said there of Wolsey taking the
Great Seal with him on that occasion.

321 **commission** body of persons charged
with a specific office
322 **Gregory de Cassado** Steevens corrects to
'Cassalis'; probably Sir Gregory di Cassalis, a member of an Italian family used by
Henry and Wolsey in negotiations in Italy,
especially with the Pope concerning the divorce. For his offer to serve Henry in dealing with Ferrara, see *Letters and Papers,
Foreign and Domestic, of the Reign of Henry
VIII*, ed. James Gairdner and R. H. Brodie
(1864–1910), vol. 3, part 2, no. 2794,
and cf. no. 3231. Many entries for de Cas-

salis, or Casalis, appear also in vol. 4.
323 **allowance** permission
325 **mere** sheer
326 **holy . . . coin** 'Wolsey had the right to
coin half-groats and half-pennies at York, as
did Archbishop Warham at Canterbury, but
by issuing a silver coin, with his initials and
cardinal's hat upon it, he "usurped the
king's prerogative"' (Foakes, citing G. C.
Brooke, *English Coins*, 3rd edn. (1950), 177).
327 **innumerable substance** measureless
wealth
329 **furnish** supply
329–31 **to prepare . . . kingdom** The charge
is that Wolsey sent money to Rome (in effect, bribes), which he collected in England, to procure for himself certain
'dignities' (i.e. titles and offices), thus
impoverishing the realm.
331 **Many more** i.e. items in the list
335 **lie open** are exposed, vulnerable

Because all those things you have done of late,
By your power legantine within this kingdom,   340
Fall into th' compass of a praemunire—
That therefore such a writ be sued against you,
To forfeit all your goods, lands, tenements,
Castles, and whatsoever, and to be
Out of the King's protection. This is my charge.   345

NORFOLK

And so we'll leave you to your meditations
How to live better. For your stubborn answer
About the giving back the great seal to us,
The King shall know it and, no doubt, shall thank you.
So fare you well, my little good lord Cardinal.   350

Exeunt all but Wolsey

CARDINAL WOLSEY

So farewell—to the little good you bear me.
Farewell, a long farewell, to all my greatness!
This is the state of man: today he puts forth
The tender leaves of hopes; tomorrow blossoms,
And bears his blushing honours thick upon him;   355
The third day comes a frost, a killing frost,
And when he thinks, good easy man, full surely

340 legantine] F4; Legatiue F1; Legantiue F2; Legatine ROWE 1709   344 Castles] F; Chattels THEOBALD   352 Farewell,] ROWE; ~? F

340 **legantine** F 'Legatiue' may be a misreading for 'Legātine' (TC). Though both are acceptable, Holinshed uses 'Legantine', the older form of the word. The reference is to Wolsey's power as a papal legate (see Introduction, p. 9).

341 **praemunire** See Introduction, p. 7. A writ of praemunire was tantamount almost to a charge of treason, since it accused a person of asserting papal jurisdiction in England, i.e. appealing to Rome instead of to English courts. Punishment consisted of forfeiture of goods and imprisonment.

342 **sued** enforced (Onions)

344 **Castles** F 'Castles' may be a misprint for Holinshed's 'cattels', which is a variant form of 'chattels'. But 'Castles' is a good climax to the series, 'goods, lands, tenements', and may allude to such palaces as Wolsey built at Hampton Court and York Place (Foakes).

350 **little good** Norfolk sarcastically emends the usual salutation, which Wolsey picks

up in the next line.

352 **Farewell** F inserts an interrogation mark, which Sisson defends (although an interrogation mark was sometimes used as an exclamation point in F). Wolsey's 'first words are an echo of Norfolk's mockery, and are spoken to the nobles as they leave. He turns to his own thoughts which play upon these *farewells* and emerge in fragments, until they flow into the full stream of imagery' (102).

353–9 **This . . . I do** Cf. Isaiah 40: 6–8: 'All flesh is grass, and all the grass thereof is as the flower of the field. The grass withereth, the flower fadeth . . . surely the people is grass', and 1 Peter 1: 24: 'For all flesh is as grass, and all the glory of man is as the flower of grass. The grass withereth, and the flower fadeth away' (Shaheen); also *Sonnet* 25 (Malone).

354 **blossoms** Possibly a verb, with 'he' understood (Maxwell).

355 **blushing** glowing

His greatness is a-ripening, nips his root;
And then he falls, as I do. I have ventured,
Like little wanton boys that swim on bladders,   360
This many summers in a sea of glory,
But far beyond my depth; my high-blown pride
At length broke under me and now has left me
Weary, and old with service, to the mercy
Of a rude stream that must for ever hide me.   365
Vain pomp and glory of this world, I hate ye!
I feel my heart new opened. O, how wretched
Is that poor man that hangs on princes' favours!
There is betwixt that smile we would aspire to—
That sweet aspect of princes—and their ruin   370
More pangs and fears than wars or women have;
And when he falls, he falls like Lucifer,
Never to hope again.

Enter Cromwell, standing amazed
                    Why, how now, Cromwell?

CROMWELL

I have no power to speak, sir.

CARDINAL WOLSEY   What, amazed

At my misfortunes? Can thy spirit wonder   375
A great man should decline?

---

362 depth;] F (~:); ~‸ OXFORD *conj.*

360 **wanton** frolicsome
  bladders Prepared bladders of an animal,
  inflated and used as floats (*OED* 3).
361 **This** A singular demonstrative before a
  plural was not uncommon: see Abbott
  §87.
362 **high-blown pride** Cf. 'bladders', 360.
364 **Weary . . . service** Wolsey had begun
  serving under Henry VII and was now
  nearly 60.
365 **rude stream** rough current
366 **Vain . . . world** Cf. 1 John 2: 15–17 and
  Book of Common Prayer: 'Dost thou forsake the devil and all his works, the vain
  pomp and glory of the world?' (Shaheen).
367 **I . . . opened** Cf. Acts 16: 14: 'Lydia . . .
  whose heart the Lord opened' (Shaheen).
367–8 **O . . . favours** Cf. Psalm 146: 2: 'Put
  not your trust in princes, nor in any child
  of man: for there is no help in them'; also

Jeremiah 17: 5, 7: 'Cursed be the man
that trusteth in man. . . . Blessed be the
man that trusteth in the Lord' (Shaheen),
and Psalm 118: 9: 'It is better to trust in
the Lord, than to put any confidence in
princes' (Humphreys).
369 **aspire** mount up
370 **their ruin** i.e. the ruin they cause
371 **pangs** Alludes to birth pangs.
372 **falls like Lucifer** Cf. Isaiah 14: 12: 'How
art thou fallen from heaven, O Lucifer,
son of the morning'; also Luke 10: 18: 'I
saw Satan, like lightning, fall down
from heaven' (Shaheen). Malone cites
Churchyard's 'Legend of Cardinal
Wolsey' in *Mirrour for Magistrates*
(1587): 'Your fault not half so great as
was my pride, | For which offence fell Lu-
cifer from the skies'.
376 **decline** fall, sink

Cromwell begins to weep

                                    Nay, an you weep

I am fall'n indeed.

CROMWELL   How does your grace?

CARDINAL WOLSEY   Why, well:

Never so truly happy, my good Cromwell.

I know myself now, and I feel within me

A peace above all earthly dignities,   380

A still and quiet conscience. The King has cured me.

I humbly thank his grace, and from these shoulders—

These ruined pillars—out of pity taken

A load would sink a navy: too much honour.

O, 'tis a burden, Cromwell, 'tis a burden   385

Too heavy for a man that hopes for heaven.

CROMWELL

I am glad your grace has made that right use of it.

CARDINAL WOLSEY

I hope I have. I am able now, methinks—

Out of a fortitude of soul I feel—

To endure more miseries and greater far   390

Than my weak-hearted enemies dare offer.

What news abroad?

CROMWELL   The heaviest and the worst

Is your displeasure with the King.

CARDINAL WOLSEY   God bless him.

CROMWELL

The next is that Sir Thomas More is chosen

Lord Chancellor in your place.

---

376 *Cromwell . . . weep*] OXFORD; *not in* F   an] and F   387–8 I . . . methinks] POPE; *as four lines divided . . .* Grace,/ . . . it./ . . . haue:/ F   389 soul$_\wedge$] POPE; ~, F

376 **an** if

379 **know myself** 'Know thyself' (Tilley K175) was a familiar proverb, deriving from Socratic philosophy and given currency by the great Renaissance humanist Erasmus in his *Adages* (1.6.95). In Sir John Davies's *Nosce Teipsum* (1599) Affliction leads the poet to a true understanding in religious terms of mind and soul (NCS). Cranmer's motto was '*Nosce teipsum et Deum*'.

383 **ruined pillars** Foakes and NCS suggest an allusion to the pillars Wolsey had carried

before him (cf. 2.4.0.11 n.), but a reference to the ruined abbeys and monasteries that followed the Reformation may also have been in the dramatist's mind (cf. 'Bare ruined choirs', *Sonnet* 73.4).

383 **taken** i.e. he has taken

387 **it** i.e. self-knowledge (379)

393 **displeasure** i.e. disgrace, falling into displeasure

394–407 **More . . . coronation** As Foakes says, chronology is severely compressed here: More was made Chancellor in 1529; Cranmer became Archbishop of

CARDINAL WOLSEY   That's somewhat sudden.   395
But he's a learned man. May he continue
Long in his highness' favour and do justice
For truth's sake and his conscience, that his bones,
When he has run his course and sleeps in blessings,
May have a tomb of orphans' tears wept on him.   400
What more?
CROMWELL   That Cranmer is returned with welcome,
Installed Lord Archbishop of Canterbury.
CARDINAL WOLSEY
That's news indeed.
CROMWELL   Last, that the Lady Anne,
Whom the King hath in secrecy long married,
This day was viewed in open as his queen,   405
Going to chapel, and the voice is now
Only about her coronation.
CARDINAL WOLSEY
There was the weight that pulled me down. O, Cromwell,
The King has gone beyond me. All my glories
In that one woman I have lost for ever.   410
No sun shall ever usher forth mine honours,
Or gild again the noble troops that waited
Upon my smiles. Go, get thee from me, Cromwell.
I am a poor fall'n man, unworthy now

408 There . . . Cromwell] POPE; *as two lines divided* downe. / F

Canterbury in 1532; and Anne was crowned in 1533. Wolsey died in 1530. NCS compares the series of messengers who bring bad news to Richard III (4.4) and Richard II (3.2); cf. also *Macbeth* (5.3). The effect of all this underscores the significance of Wolsey's fall.

396–400 **May he . . . on him** The irony of these lines may have been unintentional. Unable to support Parliament's bill, 'Submission of the Clergy', More resigned as chancellor in 1532 (see Ridley, 205). He later died a Catholic martyr.

400 **tomb . . . on him** As Johnson noted, the Chancellor by his office was the guardian of all orphans under the age of 21. He also found the expression 'a tomb of tears' very harsh. But Steevens drew comparisons to an epigram of Martial in which

the Heliades weep a tomb of tears over a viper, and to some verse of Drummond of Hawthornden, 'Tears for the Death of Moeliades' (1613): 'The Muses, Phoebus, Love, have raised of their tears, | A crystal tomb to him, through which his worth appears'.

403–4 **Anne . . . married** Cf. 41–2 n. above.

405 **in open** openly. Cf. Hall, 788, Holinshed, 929.

406 **voice** i.e. common talk, gossip

407 **coronation** (pronounced with five syllables)

408 **the weight . . . down** True only to some extent (see Introduction, p. 14).

409 **gone beyond** overreached

412 **noble troops** Cf. Holinshed, 847: dukes and earls served Wolsey at mass. Cavendish, 18–21, describes the enormous number of household staff and officers of high rank attending him.

167

To be thy lord and master. Seek the King—   415
That sun I pray may never set—I have told him
What and how true thou art. He will advance thee.
Some little memory of me will stir him—
I know his noble nature—not to let
Thy hopeful service perish too. Good Cromwell,   420
Neglect him not. Make use now, and provide
For thine own future safety.
CROMWELL (*weeping*)   O, my lord,
Must I then leave you? Must I needs forgo
So good, so noble, and so true a master?
Bear witness, all that have not hearts of iron,   425
With what a sorrow Cromwell leaves his lord.
The King shall have my service, but my prayers
For ever and for ever shall be yours.
CARDINAL WOLSEY (*weeping*)
Cromwell, I did not think to shed a tear
In all my miseries, but thou hast forced me,   430
Out of thy honest truth, to play the woman.
Let's dry our eyes, and thus far hear me, Cromwell;
And when I am forgotten, as I shall be,
And sleep in dull cold marble, where no mention
Of me more must be heard of, say I taught thee—   435
Say Wolsey, that once trod the ways of glory
And sounded all the depths and shoals of honour,
Found thee a way, out of his wreck, to rise in—
A sure and safe one, though thy master missed it.
Mark but my fall, and that that ruined me.   440
Cromwell, I charge thee, fling away ambition.
By that sin fell the angels. How can man, then,

418–19 him— | I . . . nature—not] F (*subs.*); ~. | ~ . . . ~ˏ~ OXFORD   422, 429 *weeping*]
OXFORD; *not in* F

420 **hopeful** exciting good hopes (Schmidt)
421 **Make use now** take advantage of the present opportunity
423 **forgo** renounce
425 **hearts of iron** Cf. Tilley H310.1: 'A heart of iron (would melt)' (Dent).
431 **play the woman** A common expression of the time; cf. Tilley W637.2 and *Macbeth* 4.3.232: 'O, I could play the woman with mine eyes' (Dent).

434 **dull** inert; cf. *L.L.L.* 3.1.57: 'Is not lead a metal heavy, dull, and slow?'
437 **sounded** fathomed
441 **fling away ambition** Ironical, given Cromwell's later rise under Henry, whom he served soon afterwards as Chancellor of the Exchequer in 1533, Lord Privy Seal in 1536, and Lord Chamberlain in 1539.
442 **By . . . angels** Cf. 372 and n. above. Not

The image of his maker, hope to win by it?
Love thyself last; cherish those hearts that hate thee;
Corruption wins not more than honesty.   445
Still in thy right hand carry gentle peace
To silence envious tongues. Be just, and fear not.
Let all the ends thou aim'st at be thy country's,
Thy God's, and truth's. Then if thou fall'st, O Cromwell,
Thou fall'st a blessed martyr.   450
Serve the King. And prithee, lead me in;
There take an inventory of all I have:
To the last penny 'tis the King's. My robe,
And my integrity to heaven, is all
I dare now call mine own. O Cromwell, Cromwell,   455
Had I but served my God with half the zeal
I served my King, He would not in mine age
Have left me naked to mine enemies.

452–3 have: . . . penny₍ₐ₎] F (haue, . . . penny,); ~ₐ . . . ~; CAPELL, POOLER, MAXWELL,
HUMPHREYS, NCS

only Lucifer, but legions of angels fell
with him because of the sin of pride and
ambition, as Milton portrays them in
Paradise Lost.

443 **image . . . maker** Cf. Genesis 1: 26: 'God
said, Let us make man in our image'.
win profit

444 **Love . . . last** Cf. Philippians 2: 3: 'In
meekness of mind every man esteem
other better than himself'; also
1 Corinthians 13: 5: '[Love] seeketh not
her own thing' (Shaheen).
cherish . . . thee Cf. Luke 6: 27–8: 'Love
your enemies: do well to them which hate
you. Bless them that curse you' (Shaheen).

446 **carry gentle peace** Cf. Romans 12: 18:
'As much as in you is, have peace with all
men' (Shaheen).

450 **a blessed martyr** Unlike Cranmer,
Cromwell did not die a Protestant martyr
but as Earl of Essex was executed for treason in 1540 having aroused antagonism,
like Wolsey, among the clergy and nobility, especially the Duke of Norfolk. (See
Scarisbrick, 375–80.) The half-line in F
deserves to stand for dramatic emphasis,
without 'Serve the King' moved from the
next line to fill it out, as Rowe emended it
(Foakes). R. W. Uphaus, *Beyond Tragedy:*

*Structure and Experience in Shakespeare's
Romances* (Kentucky, 1981), 126, claims
that Cromwell's rise out of Wolsey's
'wreck' associates the romances' tempest
imagery with the subsequent emergence
historically of the independent Church of
England, which Cromwell helped to establish (cf. Saccio, 23–4).

452 **take . . . have** See Cavendish, 98–9, and
Holinshed, 909. Wolsey turned over literally everything he owned. The particulars may be seen in Stow's *Chronicle*
(1631 edn., p. 546). See also the Harleian
manuscript entitled 'An Inventorie of
Cardinal Wolsey's rich Household Stuffe.
Temp. Henry VIII. The original book, as
it seems, kept by his own officers' (BL
Harleian MS 599) (Halliwell, citing
Douce).

456–8 **Had . . . enemies** Taken directly from
Holinshed, 917 (possibly adapted from
Cavendish, 178–9). There, Wolsey in his
last illness addresses not Cromwell, but
Sir William Kingston, Constable of the
Tower and captain of the guard, at
Leicester Abbey en route to London. Cf.
also Psalm 71: 9: 'Cast me not off in the
time of age; forsake me not when my
strength faileth' (Shaheen).

458 **naked** defenceless

CROMWELL
  Good sir, have patience.

CARDINAL WOLSEY   So I have. Farewell
  The hopes of court; my hopes in heaven do dwell.   460

Exeunt

4.1   *Enter the two Gentlemen meeting one another. The*
         first holds a paper

FIRST GENTLEMAN
  You're well met once again.

SECOND GENTLEMAN   So are you.

FIRST GENTLEMAN
  You come to take your stand here and behold
  The Lady Anne pass from her coronation?

SECOND GENTLEMAN
  'Tis all my business. At our last encounter
  The Duke of Buckingham came from his trial.   5

FIRST GENTLEMAN
  'Tis very true. But that time offered sorrow;
  This, general joy.

SECOND GENTLEMAN   'Tis well. The citizens,
  I am sure, have shown at full their royal minds—
  As, let 'em have their rights, they are ever forward—
  In celebration of this day with shows,   10
  Pageants, and sights of honour.

FIRST GENTLEMAN   Never greater,
  Nor, I'll assure you, better taken, sir.

SECOND GENTLEMAN
  May I be bold to ask what that contains,
  That paper in your hand?

---

460 do] F; now *conj.* G. Taylor *in TC*
    4.1] *Actus Quartus. Scena Prima.* F   0.1–2 *The first . . . paper*] OXFORD; *not in* F   3 corona-
tion?] CAPELL; Corronation. F

---

459 **have patience** Cf. 2.4.71 and n.
4.1.0.1 Enter . . . Gentlemen See 2.1 for
  their previous meeting.
3 **coronation** See Hall (798–805) for a description of Anne Boleyn's coronation in
  May 1533 and cf. Holinshed, 929–34.
8 **royal minds** devotion to the King
9 **let . . . rights** i.e. to give them their due
  forward eager, zealous

10–11 **shows . . . honour** Not only was
  Anne's coronation filled with splendour,
  but so were many seventeenth-century
  occasions, such as the installation of a
  Lord Mayor of London and the marriage
  of Princess Elizabeth in 1613, which
  audiences at the Globe would recall
  (Foakes).
12 **taken** received

FIRST GENTLEMAN　　　　　　Yes, 'tis the list

Of those that claim their offices this day　　　　　　15

By custom of the coronation.

The Duke of Suffolk is the first, and claims

To be High Steward; next, the Duke of Norfolk,

He to be Earl Marshal. You may read the rest.

　　　He offers him the paper

SECOND GENTLEMAN

I thank you, sir. Had I not known those customs,　　　20

I should have been beholden to your paper.

But I beseech you, what's become of Katherine,

The Princess Dowager? How goes her business?

FIRST GENTLEMAN

That I can tell you too. The Archbishop

Of Canterbury, accompanied with other　　　　　　25

Learned and reverend fathers of his order,

Held a late court at Dunstable, six miles off

From Ampthill, where the Princess lay; to which

She was often cited by them but appeared not.

And, to be short, for not appearance and　　　　　　30

The King's late scruple, by the main assent

Of all these learned men, she was divorced

And the late marriage made of none effect;

Since which she was removed to Kimbolton,

Where she remains now sick.

19.1 *He . . . paper*] This edition (*conj*. Capell);　*not in* F　　20 SECOND GENTLEMAN] F4 (*subs*.); I∧ F1
34 Kimbolton] F3; Kymmalton F1

14–16 **list . . . coronation** Cf. Holinshed, 930:
　'In the beginning of May, the king caused
　open proclamations to be made, that all
　men that claimed to do any service or exe-
　cute any office at the solemn feast of the
　coronation, by way of tenure, grant, or
　prescription, should put their grant three
　weeks after Easter in the Star Chamber be-
　fore Charles Duke of Suffolk, for that time
　High Steward of England, and the Lord
　Chancellor and other commissioners'.
23 **Princess Dowager** For this title, see
　3.2.70.
26 **fathers . . . order** lit., fraternity of reli-
　gious persons; here, those who held simi-
　lar rank or status, e.g. the Bishops of
　London, Winchester, Bath, Lincoln. See
　Holinshed, 929, for the account of the
　meeting at Dunstable Priory.

27 **late court** i.e. court lately
28 **Ampthill** Ampthill Castle in Bedfordshire,
　45 miles north-west of London, made
　crown property under Henry VII
　(Humphreys).
　lay lodged
29 **often . . . not** As reported by Holinshed
　(929), Katherine was summoned to the
　court but refused to attend, maintaining
　her appeal to Rome.
31 **King's late scruple** i.e. his concern about
　the validity of their marriage
　main assent general agreement
33 **of none effect** (Holinshed's term) null
34 **Kimbolton** Kimbolton (F Kymmalton)
　Castle in Huntingdonshire, where Kather-
　ine remained until her death in 1536. The
　F spelling conveys the pronunciation,
　accenting the first syllable.

SECOND GENTLEMAN   Alas, good lady!   35
  Flourish of trumpets within
The trumpets sound. Stand close. The Queen is coming.
  Enter the coronation procession, which passes over
  the stage in order and state. Hautboys, within, play
  during the procession

THE ORDER OF THE CORONATION

1. *First enter trumpeters, who play a lively flourish.*   *36.5*
2. *Then, two judges.*
3. *Then, the Lord Chancellor, with both the purse*
  containing the Great Seal and the mace borne before
  him.
4. *Then, choristers singing; with them, musicians* *36.10*
  playing.
5. *Then, the Lord Mayor of London bearing the mace,*
  followed by Garter King-of-Arms wearing his coat of
  arms and a gilt copper crown.

35.1 *Flourish . . . within*] OXFORD; *Trumpets* CAPELL; *not in* F 36 The trumpets . . . coming]
POPE; *as two lines divided* close,/ F 36.1–3 *Enter . . . procession*] OXFORD (*see ll.* 36.35–6); *Ho-*
boyes. F 36.5 *First . . . flourish*] OXFORD; *A liuely Flourish of Trumpets* F 36.7–9 *Then . . .*
him] OXFORD; *Lord* Chancellor, *with Purse and Mace before him* F 36.10–11 *Then . . .*
playing] OXFORD; *Quirristers singing. Musicke* F 36.12 *Then, the Lord*] OXFORD; *not in* F
36.13–14 *followed . . . crown*] OXFORD; *Then* Garter, *in his Coate of Armes, and on his head he wore*
a Gilt Copper Crowne F

36 **close** silent and aside
36.1–2 **passes over the stage** A. Nicoll, in
 'Passing over the Stage' (*SS* 12 (1959),
 47–55), argues that actors in processions
 such as this one entered from a door leading to the yard, then mounted the stage,
 and exited from a door in the yard at the
 opposite side; but Gurr (125) finds the argument doubtful, as no evidence exists
 for stairs from the yard to the stage. The
 actors probably entered at one of
 the stage doors and, after passing over
 the stage, left by another. Theatres had
 three or more stage doors used for en-
 trances (Gurr, 90).
36.4 **THE ORDER OF THE CORONATION**
 This procession is carefully abstracted with
 several modifications from Holinshed's
 account, 933. Various dukes, earls, and
 others are omitted, including the Earl of
 Oxford, Lord High Chamberlain, who
 carried the crown, probably to keep the

numbers within reason (Foakes). For the
same reason, the procession omits those
who came first, i.e. the esquires, knights,
and aldermen of the city, as less important than the others. Even so, it requires a
large number of supers, as at 2.4.0 (see
note).
36.13 **Garter King-of-Arms** He served under
 the Earl Marshal and was charged with
 proclaiming the sovereign's accession.
36.13–14 **coat of arms** i.e. wearing his coat
 of office emblazoned with the royal arms
 (Steevens)
36.14 **gilt copper crown** Cf. Holinshed:
 'every king of arms [there were three:
 Garter, Clarenceux, and Norroy] put on a
 crown of copper and gilt, all which were
 worn till night'. As gilt copper, they are
 distinguished from golden crowns and
 coronals that others wear. Cf. *Troilus*
 4.4.105: 'Whilst some with cunning gild
 their copper crowns'.

6. *Then, Marquis Dorset bearing a sceptre of gold, and*   36.15
   wearing on his head a demi-coronal of gold and, about
   his neck, a collar of esses. With him the Earl of
   Surrey bearing the rod of silver with the dove,
   crowned with an earl's coronet, and also wearing a
   collar of esses.   36.20

7. *Next, the Duke of Suffolk as High Steward, in his robe*
   of estate, his coronet on his head, and bearing a long
   white wand. With him the Duke of Norfolk with the
   rod of marshalship and a coronet on his head. Each
   wears a collar of esses.   36.25

8. *Then, under a canopy borne by four barons of the*
   Cinque Ports, Anne, the new Queen, in her robe. Her
   hair, which hangs loose, is richly adorned with pearl.
   She wears a crown. Accompanying her on either side
   are the Bishops of London and Winchester.   36.30

9. *Next, the old Duchess of Norfolk, in a coronal of gold*
   wrought with flowers, bearing the Queen's train.

10. *Finally, certain ladies or countesses, with plain*
    circlets of gold, without flowers.

36.15 *Then*] OXFORD; *not in* F   36.15–17 *gold, and wearing on his head . . . gold, and, about his neck, a collar of esses*] OXFORD; *Gold, on his head, . . . Gold* F   36.19–20 *and also . . . esses*] OXFORD; *Collars of Esses* F   36.21 *Next*] OXFORD; *not in* F   *as High Steward*] OXFORD; *after* 'wand', l. 36.23 F   36.24–5 *Each . . . esses*] OXFORD; *Collars of Esses* F   36.26–30 *Then, under . . . are*] OXFORD; *A Canopy, borne by foure of the Cinque-Ports, vnder it the Queene in her Robe, in her haire, richly adorned with Pearle. Crowned. On each side her,* F   36.31 *Next*] OXFORD; *not in* F   36.33 *Finally*] OXFORD; *not in* F

36.16 **demi-coronal** small coronet; cf. 36.31

36.17 **collar of esses** Ornamental gold chains of links made in the form of the letter *S*, worn as part of the insignia of knighthood (Onions).

36.18 **Surrey** Arundel in Holinshed. During the sixteenth century, the Norfolk and Arundel titles were amalgamated by marriage, and so the 14th Earl of Arundel, who succeeded in 1595, was also Earl of Surrey and of Norfolk.
  rod . . . dove his wand or staff of office (in Holinshed, made of ivory), with the dove as a symbol of peace (cf. 91, below)

36.21–2 **robe of estate** state

36.23 **Duke of Norfolk** Lord William

Howard in Holinshed, Norfolk's half-brother. The Dukes of Norfolk have been hereditary Earls Marshal since the accession of Henry VII. Anne was a niece of the third Duke.

36.26–7 **four . . . Ports** The barons of the Cinque Ports (originally Dover, Hastings, Sandwich, Hythe, and Romney, with Rye and Winchelsea added later) had the right to carry the canopy over the sovereign (see *OED*).

36.28 **hair . . . pearl** It was customary for brides to wear their hair down (cf. *Kinsmen* 5.3.0.1–2). Holinshed does not mention pearls, which were prominent in Princess Elizabeth's headdress in 1613 (Foakes).

> *The two Gentlemen comment on the procession as it*   36.35
> *passes over the stage*

SECOND GENTLEMAN

A royal train, believe me. These I know.

Who's that that bears the sceptre?

FIRST GENTLEMAN   Marquis Dorset.

And that, the Earl of Surrey with the rod.

SECOND GENTLEMAN

A bold brave gentleman. That should be   40

The Duke of Suffolk?

FIRST GENTLEMAN   'Tis the same: High Steward.

SECOND GENTLEMAN

And that, my lord of Norfolk?

FIRST GENTLEMAN   Yes.

SECOND GENTLEMAN (*seeing Anne*)   Heaven bless thee!

Thou hast the sweetest face I ever looked on.

Sir, as I have a soul, she is an angel.

Our King has all the Indies in his arms,   45

And more, and richer, when he strains that lady.

I cannot blame his conscience.

FIRST GENTLEMAN   They that bear

The cloth of honour over her are four barons

Of the Cinque Ports.

SECOND GENTLEMAN Those men are happy,   50

And so are all are near her.

I take it she that carries up the train

Is that old noble lady, Duchess of Norfolk.

36.35–6 *The two . . . stage*] OXFORD; Exeunt, *first passing ouer the Stage in Order and State, and then, A great Flourish of Trumpets*. F   41 Suffolk?] DYCE; ~. F   42 *seeing Anne*] OXFORD (*after* Johnson); *not in* F

36.35–6 Oxford's arrangement of the staging makes clearer sense of events than it appears in F and most modern editions. Obviously, the Gentlemen comment as the procession passes by them, not after it has gone out, though their dialogue follows the stage directions that describe it.

37 **train** retinue

40 **should** must

45 **all the Indies** Both the East and West In-

dies, including India and America, indicative of great riches; cf. 1.1.19–22.

46 **strains** tightly embraces

47 **blame his conscience** An allusion to scruple that afflicted Henry's conscience (31, above), but an oblique reference as well to Anne as the motive for his divorce from Katherine.

48 **cloth of honour** i.e. the canopy (36.26)

49 **Cinque Ports** See 36.26–7 n.

51 **all are** all who are

FIRST GENTLEMAN

It is. And all the rest are countesses.

SECOND GENTLEMAN

Their coronets say so. These are stars indeed—   55

⌈FIRST GENTLEMAN⌉

And sometimes falling ones.

SECOND GENTLEMAN   No more of that.

Exit the last of the procession, and then a great
flourish of trumpets within

Enter a third Gentleman in a sweat

FIRST GENTLEMAN

God save you, sir. Where have you been broiling?

THIRD GENTLEMAN

Among the crowd i'th' Abbey, where a finger

Could not be wedged in more. I am stifled

With the mere rankness of their joy.   60

SECOND GENTLEMAN

You saw the ceremony?

THIRD GENTLEMAN   That I did.

FIRST GENTLEMAN How was it?

THIRD GENTLEMAN

Well worth the seeing.

SECOND GENTLEMAN   Good sir, speak it to us.

THIRD GENTLEMAN

As well as I am able. The rich stream

Of lords and ladies, having brought the Queen   65

To a prepared place in the choir, fell off

A distance from her, while her grace sat down

To rest a while—some half an hour or so—

In a rich chair of state, opposing freely

55–6 indeed— | ⌈FIRST GENTLEMAN⌉ And] DYCE 1866 (*subs.*; *conj.* W. S. Walker); ~, | And F
56.1–2 *Exit . . . within*] OXFORD (*after* Capell); *not in* F (*but see ll.* 36.35–6)   56.3 *in a sweat*]
OXFORD; *not in* F   66, 92 choir] F (Quire)

---

55 **stars** A frequent image for nobles (Foakes).

56 **falling ones** Foakes sees a quibble on the sense 'surrendering chastity', but the more immediate reference must be to those like Wolsey and Buckingham who have recently fallen in the preceding acts.

57 **broiling** experiencing great heat (Onions)

58 **Abbey** Westminster Abbey, where cor-

onations are held.

60 **rankness** (a) exuberance; (b) foul smell. Cf. *Coriolanus* 3.1.70: 'The mutable rank-scented meinie' (Humphreys).

63 **speak** describe

66 **fell off** dropped off, stepped aside (*OED* 92b, first usage cited)

69 **opposing** exposing, displaying

The beauty of her person to the people.   70
Believe me, sir, she is the goodliest woman
That ever lay by man; which when the people
Had the full view of, such a noise arose
As the shrouds make at sea in a stiff tempest,
As loud and to as many tunes. Hats, cloaks—   75
Doublets, I think—flew up, and had their faces
Been loose, this day they had been lost. Such joy
I never saw before. Great-bellied women
That had not half a week to go, like rams
In the old time of war would shake the press   80
And make 'em reel before 'em. No man living
Could say 'This is my wife' there, all were woven
So strangely in one piece.
SECOND GENTLEMAN   But what followed?
THIRD GENTLEMAN
At length her grace rose, and with modest paces
Came to the altar, where she kneeled and saint-like   85
Cast her fair eyes to heaven and prayed devoutly;
Then rose again and bowed her to the people
When by the Archbishop of Canterbury
She had all the royal makings of a queen,
As holy oil, Edward Confessor's crown,   90
The rod and bird of peace, and all such emblems
Laid nobly on her. Which performed, the choir,
With all the choicest music of the kingdom,
Together sung *Te Deum*. So she parted,

---

80 press] F (prease)

---

72 **That . . . man** As NCS notes, the joy
   in sexual union and fruitfulness runs
   through this scene; cf. 45–6 and 78–81.
74 **shrouds** sail-ropes, standing rigging of a
   ship
76–7 **faces . . . lost** Cf. Tilley A387: 'You
   would lose your arse if it were loose'
   (Maxwell).
79 **rams** battering rams
80 **press** crowd
84 **modest** moderate, demure
87 **bowed her** 'The predilection for transitive
   verbs was perhaps one among other
   causes why many verbs, which are

now used intransitively, were used
by Shakespeare reflexively' (Abbott
§296).
89 **makings** materials that go to make
   (Onions). The modern sense, 'potential-
   ities', was not current till the nineteenth
   century (Foakes).
90 **As** such as, namely
91 **rod . . . peace** Cf. 36.18, above.
93 **music** musicians (as at *Romeo* 4.4.21)
94 *Te Deum* Hymn of thanksgiving, beginning 'We praise thee, O Lord', sung daily
   during Morning Prayer (Shaheen).
   parted departed

And with the same full state paced back again   95
To York Place, where the feast is held.
FIRST GENTLEMAN   Sir,
You must no more call it York Place—that's past;
For since the Cardinal fell, that title's lost.
'Tis now the King's and called Whitehall.
THIRD GENTLEMAN   I know it,
But 'tis so lately altered that the old name   100
Is fresh about me.
SECOND GENTLEMAN   What two reverend bishops
Were those that went on each side of the Queen?
THIRD GENTLEMAN
Stokesley and Gardiner, the one of Winchester—
Newly preferred from the King's secretary—
The other London.
SECOND GENTLEMAN   He of Winchester   105
Is held no great good lover of the Archbishop's,
The virtuous Cranmer.
THIRD GENTLEMAN   All the land knows that.
However, yet there is no great breach. When it comes,
Cranmer will find a friend will not shrink from him.
SECOND GENTLEMAN
Who may that be, I pray you?
THIRD GENTLEMAN   Thomas Cromwell,   110
A man in much esteem with th' King, and truly
A worthy friend. The King has made him
Master o' th' Jewel House
And one already of the Privy Council.

103 Stokesley] F4; *Stokeley* F1

95 **state** pomp
96 **York Place** The feast was held in Westminster Hall, according to Holinshed
(933), but York Place is named to recall
Wolsey and his fall (Foakes), perhaps
ironically alluding as well to the subsequent fall of Anne Boleyn. It was re-
named Whitehall after being taken over
by the Crown (l. 99) and expanded as
part of the King's palace at Westminster.
98 **lost** perished
101 **fresh** not faded or stale. In fact, the news
was quite stale by the time of Anne's
coronation, as Foakes says, but not in the
dramatic time of the play.

103 **Stokesley** John Stokesley, consecrated
Bishop of London in 1530, was a strong
supporter of Henry's divorce while at the
same time vigorously persecuting heret-
ics (Ridley, 202, 246).
103 **the one of Winchester** Reversed order:
Gardiner became Bishop of Winchester in
1531 (see 2.2.115 n.).
104 **preferred** promoted
105–7 **He . . . Cranmer** Gardiner's animosity
is developed fully in 5.1 and 5.2.
109 **will not** who will not
113 **Master . . . House** Appointed in April
1532, Cromwell was in charge of the
royal plate and crown jewels. In the same

SECOND GENTLEMAN

    He will deserve more.

THIRD GENTLEMAN   Yes, without all doubt.   115

    Come, gentlemen, ye shall go my way,

    Which is to th' court, and there ye shall be my guests.

    Something I can command. As I walk thither

    I'll tell ye more.

FIRST *and* SECOND GENTLEMEN   You may command us, sir.

                                Exeunt

4.2   *Three chairs. Enter Katherine Dowager, sick, led*
         between Griffith (her gentleman usher) and Patience,
         her woman

GRIFFITH

    How does your grace?

KATHERINE   O Griffith, sick to death.

    My legs, like loaden branches, bow to th'earth,

    Willing to leave their burden. Reach a chair.

        Griffith brings a chair to her. She sits

    So—now, methinks, I feel a little ease.

    Didst thou not tell me, Griffith, as thou led'st me,   5

    That the great child of honour, Cardinal Wolsey,

    Was dead?

GRIFFITH   Yes, madam, but I think your grace,

    Out of the pain you suffered, gave no ear to't.

KATHERINE

    Prithee, good Griffith, tell me how he died.

    If well, he stepped before me happily   10

    For my example.

---

119 FIRST . . . GENTLEMEN] F (*Both.*)

    4.2] *Scena Secunda*. F   0.1 *Three chairs*] OXFORD; *not in* F   3.1 *Griffith . . . sits*] This edition
(*after* Oxford); *not in* F   4 So—] ROWE; ~ˏ F   5 led'st] F (lead'st)   7 think] F2; thanke F1

sentence mentioning his appointment,
Holinshed calls him 'councillor to the
King, a man newly received into high
favour' (929). Cromwell was appointed
to the Privy Council a year earlier.

4.2.0.2 *Patience* A fictional character, with
allegorical significance: see 3.1.136 (cf.
Foakes, p. lviii). Most of the scene is invented, but see Holinshed, 939, for her
death, the visit of Caputius, and her
letter, and 917 for Wolsey's death.

2 **loaden branches** i.e. loaded with ripe
fruit

6 **child** scion, also suggesting a noble
young hero, e.g. Childe Roland; cf. *Lear*
3.4.170.

6–7 **Wolsey . . . dead** More dramatic compression: Wolsey died in 1530, Katherine
in 1536.

10 **happily** fortunately, but perhaps also
'haply', i.e. by chance (often spelled
'happily' in Shakespeare); both senses
are appropriate.

GRIFFITH   Well, the voice goes, madam.
  For after the stout Earl Northumberland
  Arrested him at York and brought him forward
  As a man sorely tainted to his answer,
  He fell sick suddenly and grew so ill   15
  He could not sit his mule.
KATHERINE   Alas, poor man.
GRIFFITH
  At last, with easy roads he came to Leicester,
  Lodged in the abbey, where the reverend abbot
  With all his convent honourably received him;
  To whom he gave these words: 'O, father abbot,   20
  An old man broken with the storms of state
  Is come to lay his weary bones among ye.
  Give him a little earth, for charity.'
  So went to bed, where eagerly his sickness
  Pursued him still; and three nights after this,   25
  About the hour of eight, which he himself
  Foretold should be his last, full of repentance,
  Continual meditations, tears, and sorrows,
  He gave his honours to the world again,
  His blessed part to heaven, and slept in peace.   30
KATHERINE
  So may he rest, his faults lie gently on him.
  Yet thus far, Griffith, give me leave to speak him,
  And yet with charity. He was a man

---

17 roads] F (Rodes)   19 convent] F (Couent)   31 So . . . him] POPE; *as two lines divided*
rest,/ F

12–16 **Earl . . . mule** For the account of
  Wolsey's arrest at Cawood Castle (ten
  miles south of York) for high treason and
  his slow and painful journey towards
  London and the Tower, see Cavendish,
  152–78, and Holinshed, 916–17.
13 **brought him forward** escorted him
14 **sorely tainted** grievously stained with
  guilt
  answer trial or punishment. Cf. *Henry V*
  2.2.140.
16 **mule** As a priest, Wolsey typically rode a
  mule, not a horse.
17 **roads** stages
  Leicester Cavendish (174–82) recounts
  Wolsey's death and his words to the

abbot at Leicester Abbey. See also Holinshed's shorter version, 917.
19 **convent** F 'Couent' is an earlier form of
  the word and may refer to the residence of
  a religious fraternity of either sex.
23 **a little earth** i.e. for a grave. 'The begging
  for this "charity" from the monks is in
  strong contrast with Wolsey's earlier
  pride' (NCS).
24 **eagerly** keenly, violently (*OED*)
26–7 **hour . . . last** (as recorded by
  Cavendish, 175)
28 **sorrows** lamentations
30 **blessed part** i.e. his soul
33–68 **He . . . God** The two accounts
  of Wolsey's character are based on

Of an unbounded stomach, ever ranking
Himself with princes; one that by suggestion   35
Tied all the kingdom. Simony was fair play;
His own opinion was his law. I' th' presence
He would say untruths and be ever double
Both in his words and meaning. He was never,
But where he meant to ruin, pitiful.   40
His promises were, as he then was, mighty;
But his performance, as he is now, nothing.
Of his own body he was ill and gave
The clergy ill example.
GRIFFITH   Noble madam,
Men's evil manners live in brass, their virtues   45
We write in water. May it please your highness
To hear me speak his good now?
KATHERINE   Yes, good Griffith,
I were malicious else.
GRIFFITH   This cardinal,
Though from an humble stock, undoubtedly
Was fashioned to much honour. From his cradle   50
He was a scholar, and a ripe and good one:

Holinshed, 917 and 922. The first (drawn from Edmund Campion and put in Griffith's mouth, later endorsed by Katherine) stresses his learning, generosity, and affability; the second (put in Katherine's), his pride, craft, and vice (Humphreys). See also Cavendish, 182.

34 **stomach** pride, arrogance
34–5 **ranking . . . princes** Cf. Holinshed, 847: Wolsey 'thought himself equal with the King'.
35 **suggestion** underhand dealings
36 **Tied . . . kingdom** brought the realm into bondage. Foakes suggests a pun on 'tithed' since Wolsey at one time proposed taxing everyone by one-tenth of their valuation (Holinshed, 874). Wolsey's taxations were notorious and burdened the populace; cf. 1.2.19–66.
Simony buying and selling of church offices, a notorious practice throughout the medieval period and a cause of the Reformation. The term derives from Acts 8: 18–20, where Simon the Samaritan offers money to the Apostles for the

power of conferring the Holy Spirit (Shaheen).
36 **fair play** upright conduct, equitable condition of intercourse or action (Onions). A Shakespearian coinage—see *K. John* 5.1.67, *Tempest* 5.1.178 (Foakes).
37 **presence** i.e. of the King
38 **double** deceitfully ambiguous (NCS). Cf. Wolsey's self-defence, 1.2.41–4.
41 **mighty** large and splendid. Cf. Tilley P602: 'Great promise, small performance' (Dent).
43 **Of . . . body** i.e. in sexual morality **ill** depraved. Cf. 3.2.296–7 (Foakes).
45–6 **Men's . . . water** Cf. Tilley I171: 'Injuries are written in brass, but benefits in water' and W114 'To write in water' (Foakes).
47 **good** i.e. virtues
50 **honour. From his cradle** Often emended, following Theobald, to 'honour from his cradle.' Since Holinshed stresses Wolsey's precocious learning (917), the F punctuation may stand.
51 **ripe** brought to perfection in growth, mature (Schmidt)

Exceeding wise, fair-spoken, and persuading;
Lofty and sour to them that loved him not,
But to those men that sought him, sweet as summer.
And though he were unsatisfied in getting—   55
Which was a sin—yet in bestowing, madam,
He was most princely: ever witness for him
Those twins of learning that he raised in you,
Ipswich and Oxford—one of which fell with him,
Unwilling to outlive the good that did it;   60
The other, though unfinished, yet so famous,
So excellent in art, and still so rising,
That Christendom shall ever speak his virtue.
His overthrow heaped happiness upon him;
For then, and not till then, he felt himself   65
And found the blessedness of being little.
And to add greater honours to his age
Than man could give him, he died fearing God.

KATHERINE

After my death I wish no other herald,
No other speaker of my living actions   70
To keep mine honour from corruption
But such an honest chronicler as Griffith.
Whom I most hated living, thou hast made me,
With thy religious truth and modesty,
Now in his ashes, honour. Peace be with him.   75
(*To her woman*) Patience, be near me still and set me lower.
I have not long to trouble thee. Good Griffith,
Cause the musicians play me that sad note

---

53 **Lofty** haughty
55 **unsatisfied in getting** never satisfied in acquisitions
58 **raised** built
you (apostrophizing Ipswich and Oxford)
59 **Ipswich and Oxford** Wolsey founded colleges in both places, using funds garnered from suppression of monasteries (Ridley, 151). At his fall, Cardinal's College, Ipswich, was dissolved, but Henry reestablished the college at Oxford as Christ Church, which still stands.
60 **Unwilling . . . it** Griffith's hyperbole; 'did' = made (cf. *Twelfth Night* 1.5.226: 'Excellently done, if God did all').
62 **art** learning. Cf. *Sonnet* 66.9 (Foakes).

62 **rising** growing (in excellence, etc.)
64 **heaped happiness** Cf. 3.2.378–81.
65 **felt** recognized, knew. Cf. 3.2.379 n.
70 **living actions** i.e. acts while alive
74 **religious** strict, conscientious (Onions)
78 **musicians** F provides no direction for musicians to enter; presumably, they were seated above the stage in one of the galleries (perhaps the lords' room: see Gurr, 91, 97–8), and at a signal from Griffith they began playing. As the music continues after the Vision vanishes, they do not enter or leave with the 'personages' who perform the dance. R. Hosley ('Was There a Music-Room in Shakespeare's Globe?', *SS* 13 (1960), 113–23)

I named my knell, whilst I sit meditating
On that celestial harmony I go to.   80
   Sad and solemn music

GRIFFITH

She is asleep. Good wench, let's sit down quiet
For fear we wake her. Softly, gentle Patience.

THE VISION

Enter, solemnly tripping one after another, six
personages clad in white robes, wearing on their heads
garlands of bays and golden visors on their faces. They
carry branches of bays or palm in their hands. They   82.5
first congé unto Katherine, then dance; and, at certain
changes, the first two hold a spare garland over her
head, at which the other four make reverent curtsies.
Then the two that held the garland deliver the same to
the other next two, who observe the same order in   82.10
their changes and holding the garland over her head.
Which done, they deliver the same garland to the last

82.4–5 *They carry*] OXFORD; *not in* F   82.6 *Katherine*] OXFORD; *her* F   82.8 *reverent*] WAR-
BURTON; *reuerend* F

argues persuasively that a music-room in
a gallery above the stage probably did not
exist at the Globe until after 1609, when
under the influence of performances at
Blackfriars Theatre, which featured
interact music, a box in the lords' room
might have easily been converted to a
music-room simply by adding a curtain.
(See 5.2.34.3 for the curtain in an upper
gallery used for other purposes.)

78 **note** tune, melody

80 **celestial harmony** Cf. *Merchant* 5.1.60–5,
where Lorenzo describes the music of the
spheres and says 'Such harmony is in
immortal souls, | But whilst this muddy
vesture of decay [the body] | Doth grossly
close it in, we cannot hear it'.

82.1 **THE VISION** No source for this episode
occurs in the chronicles, although similar supernatural events appear in other
late plays, e.g. *Pericles* Sc. 21.210–35,
Cymbeline 5.5.123 ff., and *Winter's Tale*
3.3.15–36, where Antigonus reports his
vision of Hermione telling him where to
leave and what to call her newborn infant

(Perdita). For a parallel to the funeral
oration of Marguerite of Navarre in 1550,
see E. E. Duncan-Jones, *N&Q* 206 (April
1961), 142–3, although whether the
dramatist knew of this oration is uncer-
tain (Humphreys).

82.3 **personages** Perhaps denoting sexless-
ness, as spirits (NCS).

82.4 **bays** bay leaves, symbols of triumph
and joy

   golden visors (F Vizards) Probably to
indicate spirits, as in Dekker's *Old*
Fortunatus (1600) 1.3.0 (Foakes). Gold
signifies incorruptibility, as white signifies purity; white and gold are the litur-
gical colours specified for the highest
Christian festivals, such as Christmas and
Easter.

82.5 **palm** Cf. Revelation 7: 9, where the
servants of God are 'Clothed with long
white robes, and palms in the hands'
(Shaheen).

82.6 **congé** bow, curtsy

82.7 **changes** changes in the dance move-
ments. 'The order of the dance symbol-
ises the eternal order of heaven' (NCS).

> *two, who likewise observe the same order. At which,*
> *as it were by inspiration, she makes in her sleep signs*
> *of rejoicing and holdeth up her hands to heaven. And*   82.15
> *so in their dancing vanish, carrying the garland with*
> *them. The music continues*

KATHERINE (*waking*)
Spirits of peace, where are ye? Are ye all gone,
And leave me here in wretchedness behind ye?
  Griffith and Patience rise and come forward

GRIFFITH
Madam, we are here.

KATHERINE   It is not you I call for.   85
Saw ye none enter since I slept?

GRIFFITH   None, madam.

KATHERINE
No? Saw you not even now a blessed troop
Invite me to a banquet, whose bright faces
Cast thousand beams upon me like the sun?
They promised me eternal happiness   90
And brought me garlands, Griffith, which I feel
I am not worthy yet to wear. I shall,
Assuredly.

GRIFFITH
I am most joyful, madam, such good dreams
Possess your fancy.

KATHERINE   Bid the music leave.   95
They are harsh and heavy to me.
     Music ceases

PATIENCE (*aside to Griffith*)   Do you note
How much her grace is altered on the sudden?
How long her face is drawn? How pale she looks?
And of an earthy cold? Mark her eyes!

83 *waking*] OXFORD (*after* Capell); *not in* F   84.1 *Griffith . . . forward*] OXFORD; *not in* F
92–3 I am . . . Assuredly] CAPELL; *as one line* F   96 *aside to Griffith*] This edition (*after* Capell);
not in F   99 cold] F; colour DYCE 1866 (*conj.* W. S. Walker)

87–90 **a blessed . . . happiness** Cf. Revelation   96 **heavy** annoying, wearisome (Schmidt)
19: 9: 'Blessed are they which are called   99 **earthy cold** A sign of death. Sisson, 102,
unto the Lamb's supper' and Luke 14: 15   defends the emendation 'colour' pro-
(Shaheen).   posed by W. S. Walker and adopted by
95 **leave** stop, 'leave off' (Onions)   Dyce and others as more consistent with

GRIFFITH

   She is going, wench. Pray, pray.

PATIENCE   Heaven comfort her.   100

    Enter a Messenger

MESSENGER

   An't like your grace—

KATHERINE   You are a saucy fellow—

   Deserve we no more reverence?

GRIFFITH   You are too blame,

   Knowing she will not lose her wonted greatness,

   To use so rude behaviour. Go to, kneel.

MESSENGER (*kneeling*)

   I humbly do entreat your highness' pardon.   105

   My haste made me unmannerly. There is staying

   A gentleman sent from the King to see you.

KATHERINE

   Admit him entrance, Griffith. But this fellow

   Let me ne'er see again.   *Exit Messenger*

    Enter Lord Caputius ⌈ushered by Griffith⌉

         If my sight fail not,

   You should be lord ambassador from the Emperor,   110

   My royal nephew, and your name Caputius.

CAPUTIUS

   Madam, the same, ⌈*bowing*⌉ your servant.

KATHERINE   O, my lord,

   The times and titles now are altered strangely

   With me since first you knew me. But I pray you,

   What is your pleasure with me?

---

101 An't] F (And't)   105 *kneeling*] JOHNSON; *not in* F   109, 111 *Caputius*] F (*Capuchius*)
109 *ushered by Griffith*] OXFORD (*after* Capell); *not in* F   112 *bowing*] OXFORD; *not in* F
114 With . . . pray you] ROWE 1714; *as two lines divided* me./ F

the description of Katherine's appearance. Foakes argues that emendation is
unnecessary, citing *1 Henry IV* 5.4.83,
'the earthy and cold hand of death',
and explaining that the absence of a
syllable in the line, as elsewhere in
Shakespeare, may indicate a dramatic
pause (Abbott §508).

101 **An't . . . grace** The Messenger's greet-
ing is too familiar (NCS), and he is immediately rebuked. He has also failed to
kneel, as befits someone approaching

royalty (cf. 104). In begging pardon, he
addresses Katherine as 'highness' (105)
and excuses his behaviour as occasioned
by haste (106).

102 **too blame** too blameworthy, culpable
(see *OED v.* 6). Many editors emend, 'to
blame'.

106 **staying** waiting

109 *Caputius* (F Capuchius). This is Henry
Chapuys, Charles V's ambassador. The
incident is historical; cf. Holinshed,
939.

113 **strangely** extraordinarily, extremely

CAPUTIUS   Noble lady,   115
    First mine own service to your grace; the next,
    The King's request that I would visit you,
    Who grieves much for your weakness and by me
    Sends you his princely commendations
    And heartily entreats you take good comfort.   120
KATHERINE
    O, my good lord, that comfort comes too late;
    'Tis like a pardon after execution.
    That gentle physic, given in time, had cured me;
    But now I am past all comforts here but prayers.
    How does his highness?
CAPUTIUS   Madam, in good health.   125
KATHERINE
    So may he ever do, and ever flourish
    When I shall dwell with worms and my poor name
    Banished the kingdom.—Patience, is that letter
    I caused you write yet sent away?
PATIENCE   No, madam.
KATHERINE (*to Caputius*)
    Sir, I most humbly pray you to deliver   130
    This to my lord the King.
        The letter is given to Caputius
CAPUTIUS   Most willing, madam.
KATHERINE
    In which I have commended to his goodness
    The model of our chaste loves, his young daughter—
    The dews of heaven fall thick in blessings on her—
    Beseeching him to give her virtuous breeding.   135
    She is young and of a noble modest nature.
    I hope she will deserve well—and a little
    To love her for her mother's sake, that loved him,

131 *The letter . . . Caputius*] OXFORD (*after* Malone); *not in* F

119 **commendations** compliments
128 **letter** The letter apparently fell into the hands of Polydore Vergil, who was then in England and recorded it in the twenty-seventh book of his history (Malone, who gives Herbert's translation of it, and notes that Polydore signed the divorce document).
131 **willing** willingly
133 **model** image, likeness; i.e. the Princess Mary, born in 1516
135 **virtuous breeding** good upbringing, education

Heaven knows how dearly. My next poor petition
Is that his noble grace would have some pity 140
Upon my wretched women that so long
Have followed both my fortunes faithfully;
Of which there is not one, I dare avow—
And now I should not lie—but will deserve
For virtue and true beauty of the soul, 145
For honesty and decent carriage,
A right good husband. Let him be a noble,
And sure those men are happy that shall have 'em.
The last is for my men—they are the poorest,
But poverty could never draw 'em from me— 150
That they may have their wages duly paid 'em,
And something over to remember me by.
If heaven had pleased to have given me longer life
And able means, we had not parted thus.
These are the whole contents; and, good my lord, 155
By that you love the dearest in this world,
As you wish Christian peace to souls departed,
Stand these poor people's friend and urge the King
To do me this last rite.
CAPUTIUS   By heaven I will,
Or let me lose the fashion of a man. 160
KATHERINE
I thank you, honest lord. Remember me
In all humility unto his highness.
Say his long trouble now is passing
Out of this world. Tell him, in death I blessed him,
For so I will. Mine eyes grow dim. Farewell, 165
My lord. Griffith, farewell.—Nay, Patience,
You must not leave me yet. I must to bed.
Call in more women. When I am dead, good wench,

---

139 Heaven . . . petition] ROWE 1714; *as two lines divided* deerely. / F   159 rite] OXFORD; right F

142 **both my fortunes** i.e. my prosperity and my misery
144 **now** i.e. near death. In fact, Katherine did not die until 1536 (see Introduction, p. 5), but her last appearance in the play is like a death scene, as her actions and language (e.g. 'last rite', 159) suggest.

146 **honesty** chastity
147 **noble** nobleman (since Katherine's women were also of noble rank), but also noble in character like them
154 **able** sufficient, adequate
160 **Or** or else
    fashion shape, nature
161 **honest** worthy

Let me be used with honour. Strew me over
With maiden flowers that all the world may know   170
I was a chaste wife to my grave. Embalm me,
Then lay me forth. Although unqueened, yet like
A queen and daughter to a king inter me.
I can no more.

> *Exeunt ⌜Caputius and Griffith at one door;*
> *Patience⌝ leading Katherine ⌜at another⌝*

5.1   *Enter Gardiner, Bishop of Winchester; before him, a*
Page with a torch

GARDINER
It's one o'clock, boy, is't not?

PAGE   It hath struck.

GARDINER
These should be hours for necessities,
Not for delights; times to repair our nature
With comforting repose, and not for us
To waste these times.

> *Enter Sir Thomas Lovell, meeting them*
                        Good hour of night, Sir Thomas,   5
Whither so late?

LOVELL   Came you from the King, my lord?

GARDINER
I did, Sir Thomas, and left him at primero
With the Duke of Suffolk.

---

172 forth. Although unqueened,] POPE (*subs.*); ~ (although ~) F   174.1–2 *Caputius . . .*
Patience] OXFORD; *not in* F   174.2 *at another*] OXFORD; *not in* F
  5.1] *Actus Quintus. Scena Prima.* F   0.1 *before him*] OXFORD; *after 'Torch'* F   1 o'clock]
THEOBALD 1740; a'clock F   5 *Enter . . . them*] OXFORD; *met by Sir Thomas Louell* F (*at end*
of 0.2)

---

170 **maiden flowers** i.e. as befits chastity. Cf.
    Hamlet 5.1.226–7: 'her virgin rites, |
    Her maiden strewments'.
172 **lay me forth** i.e. lay me out for burial
174 **can** i.e. do or say anything, as at *Hamlet*
    5.2.273 (Foakes)
5.1 Much of this scene and the next derives
    from John Foxe's *Acts and Monuments*,
    1693–4. A modern edition, which
    includes all the relevant material for *King*
    Henry VIII, appears in *Foxe's Book of*

Martyrs, ed. G. A. Williams (1965),
    338–41.
3 **Not for delights** 'Gardiner himself is not
    much delighted. The delight at which he
    hints, seems to be the King's diversion,
    which keeps him in attendance' (Johnson).
    repair restore
6 **Whither** where are you going
7 **primero** A popular card game at court
    and among gentlemen and gamesters,
    usually played for high stakes.

LOVELL   I must to him too
Before he go to bed. I'll take my leave.

GARDINER

Not yet, Sir Thomas Lovell: what's the matter?   10
It seems you are in haste. An if there be
No great offence belongs to't, give your friend
Some touch of your late business. Affairs that walk,
As they say spirits do, at midnight have
In them a wilder nature than the business   15
That seeks dispatch by day.

LOVELL   My lord, I love you,
And durst commend a secret to your ear
Much weightier than this work. The Queen's in
    labour—
They say in great extremity—and feared
She'll with the labour end.

GARDINER   The fruit she goes with   20
I pray for heartily, that it may find
Good time and live. But for the stock, Sir Thomas,
I wish it grubbed up now.

LOVELL   Methinks I could
Cry the 'Amen', and yet my conscience says
She's a good creature and, sweet lady, does   25
Deserve our better wishes.

GARDINER   But sir, sir,
Hear me, Sir Thomas. You're a gentleman
Of mine own way. I know you wise, religious.
And let me tell you, it will ne'er be well—
'Twill not, Sir Thomas Lovell, take't of me—   30

11 An] F (and)

8 **must** i.e. must go
11 **An** if if indeed
12 **offence** impropriety
13 **touch** hint
   late (a) recent; (b) afterhours
17 **commend** commit, entrust
18 **this work** i.e. what he is been engaged in
19 **feared** it is feared
22 **Good time** good fortune, propitious occasion. Cf. *Winter's Tale* 2.1.21: 'good time
   encounter her'.
22–3 **stock . . . grubbed up** Gardiner wishes
   that the trunk of the tree bearing the fruit
   (20) were now uprooted. Gardiner was

no friend to 'Lutherans' such as Anne.
He went along with the Reformation
politically but remained firmly Catholic in
doctrine, later serving as Queen Mary's
chancellor (Saccio, 227).

24 **Cry the 'Amen'** i.e. second your wish,
   concur
28 **mine own way** 'Mine own opinion in religion' (Johnson)
29–32 **let me . . . graves** Foxe says it was
   Gardiner himself who provoked the attack,
   but the dramatist here shows him inciting
   Lovell. Foxe does not date the attack,
   which came in 1544, though here it coin-

Till Cranmer, Cromwell—her two hands—and she
Sleep in their graves.

LOVELL   Now, sir, you speak of two
The most remarked i'th' kingdom. As for Cromwell,
Beside that of the Jewel House is made Master
O'th' Rolls and the King's secretary. Further, sir,   35
Stands in the gap and trade of more preferments
With which the time will load him. Th'Archbishop
Is the King's hand and tongue, and who dare speak
One syllable against him?

GARDINER   Yes, yes, Sir Thomas—
There are that dare, and I myself have ventured   40
To speak my mind of him, and, indeed, this day,
Sir—I may tell it you, I think—I have
Incensed the lords o'th' Council that he is—
For so I know he is, they know he is—
A most arch heretic, a pestilence   45
That does infect the land; with which they, moved,
Have broken with the King, who hath so far
Given ear to our complaint, of his great grace
And princely care, foreseeing those fell mischiefs
Our reasons laid before him, hath commanded   50
Tomorrow morning to the Council board
He be convented. He's a rank weed, Sir Thomas,

---

34 is] F; he's THEOBALD   36 more] F (moe)   37 time] F4; Lime F1   42 Sir—I may . . . you, I think—] JOHNSON (*subs.*); ~ (I ~ . . . you) I ~$_\wedge$ F   49 care,] F; ~$_\wedge$ GLOBE   50 hath] F; he hath POPE; 'hath COLLIER 1853, FOAKES

cides with Elizabeth I's birth in 1533, which derives from Holinshed's account.

33 **remarked** marked, conspicuous (Onions)
33–7 **Cromwell . . . him** As Lovell indicates, Cromwell's rise seems irresistible—and was, until his fall late in Henry's reign (see 3.2.441 n.). He eventually became the Earl of Essex shortly before his execution in 1540.
36 **gap and trade** i.e. where more preferments may be found; hence, passing to and fro as over a path (Onions); 'trade' = path; 'gap' = opening, opportunity
43 **Incensed** roused, angered. Some editors read 'insensed' = informed, after Rann's edition of 1791 (see Onions, 'insense'), but the word nowhere else appears in

Shakespeare, whereas 'incense' occurs several times in this play (NCS).

45 **arch heretic** Cranmer's Protestant sympathies were well known. He strongly supported Henry in the divorce case; and on 23 May 1533, following the trial at Dunstable, as Archbishop of Canterbury he declared that the marriage to Katherine was invalid. Five days later he pronounced the marriage to Anne as lawful (Ridley, 221).
46 **moved** angered, disturbed
47 **broken with** communicated to
49 **fell** terrible
52 **convented** summoned, as to a trial or hearing
    rank Both 'gross, overgrown' and 'virulent, poisonous' (NCS).

And we must root him out. From your affairs
I hinder you too long. Good night, Sir Thomas.

LOVELL

Many good nights, my lord; I rest your servant.   55

                        Exeunt Gardiner and Page
       ⌈*As Lovell starts to leave,*⌉ *Enter King Henry and*
       Suffolk, ⌈*as newly risen from play*⌉

KING HENRY

Charles, I will play no more tonight.

My mind's not on't. You are too hard for me.

SUFFOLK

Sir, I did never win of you before.

KING HENRY   But little, Charles,

Nor shall not when my fancy's on my play.   60

Now, Lovell, from the Queen what is the news?

LOVELL

I could not personally deliver to her

What you commanded me, but by her woman

I sent your message, who returned her thanks

In the great'st humbleness and desired your highness   65

Most heartily to pray for her.

KING HENRY   What sayst thou? Ha?

To pray for her? What, is she crying out?

LOVELL

So said her woman, and that her suff'rance made

Almost each pang a death.

KING HENRY   Alas, good lady.

55.1 *Exeunt*] ROWE (*after l.* 54; *after* 55 Capell); *Exit* F (*after l.* 54)   55.2–3 *As . . . play*] CAPELL (*subs.*); *Enter King and Suffolke* F

55 **rest** remain. Foakes defends F's placement of the stage direction, arguing that the line is spoken as Gardiner goes off, which would take some time on the wide Globe stage. But as Gardiner and his Page start to leave, Henry and Suffolk enter and their conversation begins, so there is no hiatus in the dialogue.

56 **Charles** Charles Brandon, Duke of Suffolk, an intimate of Henry's who secretly married his sister after her husband, the King of France, died. He figures prominently as Henry's companion in Rowley's *When You See Me, You Know Me*.

57 **too hard for** too powerful, getting the better of (Schmidt)

60 **fancy** inclination, attention

62 **deliver** make known

64 **who** i.e. the Queen

68 **suff'rance** suffering. Holinshed is silent on Anne's childbearing, but Rowley's play includes a scene where Jane Seymour dies in childbirth (cf. Humphreys).

SUFFOLK
  God safely quit her of her burden and   70
  With gentle travail, to the gladding of
  Your highness with an heir.
KING HENRY   'Tis midnight, Charles.
  Prithee to bed, and in thy prayers remember
  Th'estate of my poor queen. Leave me alone,
  For I must think of that which company   75
  Would not be friendly to.
SUFFOLK   I wish your highness
  A quiet night, and my good mistress will
  Remember in my prayers.
KING HENRY   Charles, good night.

                              Exit Suffolk

        Enter Sir Anthony Denny
  Well, sir, what follows?
DENNY
  Sir, I have brought my lord the Archbishop,   80
  As you commanded me.
KING HENRY   Ha? Canterbury?
DENNY
  Ay, my good lord.
KING HENRY   'Tis true: where is he, Denny?
DENNY
  He attends your highness' pleasure.
KING HENRY   Bring him to us.
                              Exit Denny

LOVELL (*aside*)
  This is about that which the Bishop spake.
  I am happily come hither.   85
        Enter Cranmer the Archbishop, ushered by Denny

78.2 *Enter . . . Denny*] CAPELL; *after l.* 79 F   83.1 *Exit Denny*] ROWE; *not in* F   85.1 *the Arch-bishop, ushered by*] OXFORD; *and* F

71 **travail** (accented on first syllable, like its doublet 'travel')
   gladding making happy
72 **midnight** i.e. the middle of the night, not twelve o'clock (cf. l. 1, above)
74 **estate** state, condition
75–6 **which . . . to** i.e. which is more suit-able for solitude
78.2 *Denny* According to Foxe, the messen-ger Henry sent to fetch Cranmer (Foakes).
79 **what follows** i.e. what's next, what have you to say
85 **happily** opportunely

KING HENRY (*to Lovell and Denny*) Avoid the gallery.
⌈*Denny begins to depart.*⌉ *Lovell seems to stay*
Ha? I have said. Be gone.
What?   *Exeunt Lovell and Denny*
CRANMER (*aside*)
            I am fearful. Wherefore frowns he thus,
'Tis his aspect of terror. All's not well.
KING HENRY
How now, my lord? You do desire to know   90
Wherefore I sent for you.
CRANMER (*kneeling*)   It is my duty
T'attend your highness' pleasure.
KING HENRY   Pray you, arise,
    My good and gracious lord of Canterbury.
Come, you and I must walk a turn together.
I have news to tell you. Come, come—give me your hand.   95
    ⌈*Cranmer rises. They walk*⌉
Ah, my good lord, I grieve at what I speak
And am right sorry to repeat what follows.
I have, and most unwillingly, of late
Heard many grievous—I do say, my lord,
Grievous—complaints of you, which, being considered,   100
Have moved us and our Council that you shall
This morning come before us, where I know
You cannot with such freedom purge yourself
But that, till further trial in those charges
Which will require your answer, you must take   105
Your patience to you and be well contented
To make your house our Tower. You, a brother of us,

86.1 *Denny . . . depart*] OXFORD; *not in* F   90–1 How . . . you] ROWE 1714; *divided* wherefore/ F
91 *kneeling*] JOHNSON; *not in* F   95 I . . . hand] POPE; *as two lines divided* you./ F
95.1 *Cranmer . . . walk*] OXFORD; *not in* F

---

86 **Avoid** leave, quit
  gallery Not the upper stage but the main
  stage where the action occurs. The 'long
  gallery' was a feature of houses of the
  period; cf. Foxe, 1694: 'the gallery where
  the King walked', and Rowley, *When You
  See Me, You Know Me*, 550 (Humphreys).
88–9 **frowns . . . terror** Cf. 3.2.205–7.
98–108 **I have . . . we thus** On Henry's shift

from first person singular to royal plural,
  see also 2.4.223–4 n.
99 **grievous** serious
101 **moved** prompted
  Council i.e. the Privy Council
103 **purge** exonerate
107–8 **You . . . proceed** you being our
  brother (i.e. fellow councillor), it is fitting
  that we act in this way

It fits we thus proceed, or else no witness
Would come against you.
CRANMER (*kneeling*)   I humbly thank your highness,
And am right glad to catch this good occasion   110
Most throughly to be winnowed, where my chaff
And corn shall fly asunder. For I know
There's none stands under more calumnious tongues
Than I myself, poor man.
KING HENRY   Stand up, good Canterbury;
Thy truth and thy integrity is rooted   115
In us, thy friend. Give me thy hand. Stand up.
Prithee, let's walk.
          Cranmer rises. They walk
                    Now, by my halidom,
What manner of man are you? My lord, I looked
You would have given me your petition that
I should have ta'en some pains to bring together   120
Yourself and your accusers, and to have heard you
Without indurance further.
CRANMER   Most dread liege,
The good I stand on is my truth and honesty.
If they shall fail, I with mine enemies
Will triumph o'er my person, which I weigh not,   125
Being of those virtues vacant. I fear nothing
What can be said against me.
KING HENRY   Know you not
How your state stands i'th' world, with the whole world?
Your enemies are many, and not small; their practices
Must bear the same proportion, and not ever   130

109 *kneeling*] JOHNSON; *not in* F   117 *Cranmer . . . walk*] OXFORD (*after* Johnson); *not in* F
halidom] F (Holydame)   123 good] F; ground RANN (*conj.* Johnson)

111 **throughly** thoroughly
111–12 **winnowed . . . asunder.** Cf. Luke
22: 31 (Geneva): 'Simon, behold Satan
hath desired you, to winnow you as
wheat', and Matthew 3: 12 (Shaheen).
113 **stands under** is subject to
115 **is** Inflection in *s* is frequent when two or
more nouns precede a verb (Abbott §336).
117 **halidom** A weak oath, originally referring to the holy relics upon which oaths
were sworn. The form 'holydame' (F) is
due to association with 'dame', the
phrase being popularly taken as 'By our

lady' (Onions).
118–57 **My . . . bid you** Henry's lines are
indebted to Foxe, 1694.
118 **looked** expected
122 **indurance** Foxe's term, meaning
imprisonment, but hardship (power of
enduring) is also possible (Foakes).
124–7 **If they . . . me** If my truth and honesty
fail me, not only my enemies, but I will
cooperate in my defeat, which matters
little to me lacking those virtues.
126 **nothing** not at all
130–2 **not ever . . . with it** The justice and

The justice and the truth o'th' question carries
The dew o'th' verdict with it. At what ease
Might corrupt minds procure knaves as corrupt
To swear against you? Such things have been done.
You are potently opposed, and with a malice   135
Of as great size. Ween you of better luck,
I mean in perjured witness, than your master,
Whose minister you are, whiles here he lived
Upon this naughty earth? Go to, go to.
You take a precipice for no leap of danger,   140
And woo your own destruction.

CRANMER   God and your majesty
Protect mine innocence, or I fall into
The trap is laid for me.

KING HENRY   Be of good cheer.
They shall no more prevail than we give way to.
Keep comfort to you and this morning see   145
You do appear before them. If they shall chance
In charging you with matters to commit you,
The best persuasions to the contrary
Fail not to use, and with what vehemency
Th'occasion shall instruct you. If entreaties   150
Will render you no remedy, ⌜*giving his ring*⌝ this ring
Deliver them, and your appeal to us
There make before them.

      Cranmer weeps

           (*Aside*) Look, the good man weeps.

---

140 precipice] F2; Precipit FI · 141 woo] F (woe)   151 *giving his ring*] OXFORD (*after* Capell);
not in F   153 *Cranmer weeps*] OXFORD; *not in* F   *Aside*] This edition; *not in* F   good man] F3;
goodman FI

truth of the matter do not always triumph
in the verdict.

132 **dew** Most editions read 'due', but the F
  spelling retains the metaphorical sense,
  'blessing, bounty' (cf. 1.3.57).
  At what ease how easily
134 **Such . . . done** (referring, perhaps, to
  Buckingham's trial?)
135 **potently** powerfully
136 **Ween you of** do you expect, imagine
137 **witness** evidence (Onions)
  your master Jesus Christ. Matthew
  26: 59–60, Mark 14: 55–7, describe the

false witnesses brought to testify against
Jesus at his trial (Shaheen).

139 **naughty** wicked
  Go to (expression of derisive incredulity)
140 **precipice** F 'Precepit' is an alternative
  form (from French *precipite*) of the newly
  introduced 'precipice' = dangerous cliff.
  Shakespeare might have written
  'precepit', though *t*/*c* confusion is common in secretary hand (Foakes).
143 **is** which is
144 **give way to** give them scope
147 **commit** i.e. to imprisonment in the
  Tower

He's honest, on mine honour. God's blest mother,
I swear he is true-hearted and a soul   155
None better in my kingdom.—Get you gone,
And do as I have bid you.   *Exit Cranmer*
                        He has strangled
His language in his tears.
          Enter the Old Lady
⌜LOVELL⌝ (*within*)   Come back! What mean you?
          ⌜*Enter Lovell, following her*⌝
OLD LADY
I'll not come back. The tidings that I bring
Will make my boldness manners. (*To the King*) Now
          good angels   160
Fly o'er thy royal head and shade thy person
Under their blessèd wings.
KING HENRY   Now by the looks
I guess thy message. Is the Queen delivered?
Say, 'Ay, and of a boy.'
OLD LADY   Ay, ay, my liege,
And of a lovely boy. The God of heaven   165
Both now and ever bless her! 'Tis a girl
Promises boys hereafter. Sir, your queen
Desires your visitation and to be
Acquainted with this stranger. 'Tis as like you
As cherry is to cherry.
KING HENRY   Lovell!
LOVELL   Sir.   170
KING HENRY
Give her an hundred marks. I'll to the Queen.   *Exit*

157–8 And . . . tears] HANMER; *divided* you./ F   158 LOVELL] HUMPHREYS; *Gent.* F
158.1 *Enter . . . her*] OXFORD (*after Capell, who combines this entry with the Old Lady's*); *not in* F
171 Give . . . Queen] POPE; *as two lines divided* Markes/ F

160 **manners** i.e. good manners. This is pre-
    sumably the same bold Old Lady as
    appeared in 2.3 with Anne.
165 **boy** The Old Lady knows that Henry has
    been hoping for a son (164) and at first
    replies accordingly, then immediately
    corrects her statement, claiming that
    boys will follow (166–7).
166–7 **her . . . hereafter** Deliberately

ambiguous; the Old Lady refers either to
Anne or Elizabeth or both.
168 **to be** i.e. and for you to be
171 **hundred marks** A mark was valued at
    two-thirds of a pound. It was a measure
    of value, not a coin, unlike the European
    mark, which was worth much less.
    (See S. K. Fisher, *Econolingua* (1985),
    93.)

OLD LADY

An hundred marks? By this light, I'll ha' more.
An ordinary groom is for such payment.
I will have more, or scold it out of him.
Said I for this the girl was like to him? I'll   175
Have more, or else unsay't; and now, while 'tis hot,
I'll put it to the issue.   *Exeunt*

5.2   *Enter pursuivants, pages, footboys, and grooms.*
            Then enter Cranmer, Archbishop of Canterbury

CRANMER

I hope I am not too late, and yet the gentleman
That was sent to me from the Council prayed me
To make great haste. All fast? What means this?
        (*Calling at the door*) Ho!
Who waits there?
            Enter a Doorkeeper
                        Sure you know me?

DOORKEEPER   Yes, my lord,

But yet I cannot help you.

CRANMER   Why?   5

---

177 *Exeunt*] CAPELL; *Exit Ladie.* F

  5.2] *Scena Secunda.* F   0.1–2 *pursuivants . . . enter*] OXFORD (*after* Steevens); *not in* F
3 *Calling at the door*] OXFORD; *not in* F   4 *Enter a Doorkeeper*] OXFORD (*after* Maxwell); *Enter Keeper* F (*after* me?)

172 **ha' more** A hundred marks was a con-
    siderable sum at that time, but the Old
    Lady is greedy for a handsomer reward.
173 **ordinary groom** (as opposed to herself, a
    lady-in-waiting)
176 **while 'tis hot** Cf. Tilley I94: 'Strike
    while the iron is hot' (Dent).
177 **put . . . issue** bring it to the point of deci-
    sion (Foakes)
5.2 Like 5.1, this scene is heavily indebted to
    Foxe's account of Cranmer's trial. Here,
    Norfolk, Cromwell, and the Lord Cham-
    berlain share what in Foxe is the Earl of
    Bedford's speech, but the development of
    Gardiner and Cromwell mostly originates
    with the dramatist (Foakes).
0.1 **pursuivants** junior officers of the her-
    alds. These and the others among whom
    Cranmer is made to wait are a means of
    humiliating Cranmer, who was deliber-

ately compelled to wait outside the council door by the members (Foxe, I694).
Cf. Butts's comment (7) and Cranmer's
recognition of the intended malice
(I3–I7).
3 **All fast** The door is locked against Cranmer. Presumably, this is one of the stage
doors, not the one through which Cranmer and the others entered. As the scene
progresses, Dr Butts enters and passes
over the stage, catching sight of Cranmer
(6–7). He then exits and ascends to the
upper stage, where he joins King Henry
(9, I8.I), and together they observe the
scene as it unfolds. At 34.4 the furniture
for the council scene is brought forward
from the discovery space, as Cranmer
waits to one side with the Doorkeeper,
until he is summoned to appear at 4I.
4 **Sure** surely

DOORKEEPER

    Your grace must wait till you be called for.

       Enter Doctor Butts

CRANMER   So.

BUTTS (*aside*)

    This is a piece of malice. I am glad

    I came this way so happily. The King

    Shall understand it presently.   *Exit*

CRANMER (*aside*)   'Tis Butts,

    The King's physician. As he passed along   10

    How earnestly he cast his eyes upon me!

    Pray heaven he found not my disgrace. For certain

    This is of purpose laid by some that hate me—

    God turn their hearts, I never sought their malice—

    To quench mine honour. They would shame to make me   15

    Wait else at door, a fellow Councillor,

    'Mong boys, grooms, and lackeys. But their pleasures

    Must be fulfilled, and I attend with patience.

       Enter King Henry and Doctor Butts at a window,

       above

BUTTS

    I'll show your grace the strangest sight—

KING HENRY   What's that, Butts?

BUTTS

    I think your highness saw this many a day.   20

KING HENRY

    Body o' me, where is it?

BUTTS (*pointing at Cranmer, below*) There, my lord.

    The high promotion of his grace of Canterbury,

---

6 *Enter Doctor Butts*] F; *after* Why? (*l.* 5) CAPELL   7 piece] F2 (Peice); Peere F1   12 found]
ROWE; sound F   17 'Mong . . . pleasures] ROWE 1714; *as two lines divided* Lackeyes./ F
19 sight—] ROWE; ~. F   21 o' me] POPE; a me F   *pointing . . . below*] OXFORD; *not in* F

---

   7 **Butts** Dr Butts, the King's physician (10),
      sees what is happening, does not address
      Cranmer, but goes directly to Henry.
  12 **found** Rowe's emendation of F 'sound' is
      not generally accepted, but long *s*/*f* con-
      fusions are not uncommon. Maxwell jus-
      tifies the metaphorical sense of 'sound' =
      fathom as well as the medical sense =
      probe. Foakes glosses 'sound' = make
      known; in NCS and Riverside 'sound' =

      proclaim.
  13 **laid** arranged (like a trap)
  17 **pleasures** wills, desires
  18.2 **above** i.e. on the upper stage or gallery
  21 **Body o' me** An oath or exclamation
      Henry also uses in Rowley's *When You*
      See Me; cf. *1 Henry IV* 2.1.26: 'God's
      body'.
  22 **high promotion** Butts's sarcasm derives
      from Foxe.

Who holds his state at door, 'mongst pursuivants,
Pages, and footboys.

KING HENRY   Ha? 'Tis he indeed.

Is this the honour they do one another?   25
'Tis well there's one above 'em yet. I had thought
They had parted so much honesty among 'em—
At least good manners—as not thus to suffer
A man of his place and so near our favour
To dance attendance on their lordships' pleasures,   30
And at the door, too, like a post with packets.
By holy Mary, Butts, there's knavery!
Let 'em alone, and draw the curtain close.
We shall hear more anon.

> *Cranmer and the Doorkeeper stand to one side.*
> *Exeunt the lackeys*
> *Above, Butts ⌈partly⌉ draws the curtain close. Below,*
> *a council table is brought in along with chairs and*
> *stools, and placed under the cloth of state. Enter the*   34.5
> *Lord Chancellor, placing himself at the upper end of*
> *the table, on the left hand, leaving a seat void above*
> *him at the table's head as for Canterbury's seat. The*
> *Duke of Suffolk, the Duke of Norfolk, the Earl of*
> *Surrey, the Lord Chamberlain, and Gardiner, the*   34.10

34.1–2 *Cranmer . . . lackeys*] OXFORD; *not in* F; *Curtain drawn*. CAPELL; *Exeunt. Scene III*. GLOBE
34.3 *Above . . . Below*] OXFORD (*after* Capell); *not in* F   34.5 *cloth of*] OXFORD; *not in* F
34.8 *at the table's head*] OXFORD; *not in* F

23 **holds his state** maintains his dignity, pomp
26 **one above 'em** Ambiguous: God or the King (Foakes).
27 **parted** shared
    honesty decency (Onions)
29 **place** rank and office
30 **dance attendance** i.e. kick one's heels in an antechamber (*OED*)
31 **post with packets** Couriers were stationed at stages along the post-road to carry the King's 'packets' to the next stage (*OED*, *post, sb.*[2] 2a).
33 **draw . . . close** The upper stage apparently had a curtain that could be closed, as here, enabling Henry and Butts to eavesdrop on the proceedings that follow. Although F has no exit here, some editors (e.g. Maxwell) begin a new scene after 34.

34.1–2 *Cranmer . . . lackeys* F gives no exit for Cranmer, who presumably remains to one side near the stage door, as if waiting outside the chamber with the Doorkeeper, as the lackeys (i.e. pursuivants and others) mentioned at 5.2.0 depart, their significance having been established. When summoned (41), Cranmer merely walks toward the councillors, whose stage furniture has been brought in through another door. (Cf. Foakes, NCS.)
34.6 *upper end* i.e. the end furthest from the door where Cranmer stands, occupied by the official of highest rank (Foakes)
34.10 *Chamberlain* At 3.2.394 Wolsey is told that Sir Thomas More has been appointed to this office, but he is left unnamed, Foakes suggests, to avoid the

Bishop of Winchester, seat themselves in order on
each side of the table. Cromwell sits at the lower end,
as secretary

LORD CHANCELLOR

Speak to the business, master secretary.   35

Why are we met in council?

CROMWELL   Please your honours,

The chief cause concerns his grace of Canterbury.

GARDINER

Has he had knowledge of it?

CROMWELL   Yes.

NORFOLK   Who waits there?

DOORKEEPER ⌈*coming forward*⌉

Without, my noble lords?

GARDINER   Yes.

DOORKEEPER   My lord Archbishop;

And has done half an hour to know your pleasures.   40

LORD CHANCELLOR

Let him come in.

DOORKEEPER (*to Cranmer*) Your grace may enter now.

Cranmer approaches the Council table

LORD CHANCELLOR

My good lord Archbishop, I'm very sorry

To sit here at this present and behold

That chair stand empty; but we all are men

In our own natures frail and capable   45

Of our flesh. Few are angels, out of which frailty

And want of wisdom you, that best should teach us,

34.12 *of the table*] OXFORD; *not in* F   *sits*] OXFORD; *not in* F   35, 111 master] STEEVENS; M. F;
Mr. ROWE   39 *coming forward*] OXFORD; *not in* F   45–6 frail‿ and . . . flesh. Few are angels,]
This edition; ~, ~ . . . flesh, few ~ ~; F

intrusion of another personality. The
scene reveals dramatic compression and
rearrangement, as the event here
occurred in 1544, long after Cromwell's
death (1540) and More's (1535); it helps
dramatize Henry's control of his realm
following Wolsey's fall.

38 **had knowledge** been informed
39 **Without** outside
43 **present** i.e. present time

44 **That chair** Cf. 34.7–8.
44–9 **we all . . . first** This passage derives
from Stokesley's speech to the clergy in
1531, as recorded in Hall, 783, and
repeated in Foxe, 959, over seven hundred pages earlier than the other material
used in this play (Foakes).
45–6 **capable . . . flesh** susceptible to the dictates of flesh and blood. Cf. *All's Well*
1.1.94–5: 'heart too capable | Of every
line and trick of his sweet favour'.

Have misdemeaned yourself, and not a little:
Toward the King first; then his laws; in filling
The whole realm by your teaching and your chaplains'—   50
For so we are informed—with new opinions,
Diverse and dangerous, which are heresies
And, not reformed, may prove pernicious.

GARDINER

Which reformation must be sudden too,
My noble lords; for those that tame wild horses   55
Pace 'em not in their hands to make 'em gentle,
But stop their mouths with stubborn bits and spur 'em
Till they obey the manège. If we suffer,
Out of our easiness and childish pity
To one man's honour, this contagious sickness,   60
Farewell all physic—and what follows then?
Commotions, uproars—with a general taint
Of the whole state, as of late days our neighbours,
The upper Germany, can dearly witness,
Yet freshly pitied in our memories.   65

CRANMER

My good lords, hitherto in all the progress
Both of my life and office, I have laboured,
And with no little study, that my teaching
And the strong course of my authority
Might go one way, and safely; and the end   70
Was ever to do well. Nor is there living—

52 Diverse] F (Diuers)   58 manège] F (mannage)

51 **new opinions** i.e. those deriving from Luther and other Protestants
52 **Diverse** F 'Diuers'. The distinction is a nice one between the senses 'various' and 'differing', but essentially making the same point. Many modern editions read 'Divers'.
53 **pernicious** deadly, fatal (i.e. to the received religion, Catholicism: Henry's break with Rome was not yet complete)
56 **Pace . . . hands** do not put them through their paces by leading them by the hand (Humphreys)
57 **stubborn** stiff, inflexible (Onions)
58 **manège** action and paces to which a horse is trained

58–63 **If we . . . state** Cf. *Troilus* 1.3.77–111 on 'The specialty of rule hath been neglected' and the anarchy that results.
58 **suffer** allow, permit
59 **easiness** indulgence (Onions)
62 **taint** corruption
63–5 **as of late . . . memories** Alluding to the disruptions Lutheranism precipitated, e.g. the Peasants' Revolt in Saxony in 1524 or the Anabaptists' in Münster in 1535, although Foxe is not specific. For dramatic compression, cf. 34.10 n.
64 **upper** higher and more inland
68 **study** deliberate effort
69 **course** planned series of actions or proceedings (*OED* 23a)

I speak it with a single heart, my lords—
A man that more detests, more stirs against,
Both in his private conscience and his place,
Defacers of a public peace than I do.   75
Pray heaven the King may never find a heart
With less allegiance in it. Men that make
Envy and crooked malice nourishment
Dare bite the best. I do beseech your lordships
That, in this case of justice my accusers,   80
Be what they will, may stand forth face to face
And freely urge against me.
SUFFOLK   Nay, my lord,
That cannot be. You are a Councillor,
And by that virtue no man dare accuse you.
GARDINER (*to Cranmer*)
My lord, because we have business of more moment,   85
We will be short with you. 'Tis his highness' pleasure
And our consent, for better trial of you,
From hence you be committed to the Tower
Where, being but a private man again,
You shall know many dare accuse you boldly,   90
More than, I fear, you are provided for.
CRANMER
Ah, my good lord of Winchester, I thank you.
You are always my good friend. If your will pass,
I shall both find your lordship judge and juror,
You are so merciful. I see your end—   95

---

72 **single** pure, without duplicity; cf. Genesis 20: 5: 'with a single heart and innocent hands have I done this'; also Ephesians 6: 5, Colossians 3: 22, Acts 2: 46. As Shaheen notes, only the Bishops' Bible has 'single heart'; most translations have 'with a pure heart' in Genesis 20: 5.

75 **Defacers** destroyers

77–9 **Men . . . best** Proverbial: cf. Tilley D432, F107: 'He finds fault with others and does worse himself' (Foakes).

80 **case of justice** case where justice is involved (Maxwell). Foakes inserts a comma after 'case'; hence 'of justice' = in fairness, according to moral right; but Maxwell compares *Cymbeline* 1.6.43, 'case of favour'.

82 **urge** pursue accusations

83 **That cannot be** Cf. 5.1.107–8, and 87–91 below.

84 **by that virtue** i.e. by virtue of that (office)

85 **business . . . moment** more pressing and important business

87 **our consent** which we have consented to

89 **being . . . again** As a prisoner in the Tower, one lost all rank and privileges.

90 **dare** who dare

93 **You . . . friend** Cranmer's sarcasm here is at first veiled, but becomes more deliberate by line 95.
will wish, desire (with the sense 'lust' implied)
pass be accepted, succeed

94 **judge and juror** ready to try as a judge and condemn as a juror (Foakes). For placement of 'both', see Abbott §420–1.

'Tis my undoing. Love and meekness, lord,
Become a churchman better than ambition.
Win straying souls with modesty again;
Cast none away. That I shall clear myself,
Lay all the weight ye can upon my patience,   100
I make as little doubt as you do conscience
In doing daily wrongs. I could say more,
But reverence to your calling makes me modest.

GARDINER

My lord, my lord, you are a sectary,
That's the plain truth. Your painted gloss discovers,   105
To men that understand you, words and weakness.

CROMWELL

My lord of Winchester, you're a little,
By your good favour, too sharp. Men so noble,
However faulty, yet should find respect
For what they have been. 'Tis a cruelty   110
To load a falling man.

GARDINER   Good master secretary,
I cry your honour mercy. You may worst
Of all this table say so.

CROMWELL   Why, my lord?

GARDINER

Do not I know you for a favourer
Of this new sect? Ye are not sound.

CROMWELL   Not sound?   115

GARDINER

Not sound, I say.

CROMWELL   Would you were half so honest!
Men's prayers then would seek you, not their fears.

96–7 **Love . . . ambition** Cf. 3.2.440–4.
98 **modesty** moderation, restraint. Cf. '**modest**', 103.
99–102 **That I . . . wrongs** All the burden you place on my patience notwithstanding, I have as little doubt that I shall clear myself of accusations as you are conscience-stricken by the wrongs you do every day.
104 **sectary** member of a (heretical) sect, schismatic (Onions)
105 **painted gloss** specious language, with a possible quibble on 'painted gloss' = false show (Foakes, citing confusion between 'gloze' = comment, and 'gloss' = brightness).
105 **discovers** discloses
106 **words and weakness** empty talk and false reasoning (Johnson)
111 **To . . . man** Cf. 'to kick a man when he's down' and 3.2.334.
112 **I . . . mercy** I beg your honour's pardon
112–13 **You . . . so** you have the least right to say so (Pooler)
115 **sound** (a) orthodox, holding to approved doctrines (NCS); (b) true, loyal, honest (Onions). Cf. 116.
116 **honest** true, having integrity

GARDINER
　I shall remember this bold language.
CROMWELL　　　　　　　　　Do.
　Remember your bold life, too.
LORD CHANCELLOR　　　　This is too much.
　Forbear for shame, my lords.
GARDINER　　　　　　　　I have done.
CROMWELL　　　　　　　　　And I.　　　　　120
LORD CHANCELLOR (*to Cranmer*)
　Then thus for you, my lord. It stands agreed,
　I take it, by all voices, that forthwith
　You be conveyed to th' Tower a prisoner,
　There to remain till the King's further pleasure
　Be known unto us. Are you all agreed, lords?　　　125
ALL THE COUNCIL
　We are.
CRANMER　Is there no other way of mercy,
　But I must needs to th' Tower, my lords?
GARDINER　　　　　　　　　What other
　Would you expect? You are strangely troublesome.
　Let some o' th' guard be ready there.
　　　　Enter the guard
CRANMER　　　　　　　　For me?
　Must I go like a traitor thither?
GARDINER (*to the guard*)　　　Receive him,　　　130
　And see him safe i' th' Tower.
CRANMER　　　　　　　Stay, good my lords.
　I have a little yet to say. Look there, my lords.
　　　　He shows the King's ring
　By virtue of that ring I take my cause
　Out of the grips of cruel men and give it
　To a most noble judge, the King my master.　　　135

---

119 LORD CHANCELLOR] CAPELL (*Chan.*); *Cham.* F　121 LORD CHANCELLOR] CAPELL (*conj.*
Theobald); *Cham.* F　126 ALL THE COUNCIL] OXFORD; *All.* F　132.1 *He . . . ring*] OXFORD
(*conj.* Capell); *not in* F　134 grips] F (gripes)

119, 121 **LORD CHANCELLOR** Capell emended
　F '*Cham.*', probably a minim misreading.
　Similar confusions are possible at 136 and
　141, but there it is not as clear that the
　presiding officer is speaking as it is here.
122 **voices** votes

128 **strangely** uncommonly, extremely
130 **Receive him** i.e. take him into custody
　(*OED, receive*, 17a). Although the Lord
　Chancellor is the presiding officer, Gar-
　diner is the true impetus of the proceed-
　ings and assumes control (NCS).

LORD CHAMBERLAIN
    This is the King's ring.
SURREY   'Tis no counterfeit.
SUFFOLK
    'Tis the right ring, by heav'n. I told ye all
    When we first put this dangerous stone a-rolling
    'Twould fall upon ourselves.
NORFOLK   Do you think, my lords,
    The King will suffer but the little finger   140
    Of this man to be vexed?
LORD CHAMBERLAIN   'Tis now too certain.
    How much more is his life in value with him!
    Would I were fairly out on't.
                              Exit King with Butts above
CROMWELL   My mind gave me,
    In seeking tales and informations
    Against this man, whose honesty the devil   145
    And his disciples only envy at,
    Ye blew the fire that burns ye. Now have at ye!
        Enter, below, King Henry frowning on them. He
        takes his seat
GARDINER
    Dread sovereign, how much are we bound to heaven
    In daily thanks, that gave us such a prince,
    Not only good and wise, but most religious: 150
    One that in all obedience makes the church
    The chief aim of his honour, and to strengthen

---

136 CHAMBERLAIN] F (*Cham*.); *Chan⟨cellor⟩*. BOSWELL   143 *Exit . . . above*] OXFORD; *not in* F
147.1 *below*] OXFORD (*conj*. Sisson, *after* burns ye); *not in* F   148 Dread . . . heaven] POPE; *as
two lines divided* Soueraigne/ F

138–9 **When . . . ourselves** Cf. Tilley S889
and Proverbs 26: 27: 'He that diggeth a
pit shall fall therein, and he that rolleth
a stone, it shall return unto him'. The
reference to Proverbs is not in Foxe (Shaheen).
142 **in value with** valued by, esteemed by
143 **gave me** misgave me, made me suspect
144 **tales** stories, gossip
    informations accusations (*OED* 4)
147 **Ye . . . burns ye** Cf. Ecclesiasticus 28: 12:
    'If thou blow the spark, it shall burn',

and Tilley F251: 'Do not blow the fire
thou wouldst quench' (Shaheen).
147.2 **his seat** i.e. the seat under the cloth of
state (34.5). Sisson, 104, says Henry's
entrance should come after 'burns ye'
since Cromwell evidently speaks his last
four words as Henry appears and takes
his place; but Cranmer may speak as he
sees Henry approach.
151–2 **makes . . . honour** i.e. makes it his
main object to benefit the church
(Foakes)

That holy duty, out of dear respect
His royal self in judgement comes to hear
The cause betwixt her and this great offender.   155
KING HENRY
You were ever good at sudden commendations,
Bishop of Winchester. But know I come not
To hear such flattery now, and in my presence
They are too thin and base to hide offences.
To me you cannot reach. You play the spaniel   160
And think with wagging of your tongue to win me.
But whatsoever thou tak'st me for, I'm sure
Thou hast a cruel nature and a bloody.
(To Cranmer) Good man, sit down.
        Cranmer takes his seat at the head of the Council table
                        Now let me see the proudest,
He that dares most, but wag his finger at thee.   165
By all that's holy, he had better starve
Than but once think this place becomes thee not.
SURREY
May it please your grace—
KING HENRY   No, sir, it does not please me.

---

153 duty, . . . respect‸] This edition; ~‸ . . . ~, F; ~, . . . ~, THEOBALD   159 base] F; bare
SINGER *(conj.* Malone)   164 *Cranmer . . . table*] OXFORD; *not in* F   proudest,] COLLIER; ~‸ F
167 this] F4; his F1

---

153 **dear respect** zealous regard (for the
  church)
156 **sudden commendations** quick, extem-
  poraneous compliments
159 **They** i.e. the 'commendations' (156)
160 **To . . . reach** i.e. your flattery cannot
  touch me (cf. 2.2.88). Some editors follow Johnson and place a comma after
  'reach', connecting the clause to what
  follows, arguing that it cannot stand
  alone (Maxwell), and F's punctuation,
  which places a comma after 'offences', is
  clearly wrong. But 'It . . . reach' provides
  a good transition between the 'flattery' of
  158 and the spaniel image that follows
  (NCS).
  the spaniel Shakespeare disliked dogs,
  especially their fawning behaviour.
  See Caroline Spurgeon, *Shakespeare's
  Imagery and What It Tells Us* (Cambridge,
  1935; repr. 1971), 195–9. Cf. Tilley
  S704: 'As flattering (fawning) as a

spaniel', and *Antony* 4.12.20–1: 'The
  hearts | That spanieled me at heels'.
164–5 **proudest, | He** Foakes follows F,
  omitting any punctuation after
  'proudest', arguing that 'He' is a noun
  (= man), and citing *Shrew* 3.3.106. But
  'proudest' may stand as a noun, with 'He
  that dares most' in apposition, clarifying
  and extending its significance. Cf. *Much
  Ado* 4.1.194: 'The proudest of them shall
  well hear of it', and Abbott §216, where
  the punctuation used here is defended
  against the 'intolerably harsh' reading
  that omits the comma.
166 **starve** die
167 **this place** i.e. the chair at the head of the
  table, or the office of privy councillor
  itself, in which case F 'his' may stand
  (Malone, Foakes). But as Humphreys
  says, Henry has just told Cranmer to
  sit down (164), and F's wording is
  awkward.

I had thought I had had men of some understanding
And wisdom of my Council, but I find none.   170
Was it discretion, lords, to let this man,
This good man—few of you deserve that title—
This honest man, wait like a lousy footboy
At chamber door? And one as great as you are?
Why, what a shame was this! Did my commission   175
Bid ye so far forget yourselves? I gave ye
Power as he was a Councillor to try him,
Not as a groom. There's some of ye, I see,
More out of malice than integrity,
Would try him to the utmost, had ye mean;   180
Which ye shall never have while I live.
LORD CHANCELLOR   Thus far,
My most dread sovereign, may it like your grace
To let my tongue excuse all. What was purposed
Concerning his imprisonment was rather—
If there be faith in men—meant for his trial   185
And fair purgation to the world than malice,
I'm sure, in me.
KING HENRY   Well, well, my lords, respect him,
Take him, and use him well; he's worthy of it.
I will say thus much for him: if a prince
May be beholden to a subject, I   190
Am for his love and service so to him.
Make me no more ado, but all embrace him.
Be friends, for shame, my lords. —My lord of Canterbury,
I have a suit which you must not deny me:
That is a fair young maid that yet wants baptism;   195
You must be godfather and answer for her.
CRANMER
The greatest monarch now alive may glory

---

180 mean] F (meane); means POPE   192 him] F; *not in* JOHNSON   195 That is] OXFORD;
~ ~, F; There is ROWE

170 **of** on. Like much of this speech, the
wording derives from Foxe. (See Introduction, pp. 41–2, for parallels to 169–80.)
175 **shame** disgrace
   my commission Cf. 5.1.99–107.
177 **try** (a) put on trial; (b) afflict (Foakes)

180 **mean** means. Cf. *Measure* 2.4.95: 'No
earthly mean to save him'.
182 **like** please
186 **purgation** action of clearing (oneself)
from the accusation or suspicion of guilt
(Onions)

In such an honour; how may I deserve it,
That am a poor and humble subject to you?

KING HENRY Come, come, my lord—you'd spare your   200
spoons. You shall have two noble partners with you—
the old Duchess of Norfolk and Lady Marquis Dorset.
Will these please you?—
Once more, my lord of Winchester, I charge you:
Embrace and love this man.

GARDINER   With a true heart   205
And brother-love I do it.
        Gardiner and Cranmer embrace

CRANMER (*weeping*)   And let heaven
Witness how dear I hold this confirmation.

KING HENRY
Good man, those joyful tears show thy true heart.
The common voice, I see, is verified
Of thee which says thus, 'Do my lord of Canterbury   210
A shrewd turn, and he's your friend for ever.'
Come, lords, we trifle time away. I long
To have this young one made a Christian.
As I have made ye one, lords, one remain:
So I grow stronger, you more honour gain.   *Exeunt*   215

5.3   *Noise and tumult within. Enter Porter with rushes
        and his Man with a broken cudgel*

PORTER (*to those within*) You'll leave your noise anon, ye

---

206 brother-love] MALONE; Brother; loue F1; Brothers love F2   206 *Gardiner . . . embrace*]
OXFORD (*after* Johnson); *not in* F   206 *weeping*] OXFORD; *not in* F   208 heart] F2; hearts F1
    5.3] *Scena Tertia.* F; *Scene IV.* GLOBE   0.1–2 *with rushes . . . cudgel*] OXFORD; *and his man* F
1–10] *as prose* F; *as verse, divided . . .* noise/ . . . court/ . . . gaping./ . . . larder./ . . . rogue:/
. . . in?—/ . . . ones;/ . . . 'em.—/ . . . christnings?/ CAPELL; *as verse, divided . . .* take/ . . .
slaves?/ . . . gaping./ . . . larder./ . . . rogue!/ . . . in?/ . . . ones,/ . . . heads./ . . . look / OXFORD

200–1 **spare your spoons** Henry teases Cran-
    mer that he is trying to avoid the expense
    of a christening gift of silver spoons, usu-
    ally twelve to a set with the figure of an
    apostle on the handles. See Halliwell,
    208–9, for a discussion and illustration of
    christening spoons.
201 **partners** co-sponsors. The switch to
    prose in these lines may signal a brief drop
    in tension and formality.

209 **voice** opinion
211 **shrewd** bad, malicious. The saying
    comes from Foxe, 1691.
213 **made a Christian** i.e. christened,
    baptized
5.3.0.1 **within** behind the stage wall
    rushes See 7–8, below (*TC*).
0.2 **broken cudgel** See 18–19 below (*TC*).
    1 **to those within** The inserted directions
    here and later (l. 8) suggest that the

rascals. Do you take the court for Paris Garden? Ye rude
slaves, leave your gaping.

ONE (*within*) Good master porter, I belong to th' larder.

PORTER Belong to th' gallows, and be hanged, ye rogue! Is   5
this a place to roar in? (*To his man*) Fetch me a dozen
crab-tree staves, and strong ones. ⌜*Raising his rushes*⌝
These are but switches to 'em. (*To those within*) I'll
scratch your heads. You must be seeing christenings? Do
you look for ale and cakes here, you rude rascals?   10

MAN

Pray, sir, be patient. 'Tis as much impossible,
Unless we sweep 'em from the door with cannons,
To scatter 'em as 'tis to make 'em sleep
On May-day morning, which will never be.
We may as well push against Paul's as stir 'em.   15

PORTER How got they in, and be hanged?

MAN

Alas, I know not. How gets the tide in?
As much as one sound cudgel of four foot—
       He raises his cudgel
You see the poor remainder—could distribute,
I made no spare, sir.

---

2 Paris] F4; Parish F1   4, 26 ONE (*within*)] FOAKES; *Within*. F   4, 26, 27 master] MALONE;
Mr. F3; M. F1   7 *Raising his rushes*] OXFORD; *not in* F   15 Paul's] F4; Powles F1   18.1 *He
. . . cudgel*] OXFORD (*conj.* Capell, *after* remainder, *l.* 19); *not in* F

crowd is 'within', as the speech at 26
also suggests. But it is possible that the
Porter addresses the theatre audience:
see 84–7 n. below.

1 **leave** stop, cease. 'The enthusiastic and
riotous crowd which the Porter and his
Man are trying to hold back seem to have
gathered at a doorway or gate [to the
palace] through which the procession
must pass on its way back from the christening' (NCS). For suggestions on staging
this scene, see 84–7 n. below.

2 **Paris Garden** F's 'Parish Garden' is an
alternative spelling for the bear- and bull-
baiting ring near the Globe, supposedly
named after Robert de Paris, who had a
house there in Richard II's time (Malone,
citing Thomas Blount, *Glossographia*,
4th edn. (1674)). Cf. modern football
crowds.

2 **rude** ignorant, uncivilized

3 **gaping** bawling, shouting

4 **belong . . . larder** work in the pantry

7 **crab-tree** Crab-apple trees were proverbi-
ally hard; cf. Tilley C787.

8 **switches to 'em** The rushes or rods he
holds are twigs compared to them.

10 **ale and cakes** Festive fare, as at *Twelfth
Night* 2.3.111.

14 **May-day morning** 1 May at dawn, when
young people went to gather hawthorn
and other branches to decorate their
doorways and dew to aid their complex-
ions in preparation for the festivities that
followed, such as Maypole dancing and
love-making.

15 **Paul's** St Paul's Cathedral

16 **and be hanged** A curse, as at *1 Henry IV*
2.2.5.

18–20 **As . . . spare, sir** The Porter's Man
says he did his best to disperse the crowd

PORTER   You did nothing, sir.   20

MAN I am not Samson, nor Sir Guy, nor Colbrand, to mow
     'em down before me; but if I spared any that had a head
     to hit—either young or old, he or she, cuckold or
     cuckold-maker—let me ne'er hope to see a chine again.
     And that I would not for a cow, God save her!   25

ONE (*within*) Do you hear, master porter?

PORTER I shall be with you presently, good master puppy.

     (*To his man*) Keep the door close, sirrah.

MAN What would you have me do?

PORTER What should you do, but knock 'em down by th'   30
     dozens? Is this Moorfields to muster in? Or have we some
     strange Indian with the great tool come to court, the
     women so besiege us? Bless me, what a fry of fornication
     is at door! On my Christian conscience, this one
     christening will beget a thousand. Here will be father,   35
     godfather, and all together.

MAN The spoons will be the bigger, sir. There is a fellow
     somewhat near the door, he should be a brazier by his

21–5 I . . . her] *as prose* POPE; *as verse, divided* . . . *Colbrand,*/ . . . *any*/ . . . *old,*/ . . . *-maker:*/
. . . *againe,*/ F   27–8 I . . . sirrah] *as prose* MAXWELL; *as verse, divided Puppy,*/ F   27 puppy]
MALONE; *Puppy* F   29–30 What . . . do] *as prose* ROWE; *as verse, divided* doe?/ F   30–63 but
. . . come] *as prose* F; *as verse* CAPELL   32 tool] POPE; *Toole* F; Tool ROWE

with his four-foot long cudgel, which
broke in pieces with his unsparing effort.

21 **Samson** The Israelites' strong man
who slaughtered a thousand Philistines
with the jawbone of an ass: see Judges
15: 15–16 (Shaheen).
Sir Guy, nor Colbrand Sir Guy of War-
wick slew the Danish giant Colbrand at
Winchester, as Drayton recounts in his
Poly-Olbion (1613), Song 12 (Johnson).

24 **see a chine** Various explanations have
been offered, but the expression probably
refers to the backs of those the Man has
been cudgelling (Foakes); the 'chine' is a
joint consisting of the whole or part of the
back of an animal (*OED sb.*² 3). But the
context ('cuckold', 'cuckold-maker',
'cow') suggests a quibble on a slang
expression for the vagina, since 'chine'
may also mean 'a fissure or crack in the
skin' (*OED sb.*¹ 1b). See Hilda Hulme,
Explorations in Shakespeare's Language
(1962), 126–9, for further discussion of

this passage, and notes to 25 and 32–6.

25 **I . . . her** Perhaps a common phrase, with
'cow' in a bawdy sense. Foakes cites *The
Tell-Tale* (Dulwich College ms. XX), 20:
'*Victo[ria]*: . . . rather than my bewty
should play the villaine . . . thus would I
mangle yt. *Julio*: not for a cow god save
her'.

31 **Moorfields** Like the Paris Garden (l. 2),
Moorfield Gardens beyond Moorgate was
another place where Londoners crowded
on holidays.
muster gather, assemble (*OED v.* 4)

32–6 **strange Indian . . . together** American
Indians were exhibited in London as
curiosities. The 'great tool' is a bawdy
reference to the penis, attracting women;
hence, the 'fry of fornication' (products
of intercourse, bastards) besiege the
palace, with the expected result of a
multitude of births ensuing.

37 **spoons** christening spoons (cf. 5.2.200)

38 **brazier** worker in brass (whose occupa-
tion required using extreme heat)

face, for o' my conscience twenty of the dog-days now
reign in's nose. All that stand about him are under the   40
line; they need no other penance. That fire-drake did I
hit three times on the head, and three times was his nose
discharged against me. He stands there like a mortar-
piece, to blow us. There was a haberdasher's wife of
small wit near him that railed upon me, till her pinked   45
porringer fell off her head, for kindling such a combus-
tion in the state. I missed the meteor once and hit that
woman, who cried out 'Clubs!', when I might see from
far some forty truncheoners draw to her succour, which
were the hope o'th' Strand, where she was quartered.   50
They fell on. I made good my place. At length they came
to th' broomstaff to me. I defied 'em still, when suddenly
a file of boys behind 'em, loose shot, delivered such a
shower of pebbles that I was fain to draw mine honour in
and let 'em win the work. The devil was amongst 'em, I   55
think, surely.

PORTER These are the youths that thunder at a playhouse
and fight for bitten apples, that no audience but the
tribulation of Tower Hill or the limbs of Limehouse, their
dear brothers, are able to endure. I have some of 'em in   60

44 blow us] F1; blow us up F3

39 **dog-days** The dog-days of summer (from
mid-July to mid-August) were from ancient
times regarded as the hottest and unhealth-
iest days of the year. Their name derives
from the dog-star, Sirius, which rises about
the same time as the sun in August.

40–1 **under the line** on the Equator

41 **fire-drake** fiery dragon or meteor (cf. 47);
also a firework (*OED*)

43–4 **mortar-piece** a small cannon with a
large bore

44 **blow us** (a) blow us out of the way;
(b) blow us up (NCS)

44–5 **haberdasher's wife . . . wit** a female
dealer in cheap witticisms (Pooler)

45–6 **pinked porringer** A round cap ornamented with small holes or scalloped
('pinked'), resembling an upturned dish
or basin.

47 **state** commonwealth, assembly
meteor i.e. the brazier ('fire-drake', 41)

48 **Clubs!** Rallying cry to summon apprentices to a fight.

49 **truncheoners** cudgel-bearers (a coinage)

50 **hope o'th' Strand** boys or men of the
Strand, a fashionable London street at
this time

51 **fell on** attacked
made good i.e. held

52 **to th' broomstaff** to close quarters;
'broomstaff' = broom handle

53 **loose shot** marksmen not attached to a
company (*OED, loose, a.* 1k)

54 **fain** obliged

55 **work** fortification (Onions)

57–8 **youths . . . apples** apprentices or
groundlings who quarrel over partly
eaten fruit

59 **tribulation . . . Hill** troublemakers around
Tower Hill, a rough neighbourhood
where public executions were held
limbs of Limehouse Limehouse was
another rough district, a dockyard area,
where sailors were recruited. The wordplay depends on the pronunciation of
'Limehouse' with a short *i* (see Kökeritz,
78) and continues with *limbo patrum* (61);
'limbs' = members, with an echo of

limbo patrum, and there they are like to dance these three
days, besides the running banquet of two beadles that is
to come.

    Enter the Lord Chamberlain

LORD CHAMBERLAIN

Mercy o' me, what a multitude are here!

They grow still, too; from all parts they are coming,   65

As if we kept a fair here! Where are these porters,

These lazy knaves? (*To the Porter and his man*) You've

    made a fine hand, fellows!

There's a trim rabble let in: are all these

Your faithful friends o'th' suburbs? We shall have

Great store of room, no doubt, left for the ladies   70

When they pass back from the christening!

PORTER   An't please your honour,

We are but men, and what so many may do,

Not being torn a-pieces, we have done;

An army cannot rule 'em.

LORD CHAMBERLAIN   As I live,

If the King blame me for't, I'll lay ye all   75

By th' heels, and suddenly—and on your heads

Clap round fines for neglect. You're lazy knaves,

And here ye lie baiting of bombards when

Ye should do service.

    Flourish of trumpets within

                Hark, the trumpets sound.

71 An't] CAPELL; And't F   79 *Flourish . . . within*] OXFORD; *not in* F

'limb of Satan' (Foakes). Cf. F 'white-
limb'd' (= whitelimed), *Titus* 4.2.97
(Cercignani, 312).

61 *limbo patrum* Slang term for 'prison',
deriving from the place near Hell where
the souls of the just but unbaptized (e.g.
the patriarchs) were held till Judgement
Day. In *Black Book* (1604; ed. Bullen,
viii. 12) Thomas Middleton plays on
'Limbo'–'Lime-street' (Foakes).

62–3 **running . . . come** The 'light refreshment' after their entertainment in prison
will be a whipping through the streets by
two officers with the power to punish
offenders.

67 **You've . . . hand** You have done well
(ironic); cf. Tilley H99: 'To make a fair

hand of a thing' and *Coriolanus* 4.6.123
(Dent).

68 **trim** fine

69 **suburbs** Rowdy districts outside London
jurisdiction.

70 **Great store** plenty (cf. 1 n. above)

72 **We . . . men** Cf. Tilley M541: 'Men are
(but) men' (Dent).

74 **rule** control

75 **If** Even if

75–6 **lay . . . heels** put you in fetters or in the
stocks

77 **Clap round** impose heavy

78 **baiting** worrying, harassing (like dogs
baiting a bear)
bombards drunkards (from the leather
jug used for liquor; cf. *1 Henry IV*
2.5.456: 'that huge bombard of sack')

They're come already from the christening.   80
Go break among the press and find a way out
To let the troop pass fairly, or I'll find
A Marshalsea shall hold ye play these two months.
            As they leave, the Porter and his man call within

PORTER

Make way there for the Princess!

MAN   You great fellow,

Stand close up, or I'll make your head ache.   85

PORTER

You i'th' camlet, get up o'th' rail,
I'll peck you o'er the pales else.   *Exeunt*

5.4   *Enter trumpeters, sounding. Then two aldermen, the*
           Lord Mayor of London, Garter King-of-Arms,
           Cranmer the Archbishop of Canterbury, the Duke of
           Norfolk with his marshal's staff, the Duke of Suffolk,

83.1 *As . . . within*] OXFORD; *not in* F

  5.4] *Scena Quarta.* F; *Scene V.* GLOBE   0.1 *trumpeters*] OXFORD; *Trumpets* F   0.2 *of London*]
OXFORD; *not in* F   *King-of-Arms*] OXFORD; *not in* F

81 **press** crowd

83 **Marshalsea** prison in Southwark
    hold ye play keep you engaged, busy

84–7 **You . . . else** J. W. Saunders ('Vaulting
    the Rails', *SS* 7 (1954), 69–81) argues
    that the Man addresses a member of the
    audience on the 'rail', l. 86 (the stage
    railing). As in modern productions of
    some plays, this would briefly engage the
    audience as part of the cast (obviating the
    need for supers) and would doubtless pro-
    voke laughter. Saunders says, 'Many
    dramatists and players exploited the
    interconnexion between stage and audi-
    torium, not only by way of extempore
    pleasantries, by simulating the presence
    of multitudes and treating groundlings as
    an extension of the stage-crowd in scenes
    describing battles, armies and mobs, but
    also by more direct reference' (70). Some
    of the Porter's yells to the crowd earlier
    may have been aimed at the Globe audi-
    ence itself, as Saunders contends—con-
    tinuing a practice from earlier miracle
    and mystery plays (and revived in some
    stagings of plays at the reconstructed
    Globe. Cf. also W. Smith's *Hector of Ger-
    many* (1615) (not included by Saunders),
    where a direction reads 'Sit on the

Railes' (Foakes), and Glynne Wickham,
'The Stage and Its Surroundings', in *The
Third Globe*, ed. C. Walter Hodges *et al.*
(Detroit, 1981), 137–8, who says rails
were on stages in some theatres and perhaps at the Globe (Gurr, 88, also says
rails appeared on some stages). Hodges
(*The Globe Restored* (New York, 1973),
90–1) draws the Globe stage with a
railing, but the reconstructed Globe on
the Bankside has no rails. Two illustrations (from 1632 and 1640), reproduced
in A. Nicoll, *The Development of the
Theatre*, 5th edn. (1966), 98, show rails
on stages.

85 **close up** close up against the others or
    against the wall

86 **camlet** fine cloth (of silk or other costly
    material)
    o' of (i.e. off)

87 **peck . . . pales** pitch you over the rails
    ('pales' = palings)

5.4 For the christening scene, see Holin-
    shed, 934, and Hall, 805–6, neither of
    whom mentions Cranmer's prophecy
    (17–55, 56–62).

0.2 **Garter King-of-Arms** See 4.1.36.13 n.

0.4 **marshal's staff** i.e. as Earl Marshal
    (4.1.36.23–4)

> *two noblemen bearing great standing bowls for the*   0.5
> *christening gifts; then four noblemen bearing a*
> *canopy, under which is the Duchess of Norfolk,*
> *godmother, bearing the child Elizabeth richly habited*
> *in a mantle, etc., whose train is borne by a lady. Then*
> *follows the Marchioness Dorset, the other godmother,*   0.10
> *and ladies. The troop pass once about the stage and*
> *Garter speaks*

GARTER Heaven, from thy endless goodness send prosper-
ous life, long, and ever happy, to the high and mighty
Princess of England, Elizabeth.

> *Flourish. Enter King Henry and guard*

CRANMER (*kneeling*)
And to your royal grace and the good Queen!
My noble partners and myself thus pray   5
All comfort, joy, in this most gracious lady
Heaven ever laid up to make parents happy,
May hourly fall upon ye.

KING HENRY   Thank you, good lord Archbishop.
What is her name?

CRANMER   Elizabeth.

KING HENRY   Stand up, lord.

> *Cranmer rises*
> (*To the child*) With this kiss take my blessing.
> *He kisses the child*

God protect thee,   10
Into whose hand I give thy life.

CRANMER   Amen.

KING HENRY (*to Cranmer, old Duchess, and Marchioness*)
My noble gossips, you've been too prodigal.

0.8 *Elizabeth*] OXFORD; *not in* F   0.9 *whose*] OXFORD; *not in* F   1–3 Heaven . . . Elizabeth]
as prose CAPELL; *as four verse lines divided* . . . Heauen/ . . . life,/ . . . Mighty/ F   4 *kneeling*] JOHN-
SON; *not in* F   9.1 *Cranmer rises*] OXFORD; *not in* F   10 *He kisses the child*] JOHNSON (*after l.* 9);
not in F

0.5–6 **two noblemen . . . gifts** Holinshed
(934) and Hall (805–6) name the personnel and the gifts.

0.5 **standing bowls** large bowls that rest on
legs or bases

0.9 **mantle** The mantle was of purple velvet
with a long train furred with ermine, supported by the Earl of Wiltshire on the
right and the Earl of Derby on the left,

between the child and the Countess of
Kent, who held the end of the train
(Holinshed, 934).

1–3 **Heaven . . . Elizabeth** The customary
ceremonial formula, similar to the one
used at the wedding of Princess Elizabeth
in 1613.

5 **partners** fellow sponsors

12 **gossips** godparents (from 'god-sip' =

I thank ye heartily. So shall this lady,
When she has so much English.

CRANMER   Let me speak, sir,

For heaven now bids me, and the words I utter   15
Let none think flattery, for they'll find 'em truth.
This royal infant—heaven still move about her—
Though in her cradle, yet now promises
Upon this land a thousand thousand blessings,
Which time shall bring to ripeness. She shall be—   20
But few now living can behold that goodness—
A pattern to all princes living with her,
And all that shall succeed. Sheba was never
More covetous of wisdom and fair virtue
Than this pure soul shall be. All princely graces   25
That mould up such a mighty piece as this is,
With all the virtues that attend the good,
Shall still be doubled on her. Truth shall nurse her,
Holy and heavenly thoughts still counsel her.
She shall be loved and feared. Her own shall bless her;   30
Her foes shake like a field of beaten corn,
And hang their heads with sorrow. Good grows with her.
In her days every man shall eat in safety
Under his own vine what he plants and sing
The merry songs of peace to all his neighbours.   35
God shall be truly known, and those about her
From her shall read the perfect ways of honour

23 Sheba] F (Saba)   32 And . . . her] ROWE 1714; *as two lines divided* sorrow:/ F   37 ways]
F4; way FI

God-related, i.e. spiritually akin to child
and parents: Foakes)
12 **prodigal** i.e. in christening gifts

17 **heaven . . . her** God be always near her;
cf. *First Part of the Contention* (*2 Henry VI*)
3.3.19: 'O Thou eternal mover of the
heavens' (Foakes).
23 **Sheba** The Queen of Sheba, who heard of
King Solomon's great wisdom and tested
it with 'hard questions': see 1 Kings
10: 1–8. Shakespeare used the spelling of
the Latin Vulgate, 'Saba', repeated by
most English bibles (Shaheen).

26 **mould up** create, go to form
piece person. Cf. *Tempest* 1.2.56: 'Thy
mother was a piece of virtue'.

30 **own** i.e. own people

33–5 **every man . . . neighbours** Cf. 1 Kings
4: 25: 'Judah and Israel dwelt without
fear, every man under his vine and under
his fig tree'; also 1 Kings 4: 20, Micah
4: 4, etc. (Shaheen). The golden age was
a favourite reference in relation to the
peace of James I's reign (Foakes).

36 **God . . . known** true religion shall prevail
(Humphreys)

37 **read** learn

And by those claim their greatness, not by blood.
Nor shall this peace sleep with her but, as when
The bird of wonder dies—the maiden phoenix—   40
Her ashes new create another heir
As great in admiration as herself,
So shall she leave her blessedness to one,
When heaven shall call her from this cloud of darkness,
Who from the sacred ashes of her honour   45
Shall star-like rise as great in fame as she was,
And so stand fixed. Peace, plenty, love, truth, terror,
That were the servants to this chosen infant,
Shall then be his and like a vine grow to him.
Wherever the bright sun of heaven shall shine,   50
His honour and the greatness of his name
Shall be, and make new nations. He shall flourish
And like a mountain cedar reach his branches
To all the plains about him. Our children's children
Shall see this and bless heaven.

KING HENRY   Thou speakest wonders.   55

CRANMER

She shall be to the happiness of England
An agèd princess. Many days shall see her,
And yet no day without a deed to crown it.
Would I had known no more. But she must die—

---

38 **claim . . . blood** Cf. *All's Well* 2.3.118–42, where the King of France similarly proclaims the superiority of virtue over inherited title as true 'honour'.

40 **maiden phoenix** The fabulous Arabian bird was the only one of its kind. She lived unmated, and when she died, out of her ashes (45) rose another bird. This symbolized both the uniqueness of a monarch and his or her linking together precursors and successors. Poets used it in reference to Queen Elizabeth, whose spirit continued in James I ('another heir', 41) and, by extension, Princess Elizabeth (see Foakes, p. xxiv).

42 **admiration** causing wonder

44 **cloud of darkness** i.e. earthly existence. Cf. 2 Samuel 22: 29: 'the Lord will lighten my darkness' (Foakes) and Isaiah 9: 2: 'The people that walked in darkness have seen a great light'.

47 **stand fixed** like a fixed star. Cf. *Sonnet* 116.5: '[Love] is an ever fixèd mark'.

51–2 **His honour . . . nations** Cf. Genesis 17: 4–6: 'Thou shalt be a father of many nations . . . Thy name shall be Abraham: for a father of many nations have I made thee. Also I will make thee exceeding fruitful, and will make nations of thee: yea, Kings shall proceed of thee' (Shaheen).

52–4 **He shall . . . him** Cf. Psalm 92: 11–12: 'The righteous shall flourish like a palm tree and shall spread abroad like a cedar in Libanus. Such as be planted in the house of the Lord shall flourish'; also Ezekiel 17: 22–3, 31: 3 (Shaheen).

52 **new nations** Alludes perhaps to the settlement of Virginia, for which a lottery was held in 1612 (Malone).

57 **agèd princess** Elizabeth I died in 1603 at the age of 69.

She must, the saints must have her—yet a virgin.   60
A most unspotted lily shall she pass
To th' ground, and all the world shall mourn her.
KING HENRY O Lord Archbishop,
Thou hast made me now a man. Never before
This happy child did I get anything.   65
This oracle of comfort has so pleased me
That when I am in heaven I shall desire
To see what this child does, and praise my maker.
I thank ye all. To you, my good Lord Mayor,
And your good brethren, I am much beholden.   70
I have received much honour by your presence,
And ye shall find me thankful. Lead the way, lords.
Ye must all see the Queen, and she must thank ye.
She will be sick else. This day, no man think
H'as business at his house, for all shall stay: 75
This little one shall make it holiday.

⌈*Flourish.*⌉ *Exeunt*

Epilogue   *Enter Epilogue*
EPILOGUE
'Tis ten to one this play can never please
All that are here. Some come to take their ease
And sleep an act or two; but those, we fear,
We've frighted with our trumpets; so, 'tis clear,
They'll say 'tis naught. Others, to hear the city   5
Abused extremely and to cry 'That's witty!'—
Which we have not done neither; that, I fear,

---

60 her—yet a virgin.] This edition; ~; ~ ~ ~, F; ~ₐ ~ ~ ~; THEOBALD   70 your] THEOBALD
(*conj.* Thirlby); you F   75 H'as] POPE; 'Has F   76 holiday] CAPELL; Holy-day F; holy day
JOHNSON   76.1 *Flourish*] OXFORD; *not in* F
  Epilogue 0.1–1 *Enter . . .* EPILOGUE] OXFORD; THE EPILOGVE. F

64 **made . . . man** ensured my prosperity
(*OED, man, sb.*¹ 7) (Foakes)
65 **get** (a) achieve; (b) beget
66 **oracle** Cf. 3.2.105.
70 **your** Theobald's emendation is doubtless
correct, explaining that aldermen were
never the King's 'brethren'; cf. *Henry V*
5.0.25: 'The Mayor and all his brethren'.
74 **sick** unhappy
76 **holiday** F Holy-day; both senses are
operative.
Epilogue 0.1 *Enter Epilogue* No designated

speaker is named, though usually the
King speaks the epilogue, but in Davies's
RSC production (1983) the woman who
held the baby stepped forward and
spoke it.
5 **naught** worthless
5–6 **the city . . . witty** Satirical city comedies
were becoming popular, especially in private theatres, and abuse of citizens was a
stock theme, as in Nathan Field's *Woman
is a Weathercock* (1612) (Foakes).
7 **that** so that

All the expected good we're like to hear
For this play at this time is only in
The merciful construction of good women,   10
For such a one we showed 'em. If they smile,
And say ''Twill do', I know within a while
    All the best men are ours; for 'tis ill hap
    If they hold when their ladies bid 'em clap.   *Exit*

---

14 *Exit*] OXFORD; *not in* F

8 **expected good** anticipated praise
10 **construction** interpretation
13 **best . . . ours** Cf. *2 Henry IV* Epi. 20–3 and
   As You Like It Epi. 11–16, where the
   appeal is again to the women first, then
   the men, as Steevens indicated.

13 **ill hap** bad luck
14 **hold** hold back, refrain. On the
   Epilogue's relation to Shakespeare's
   sonnet structure, and especially Sonnet
   126, see Barbara Hodgdon, *The End
   Crowns All* (Princeton, 1991), 229–31.

INDEX

The index includes words glossed in the Commentary, except for extended phrases and those that simply refer to explanations of stage directions or the antecedents of pronouns. References to the sources in Holinshed, Hall, Cavendish, and Foxe are also included, as are references to biblical allusions, proverbial expressions, and puns, quibbles, and other ambiguities. Word definitions that supplement the *OED* are marked with an asterisk.